DECEPTION, CENTRALIZATION, MANIPULATION & BETRAYAL:

The Complex Leadership of

ABIY AHMED ALI

DR. MEKONNEN H. BIRRU

ንጉሠና እሳቱ ......

***

A crown of peace upon his head, yet blood upon his hands,
He spoke of unity, but divided countless lands.

The Nobel's light adorned him, the world's applause was near,
Yet in the hills of Tigray, Oromia and Amharia, the drums of war
rang clear.

Streets of Addis shimmer, towers pierce the sky,
But shadows veil the alleys where broken voices cry.

With silver words he fashions dreams, with iron chains he binds,
A master of deception, ensnaring hearts and minds.

Hope once rose to greet him, now trust has turned to dust,
A leader clothed in glory, betrayed by his own lust.

***

***

This book is dedicated to the Ethiopians who have been deceived, displaced, harmed, or killed under the leadership of Abiy Ahmed Ali and the EPRDF. May their suffering be remembered, and their voices never silenced.

***

PREFACE

Abiy Ahmed Ali: A Leader of Contradictions

Abiy Ahmed, Prime Minister of Ethiopia since 2018, emerged onto the global stage as a figure of dazzling promise and deep paradox. To some, he appeared as a visionary reformer, a man destined to heal Ethiopia's divisions and usher in a new era of unity. To others, he quickly revealed himself as a self-serving leader, whose ambition often cloaked cruelty and whose every achievement was shadowed by contradictions. His meteoric rise to power, his pledge of democratic reforms, and his unexpected peace accord with Eritrea won him international admiration, culminating in the Nobel Peace Prize of 2019. Yet his years in power have been scarred by internal wars, most notably in Tigray and Amhara, and by his inability or unwillingness to halt the country's descent into deepening ethnic fragmentation.

At the heart of Abiy's political vision lies the philosophy of *Medemer* (Synergy), an idea that emphasizes unity, collective responsibility, and self-reliance. On paper, it promised a reconciliation of Ethiopia's fractured identities, a grand synthesis of the many into a single strong whole. But in practice, *Medemer* has collided with the harsh realities of governance. Critics contend that beneath the rhetoric lies an obsession with image over substance, a government increasingly authoritarian, militarized, and bent more on consolidating control than empowering citizens. The Prosperity Party, Abiy's creation, was presented as a vehicle of reform; yet for many Ethiopians, it has become a symbol of centralization, loyalty to one man, and the silencing of dissent.

Despite his claims of modernization, Abiy's Ethiopia has been marked by a steady erosion of democratic practice. Opposition voices have been stifled, protests crushed, and media freedom curtailed. His global posture, fluent in the language of reform, eager for international validation, has often overshadowed the stark realities on the ground: broken institutions, ethnic bloodshed, and a nation teetering between authoritarianism and anarchy. The contradiction is glaring: the statesman who won accolades abroad as a peacemaker has become, for many at home, the architect of war and repression.

Abiy's background helps explain his style. His early career was forged in the military and within the Oromo People's Democratic Organization (OPDO), experiences that gave him discipline, tactical skill, and a taste for control. His elevation to prime minister was, at first, hailed as the dawn of something new, especially for the Oromo, Ethiopia's largest ethnic group, who had long felt marginalized. Yet the promise of representation soon gave way to disappointment. The reality of his leadership has been more complex, less liberating than imagined, raising pressing questions about whether his reformist image was genuine or merely a mask for a more self-interested agenda.

This book explores the enigma of Abiy Ahmed: a leader whose ambition is matched only by the devastation it has left in its wake. His early acts, releasing political prisoners, opening political space, projecting optimism, convinced millions that Ethiopia was on the verge of renewal. But as the years unfolded, those hopes began to wither. Wars in the north, suppression of dissent, and the tightening grip of state power revealed the cost of his vision. His contradiction is not subtle: a man who vowed to bring peace but waged war; a leader who promised freedom but fostered fear; a statesman who sought international prestige even as his country fractured beneath him.

The duality of Abiy's leadership is now written across the nation itself. Ethiopia's capital city, Addis Ababa, gleams with construction and beautification projects, yet its streets are haunted by the invisible scars of displacement, betrayal, and repression. His speeches, soaring in rhetoric and heavy with dreams of unity, once inspired millions but now ring hollow for many, overshadowed by the violence, distrust, and uncertainty that define his rule. A generation of Ethiopians has been left suspended between the hope they once carried and the disillusionment that now weighs upon them.

This book will probe both the promise and the peril of Abiy Ahmed's rule. It will examine the cost of his ambition: how his determination to reshape Ethiopia has created as much chaos as reform, and how the hope he once stirred has curdled into despair. It will ask whether his story is one of genuine failure or of betrayal by design, whether he is a man trapped by circumstance or one who willingly sacrificed principle for power.

Abiy Ahmed's story is not just the story of a leader; it is the story of Ethiopia at a crossroads. It is the tale of a nation poised between a bright future and a dark present, of a people caught between longing for unity and living with division. His legacy, part triumph, part tragedy, forces us to ask: can the dreams of one man, tainted by cruelty and deception, ever yield true prosperity for a wounded nation? Or are Ethiopia's wounds too deep, its fractures too sharp, for even the most determined vision to heal?

This is the story of Abiy Ahmed Ali: his rise, his lies, his ambitions, and the devastating price paid by his people.

***

DECEPTION, CENTRALIZATION, MANIPULATION & BETRAYAL...

INTRODUCTION

Ethiopia, located in the Horn of Africa, is one of the most historically and culturally significant nations in Africa. With a history that stretches back over 3,000 years, Ethiopia is a land where ancient civilizations flourished, and a country that has resisted colonization in a way few others have. It is a nation that was able to maintain its sovereignty against external forces, particularly during the Scramble for Africa in the late 19th century. This book explores Ethiopia's historical development, from its ancient kingdoms to its resistance against European colonialism, its struggles with internal political upheavals, and its current state under the leadership of Prime Minister Abiy Ahmed.

＊

A Historical and Cultural Overview of Ethiopia

Ethiopia, one of the oldest countries in Africa, has long been a cradle for diverse civilizations, cultures, and religions. It is believed to be the site of the legendary Kingdom of D'mt, which emerged around the 10th century BCE in the highlands of what is now northern Ethiopia. Over time, the kingdom expanded its influence, becoming one of the major players in the ancient world. The subsequent rise of the Aksumite Empire cemented Ethiopia's role as a major political and economic power in the region. The Aksumites, based in the city of Aksum, controlled vital trade routes that connected Africa with Europe, Arabia, and Asia. This period in Ethiopian history, stretching from the 4th century CE to around the 7th century CE, marks the height of Ethiopia's ancient civilization.

In addition to its military and economic successes, Ethiopia became one of the first nations in the world to officially adopt Christianity, a defining moment that still shapes its culture, religious practices, and national identity today. The influence of Christianity continued to spread throughout Ethiopia, becoming intertwined with the nation's political, social, and cultural evolution.

In terms of biblical significance, Ethiopia (referred to as Cush in ancient texts) holds an essential place in the Old and New Testaments. The role of Ethiopia in biblical texts reflects its complex relationship with ancient Israel and its symbolic importance. In the Old Testament, Ethiopia is mentioned numerous times, reflecting its prominence in the ancient world. For instance, in Genesis 2:13, the land of Ethiopia is described as one of the regions surrounding the Garden of Eden, symbolizing its early importance in the biblical narrative. The kingdom of Cush, often identified with Ethiopia, is also mentioned in the context of military conflicts, such as the military leader Zerah in 2 Chronicles 14:9, whose vast army posed a serious threat to the Kingdom of Judah.

In the New Testament, Ethiopia is represented as a center of wisdom and Christianity. One of the most significant references is the story of the Ethiopian Eunuch in the Book of Acts, who becomes one of the first Gentile converts to Christianity after his encounter with Philip the Evangelist. This conversion story symbolizes Ethiopia's early role in the spread of Christianity, a connection that remains central to Ethiopian identity today.

***

Ethiopia's Ancient Civilizations

Ethiopia's civilization stretches back millennia, with its early roots in the Kingdom of D'mt (circa 10th century BCE). Located in the northern highlands, D'mt's strategic position allowed it to facilitate trade between sub-Saharan Africa, the Red Sea, and the Arabian Peninsula. D'mt laid the foundation for the rise of the more powerful Aksumite Empire.

The Aksumite Empire, which flourished from the 4th century CE to the 7th century CE, was a highly advanced civilization. At its peak, the empire expanded across parts of modern-day Ethiopia, Eritrea, Sudan, and the Arabian Peninsula. Aksum was a major trading hub, connecting Africa to the Mediterranean and India, and became the first African kingdom to mint its own coins, showcasing its economic power.

King Ezana, one of the most influential rulers of the Aksumite Empire, is credited with making Christianity the state religion in the 4th century, which set Ethiopia apart from other African nations and tied it to the broader Christian world. The Kingdom of Aksum also constructed impressive architectural works, including the famous obelisks that still stand today as testament to the empire's grandeur.

As the Aksumite Empire declined around the 7th century, weakened by the rise of Islam and changing trade routes, Ethiopia entered a period of fragmentation and political instability. Despite this, the country would remain an independent power and continue to develop its unique Christian traditions.

****

The Rise of the Solomonic Dynasty

After the fall of Aksum, Ethiopia experienced political fragmentation and intermittent warfare. In the 10th century, the Zagwe dynasty came to power. This period saw the construction of the famous rock-hewn churches of Lalibela, which remain among Ethiopia's most important cultural landmarks. These churches, carved out of solid rock, were a testament to Ethiopia's deep connection to Christianity and to its historical period of relative stability and religious devotion.

The Zagwe dynasty was eventually replaced in the 13th century by the Solomonic dynasty, which claimed descent from the biblical King Solomon and the Queen of Sheba. This royal lineage gave the Solomonic rulers a sense of divine legitimacy and helped solidify Ethiopia's connection to both biblical tradition and the broader Christian world. The Solomonic emperors expanded Ethiopia's territories, fortified its military, and built impressive churches, monasteries, and palaces, thereby contributing to the rich cultural heritage of the country.

However, the Solomonic dynasty also faced significant challenges, including political division, invasions from neighboring empires such as the Ottoman Turks, and internal conflicts that ultimately weakened their control. Despite these setbacks, the Solomonic monarchy continued to represent Ethiopian unity and the strength of the Ethiopian Orthodox Church until the early 20th century.

***

The Battle of Adwa: Ethiopia's Victory Against Colonialism

One of the defining moments in Ethiopia's modern history was the Battle of Adwa in 1896. At this pivotal battle, Emperor Menelik II led Ethiopian forces to a resounding victory against the Italian colonial army. Menelik's victory secured Ethiopia's sovereignty and set a precedent for African resistance against European colonial powers. The defeat of Italy was not only a triumph for Ethiopia but also a symbol of resistance for all of Africa, making it one of the few African nations to remain independent during the Scramble for Africa.

The Battle of Adwa had significant repercussions. It demonstrated that an African nation could successfully resist European imperialism, providing a sense of pride and unity across the continent. The victory also positioned Ethiopia as a beacon of African independence and solidarity in the face of European domination. Menelik II's leadership and the unity of the Ethiopian people were crucial factors in this success, and the battle remains an integral part of Ethiopia's national identity.

***

Ethiopia in the 20th Century: From the Monarchy to the Derg Regime:

Despite the victory at Adwa, Ethiopia faced many challenges in the 20th century, particularly in the mid-1900s, when the country underwent significant political changes. In 1974, after decades of growing discontent with Emperor Haile Selassie's rule, a military coup led by the Derg (a Marxist-Leninist regime) overthrew the monarchy. The Derg, under the leadership of Colonel Mengistu Haile Mariam, implemented socialist policies that included land redistribution and the nationalization of private property. These policies, however, led to widespread economic hardship, political repression, and violent purges that decimated the political opposition.

The 1980s were marked by devastating famine, civil wars, and political unrest. The Derg's inability to address Ethiopia's problems ultimately led to its downfall. In 1991, the Tigray People's Liberation Front (TPLF), a major rebel group, led a successful campaign to overthrow the Derg regime, resulting in the establishment of the Ethiopian People's Revolutionary Democratic Front (EPRDF).

***

The Eritrean Question: Federation, Annexation, Struggle, and the Assab Dilemma

Eritrea's modern history has been shaped by the overlapping forces of colonialism, federation, annexation, and liberation war. Its fate has also been inseparably tied to Ethiopia's quest for maritime access and national unity. To fully understand the Eritrean issue, one must trace the chronology of events that unfolded between the late nineteenth century and the present day, with particular focus on the federation of 1952, the annexation of 1962, the long independence struggle, and the unresolved contention over the Red Sea port of Assab.

Italian Colonization and the Seeds of Division

Eritrea emerged as a distinct political entity under Italian colonial rule. In 1869, the Italian Rubattino Shipping Company purchased the small port of Assab from local chiefs, and by 1882, Italy had annexed it as the foothold of its colonial ambitions. This marked the beginning of Italy's expansion in the Horn of Africa, which culminated in the declaration of Eritrea as an Italian colony in 1890. Massawa, Assab, and other ports along the Red Sea coast became integral to Italian trade and military strategy.

For Ethiopia, this colonial occupation meant the loss of direct sovereignty over its historic access to the sea. Although Emperor Menelik II secured Ethiopia's independence through victory at Adwa in 1896, the Red Sea remained under foreign control. Italy continued to consolidate Eritrea as a colony, while Ethiopia was forced to rely on complicated arrangements for trade through neighboring territories.

During World War II, Italy was defeated in East Africa by British and Ethiopian forces. From 1941 to 1952, Eritrea was administered by Britain. The question of Eritrea's future became a subject of heated debate, as Britain, the United States, the Soviet Union, and other powers weighed their strategic interests in the Red Sea. The newly created United Nations assumed responsibility for determining Eritrea's political destiny.

On December 2, 1950, the UN General Assembly adopted Resolution 390 A (V), which created a federation between Eritrea and Ethiopia. The resolution took effect on September 15, 1952. Eritrea was to have its own parliament, official languages (Tigrinya and Arabic), and a flag, while Ethiopia would control defense, foreign affairs, and finance. The arrangement was a compromise designed to balance Eritrea's aspirations for self-rule with Ethiopia's demand for sovereignty and access to the sea.

The federation, however, proved fragile. Emperor Haile Selassie viewed it as a temporary inconvenience rather than a permanent arrangement. Over the following decade, he systematically eroded Eritrea's autonomy. Political parties were restricted, labor unions were suppressed, and Eritrean institutions were dismantled. In 1962, in violation of the UN resolution, Haile Selassie formally dissolved the federation and annexed Eritrea as Ethiopia's 14th province.

This unilateral annexation was one of Haile Selassie's gravest mistakes. At a time when African nations were gaining independence, Eritrea, after tasting autonomy, was being absorbed against its will. The annexation ignited resistance. In September 1961, even before the formal annexation, the Eritrean Liberation Front (ELF) had launched an armed struggle from bases in Sudan.

The annexation in 1962 intensified the rebellion, transforming Eritrea into the theater of one of Africa's longest wars.

When Haile Selassie was overthrown in September 1974 by the Marxist-Leninist Derg regime, many Eritreans hoped the new rulers would grant autonomy or independence. Instead, the Derg, led by Colonel Mengistu Haile Mariam, rejected Eritrean self-determination and launched massive military offensives to crush the rebellion. Backed by the Soviet Union and Cuba, Ethiopia deployed tens of thousands of troops into Eritrea during the late 1970s.

Despite temporary successes, the Ethiopian army could not defeat the insurgency. The Eritrean People's Liberation Front (EPLF), formed in the early 1970s after splitting from the ELF, grew into a highly disciplined force. Key victories, such as the Battle of Afabet in March 1988, marked turning points. In that battle, the EPLF annihilated an entire Ethiopian division, capturing thousands of troops and massive stockpiles of weapons. The defeat demonstrated the weakening grip of the Derg.

By the late 1980s, Ethiopia was fighting on multiple fronts. In addition to the EPLF in Eritrea, the Tigray People's Liberation Front (TPLF) waged war in northern Ethiopia, and other insurgent groups operated in Oromia and elsewhere. The Ethiopian state was collapsing under famine, economic failure, and political repression.

On May 28, 1991, the Derg was overthrown by the Ethiopian People's Revolutionary Democratic Front (EPRDF), a coalition led by the TPLF. Simultaneously, the EPLF advanced into Asmara, liberating the Eritrean capital on May 24, 1991. For Eritreans, this date became their day of independence.

The 1993 Referendum: Freedom or Slavery

Following the Derg's collapse, the EPRDF government in Ethiopia, under Meles Zenawi, agreed to allow Eritreans to decide their future in a referendum. In April 1993, a UN-supervised referendum was held, offering Eritreans only two stark choices: "Freedom" or "Slavery." This phrasing, criticized by many Ethiopians as manipulative, made any option short of independence politically untenable. On April 23–25, 1993, more than 99 percent of Eritreans voted for freedom.

On May 24, 1993, Eritrea officially declared independence, and Ethiopia became a landlocked nation, the largest in the world without direct access to the sea.

The Assab issue, in particular, remains unresolved. Many Ethiopians argue that Eritrea's independence was accepted too hastily by the TPLF-led government without securing permanent maritime rights. Assab is seen as historically Ethiopian, integral to the nation's economic survival, and unfairly "given away." For Eritreans, however, Assab is inseparable from the sovereignty they fought for during their 30-year war of independence.

Today, Ethiopia remains one of the few ancient civilizations without a coastline, a fact that shapes both its economy and its national psyche. The "Assab question" continues to stir debate among Ethiopians, who regard the port as a lost inheritance. The unresolved legacy of federation, annexation, war, and referendum demonstrates how Haile Selassie's 1962 decision to dismantle the federation set in motion a chain of events that no imperial or Marxist regime could reverse. The Eritrean issue is not just a story of separation but a narrative of missed opportunities, mistrust, and enduring contention that continues to define politics in the Horn of Africa.

The EPRDF Era and Ethnic Federalism

Under the EPRDF, Ethiopia formally adopted the 1995 Constitution of the Federal Democratic Republic of Ethiopia (FDRE), which established a federal system explicitly organized along ethno-linguistic lines. Article 39 of the Constitution granted each "Nation, Nationality, and People" the right to secession, including the power to establish its own regional state and, if desired, to secede from the federation altogether. This was unprecedented in African constitutional law, as it not only recognized ethnic self-determination but also codified a legal right to independence. The Constitution divided Ethiopia into nine regional states, known as

"National Regional States," each with its own constitution, official language, regional council, and regional security forces. These regions, such as Tigray, Oromia, Amhara, and Somali, were granted extensive autonomy on paper, including legislative, executive, and judicial powers.

In practice, however, the Tigrayan People's Liberation Front (TPLF), as the dominant faction within the EPRDF coalition, exercised disproportionate control over the federal apparatus. While Article 50 of the Constitution emphasized a federal structure with a clear separation of powers between federal and regional authorities, power remained centralized through party mechanisms rather than constitutional institutions. The EPRDF maintained strict control over electoral bodies, the judiciary, and the military, effectively undermining the federal balance envisioned in the Constitution.

During the 2005 elections, Ethiopia witnessed its most competitive multi-party contest, with opposition parties, such as the Coalition for Unity and Democracy (CUD), making unprecedented gains. Although the National Election Board of Ethiopia (NEBE) was legally mandated by Article 102 of the Constitution to ensure impartiality, widespread reports of irregularities, intimidation, and fraud undermined the credibility of the process. When protests erupted in Addis Ababa and other cities, the government invoked security provisions under Article 93, which allows the Council of Ministers to declare a state of emergency in times of threat. The result was a violent crackdown, with security forces killing nearly 200 protesters and detaining thousands, including opposition leaders and journalists.

Thus, while the federal system enshrined in the Constitution was legally framed as one of the most radical experiments in ethnic self-rule, the authoritarian tendencies of the EPRDF, the party's dominance over state institutions, and its unwillingness to allow genuine political pluralism entrenched both ethnic division and central control. The contradictions between the written law and the political reality sowed seeds of long-term instability, even as Ethiopia experienced double-digit economic growth in sectors such as construction, telecommunications, and infrastructure development.

***

Abiy Ahmed's Reforms and the Challenges of Nation-Building:

In 2018, Abiy Ahmed rose to the position of Prime Minister of Ethiopia, and for a moment it seemed as if a new chapter of hope had been opened in the long and troubled history of the Horn of Africa. His appointment carried with it the fragrance of renewal, a promise whispered across mountains and valleys, a long-awaited sigh of relief for a people weary of authoritarianism and war. Almost immediately, Abiy moved with startling boldness, releasing political prisoners whose voices had been silenced, extending a hand to exiled opposition leaders who had been banished to foreign shores, and calling for national reconciliation as if he were trying to heal centuries of fractured trust with a single breath. His most celebrated triumph was the peace agreement with Eritrea, a gesture that closed the scar of a twenty-year conflict which had drained lives, resources, and dreams. The world, captivated by this narrative of peace, crowned him with the Nobel Peace Prize in 2019, a laurel that carried both honor and the heavy burden of expectation.

Yet the glitter of reform soon revealed fractures beneath its surface. The very openness that promised unity unearthed the long-suppressed fault lines of Ethiopia's ethnic politics. The eruption of the Tigray conflict in 2020 exposed the fragility of Abiy's project, raising bitter questions about whether his words of reconciliation were a vision sincerely held or a mask worn for power's sake. The war devastated towns and villages, displaced millions, and drenched the soil with the tears of the innocent. Humanitarian catastrophe became the daily reality of countless families, and the optimism of 2018 seemed like a distant mirage swallowed by the desert of conflict.

Abiy's Ethiopia thus became a paradox, a land suspended between lofty promises and haunting betrayals. The Prime Minister cloaked himself in the language of peace and unity, speaking of harmony as if it were within reach, yet his grip on power tightened with each passing year. He invoked the rhetoric of national strength while centralizing authority in ways that silenced dissent and undermined the delicate autonomy of Ethiopia's regions. The vision of a harmonious federation, where diverse ethnicities would walk hand in hand, often collided with the grim reality of suppressed voices, the Oromo, the Amhara, the Tigrayans, and others whose songs of belonging were drowned by the drums of war and the iron weight of political control. Across the land, the word "unity" echoed in speeches and posters, but to many ears it sounded more like a command than an invitation, accompanied by the silence of broken communities.

In Addis Ababa, the capital city, this paradox was etched into stone and steel. The government's vision materialized in grand infrastructural projects, skyscrapers climbing toward the sky, expansive highways stretching like veins of progress, and ambitious schemes of urban beautification. These were meant to symbolize modernity, to announce Ethiopia's arrival as a nation striding confidently into the future. Yet behind this shimmering facade lay another Ethiopia, fragmented and restless, where unity was more performance than substance. The beautification of Addis Ababa became not merely an architectural endeavor but also a political narrative, a way of constructing a visual myth that masked the raw wounds of displacement, resentment, and unrest in the countryside. The polished marble of the capital stood as a monument to aspiration, even as villages were reduced to ash in the north and families were fractured by grief in the west.

Meanwhile, armed resistance brewed and multiplied. The Oromo Liberation Front, once hailed as an ally in Abiy's meteoric rise, now stood in bitter opposition to his policies, denouncing the erosion of the very freedoms they had fought to win. The Amhara militia known as Fano emerged as a force of its own, reflecting the deepening cracks of ethnic polarization. In this shifting terrain, Abiy's calls for unity sounded increasingly hollow, like a bell rung in an empty cathedral. To maintain his grip, he turned to deception and propaganda, painting his crackdowns on dissenters as necessary acts of national defense. The rhetoric of stability masked the violence of suppression; the poetry of unity became the prose of control. Truth itself seemed to bend beneath the weight of his narratives, leaving citizens uncertain whether they were witnessing reform or simply the rebirth of tyranny in a new garment.

Thus Ethiopia stands at a crossroads, caught between the glittering promise of 2018 and the bitter trials that followed. The peace once celebrated in Oslo now lies tarnished, the dream of reconciliation entangled with the reality of division. Addis Ababa gleams like a jewel, a city beautified to project strength and progress, yet it also casts a long shadow that reminds Ethiopians of the price paid in blood, displacement, and silence. The nation's future remains suspended in uncertainty. Will Abiy Ahmed's vision eventually crystallize into a durable unity, a reconciliation that heals Ethiopia's wounds? Or will the weight of deception, authoritarianism, and unresolved ethnic rivalries unravel the fragile threads holding the country together?

Only time will tell whether Abiy Ahmed's Ethiopia will be remembered as a story of renewal betrayed, or as a painful crucible through which the nation was reborn.

***

CHAPTER 1

The Rise of Abiy Ahmed: Ambition in Action

A Humble Beginning

Abiy Ahmed was born on August 15, 1976, in the small town of Beshasha, located in the Oromia region of Ethiopia. At the time of his birth, Ethiopia was still living under the shadow of the Derg, a brutal military dictatorship that had been in power since 1974. The country had been scarred by years of political violence, economic instability, and human rights abuses. Under the Derg regime, led by Mengistu Haile Mariam, Ethiopia witnessed atrocities such as the Red Terror, during which thousands were executed or disappeared. This was the backdrop against which Abiy entered the world, a nation deeply divided and struggling with the weight of its turbulent history.

Abiy Ahmed's father, Ahmed Ali, was a Muslim Oromo farmer from the town of Beshasha in Ethiopia. As a typical figure of his ethnic group, Ahmed Ali's life was rooted in the agricultural practices of the Oromo people, a community often marginalized in Ethiopia's political history. The fact that Abiy's father was a farmer rather than a military officer or political leader, as some might expect from the background of a prominent political figure, is significant in understanding the early foundation of Abiy's worldview and leadership style.

Abiy was the 13th child of Ahmed Ali, who had multiple wives, and his mother, Tezeta Wolde, was of Amhara origin, although some sources indicate that she had converted to Islam after marrying Abiy's father. This mixture of cultures and religions, Abiy's mother being Christian and of Amhara descent, his father being Muslim and of Oromo descent, created a unique context for Abiy's upbringing. This complex familial and ethnic background likely influenced the way Abiy viewed Ethiopia's ethnic and religious diversity, but it also set the stage for his later political ambitions but controversial mixture of ethnic and national identity.

Despite this complex heritage, Abiy's relationship with his father is not one marked by open admiration or public recognition. Abiy has kept his personal relationship with his father relatively private, and there is little evidence that he speaks fondly or seeks to emulate his father's lifestyle. Abiy's father was not involved in the military or political circles, which often tend to play a key role in shaping Ethiopian leaders. Instead, he was a figure of local, rural life, focused on farming and community-based existence, representing a way of life that Abiy, as a national leader, has distanced himself from. While there is no explicit evidence of a strained or particularly close relationship between father and son, it's clear that Abiy's vision for Ethiopia diverges from his father's more traditional and localized existence.

Abiy Ahmed's leadership approach is not rooted in a deep commitment to ethnic reconciliation or an overt desire to heal the historical divisions that have long plagued Ethiopia. Instead, his political persona is shaped by a more personal ambition: to forge a nation that is united under his leadership and guided by his ideals, his desires, and his sense of purpose. Central to this vision is the beauty and serenity of his hometown, Beshasha, a place that seems to hold profound personal significance for him. This rural town, with its stunning landscapes, may serve as a metaphor for the ideal Ethiopia he seeks to create, one that is beautiful, unified, and orderly, yet centered around his personal legacy. Abiy's vision seems less about reconciling the fragmented ethnic communities of Ethiopia and more about uniting them in service of a national identity shaped by his personal ambition and leadership style.

While his father, Ahmed Ali, came from the Oromo ethnic group and lived a life that was emblematic of the traditional rural concerns and struggles of the Oromo people, Abiy's public persona and political trajectory do not seem to reflect a direct celebration of his father's background or the deeper traditions of the Oromo community. His father's life, rooted in the rural, agrarian ethos, was one of hard work and resilience, characteristics that no doubt shaped Abiy's early years. However, Abiy's political identity does not appear to be specifically molded by the traditional values or struggles of the Oromo people, nor does it prioritize ethnic unity in the way that some of his predecessors might have.

Instead, Abiy's leadership seems to revolve around a vision of a unified Ethiopia that transcends ethnic boundaries but does so on terms that are largely shaped by Abiy himself. His approach to politics is less about addressing the deep historical grievances between Ethiopia's many ethnic groups and more about uniting them under a singular, centralized narrative that emphasizes his personal aspirations and his belief in Ethiopia's potential. This approach can be seen in his ambitious reforms, his focus on modernization, and his self-assured, almost iconoclastic leadership style.

Abiy has often framed his role as a leader of transformation, emphasizing Ethiopia's natural beauty, its historical significance, and its future potential, but his vision is consistently aligned with his own personal legacy. Rather than seeking reconciliation through dialogue between Ethiopia's ethnic groups, his approach seems more focused on projecting an image of national unity through his own leadership and the centralization of power. This is not to say that Abiy rejects the notion of unity altogether; rather, his unity is one forged through his leadership, his narrative, and his ability to inspire devotion to his vision of Ethiopia's future.

A key aspect of this vision is how Abiy has portrayed himself as the man capable of overcoming Ethiopia's historical ethnic divisions, but his focus appears to be more on creating a strong, centralized state rather than promoting true ethnic reconciliation. He envisions a nation where the challenges of ethnic conflict are set aside in favor of a modern Ethiopia united under his guidance. For Abiy, this is not just about resolving ethnic grievances, but about forging a nation where his legacy as the unifying force is firmly established in the history of Ethiopia.

In many respects, Abiy's vision for Ethiopia reflects his own personal desires and the strong connection he feels to his hometown of Beshasha. His ties to the town, which represents a simpler, peaceful way of life, seem to inform his ideal of Ethiopia: a beautiful, unified country that harmonizes with its natural surroundings. This connection to nature and beauty is a hallmark of Abiy's public persona, and it contrasts sharply with the deeply political and divisive nature of the ethnic conflicts that have characterized Ethiopian politics for decades. His narrative does not aim to simply resolve ethnic tensions, but to transcend them, focusing instead on a vision of Ethiopia as a land of opportunity, beauty, and peace under his leadership.

This desire to transcend the ethnic divisions of Ethiopia is both a strength and a potential weakness in Abiy's leadership. On one hand, his ability to project a vision of unity has earned him praise internationally, culminating in his receiving the Nobel Peace Prize. However, his reluctance to fully embrace the complexities of Ethiopia's ethnic divisions has also led to criticisms. Critics argue that Abiy's approach has sometimes led to policies that exacerbate tensions rather than heal them, as his desire to consolidate power under a unified national narrative can overlook the intricacies of ethnic politics and the importance of addressing the specific needs and grievances of the country's diverse communities.

Abiy's public rhetoric often centers on themes of national pride and unity, but this rhetoric is heavily tied to his own identity as the figure leading Ethiopia into a new era. The emphasis on his personal legacy as the catalyst for Ethiopia's future is clear. His vision of Ethiopia, while filled with ambition and optimism, tends to place him at the center, rather than fostering a more inclusive, grassroots approach to unity. This approach is not necessarily about inclusivity in a traditional sense; it is about shaping Ethiopia in a way that reflects his own vision of leadership, and this vision is rooted in his personal experiences, especially in his hometown of Beshasha, and his belief in the natural and moral beauty of his country.

In this sense, Abiy's leadership can be understood as less about ethnic inclusivity and more about crafting a legacy that is deeply tied to his personal experiences, his view of Ethiopia's potential, and his desire to leave an indelible mark on the nation's history. He seeks to unify Ethiopia under a singular narrative that reflects his own identity as a leader, and in doing so, he shapes the country's future not as a mere reflection of its diverse peoples, but as a manifestation of his vision and legacy.

***

The Oromo Identity: A Complex Heritage

Abiy Ahmed's Oromo heritage is perhaps one of the most crucial elements of his identity, both personally and politically. He has consistently emphasized his roots in the Oromo community, pushing back against critics who have attempted to undermine or erase his Oromummaa (Oromo identity). This aspect of his identity is not merely a matter of ethnic pride; it is a defining feature of his leadership and political vision. For centuries, the Oromo people have faced marginalization in Ethiopia, their language, culture, and political power historically sidelined by successive regimes. Abiy's rise to the position of Prime Minister has been seen by many as a historic moment for the Oromo community, an opportunity to shift the narrative and bring them into the political mainstream.

However, Abiy's relationship with his Oromo identity is multilayered and complex. On the one hand, his leadership can be viewed as a response to the decades of exclusion and oppression that the Oromo people endured. His political rise, coupled with his public statements on the importance of recognizing and embracing Oromo identity, resonated deeply with those who viewed his ascension as a breakthrough. Abiy became a symbol of hope for many Oromos, as his leadership suggested that they might finally have a voice in the governance of the country. This sense of pride and empowerment is central to his political persona, and he has often used his Oromo identity as a source of legitimacy in his leadership.

At the same time, Abiy has sought to transcend the ethnic divisions that have long plagued Ethiopia. His vision for the country has been one of unity, a unified Ethiopia that can move past the deep ethnic and regional cleavages that have characterized its modern history. This ambition, however, has led to a paradox in his leadership. While Abiy has positioned himself as a leader for all Ethiopians, he has also been criticized for not sufficiently addressing the specific needs and grievances of the Oromo community, the very group that elevated him to power.

Abiy's political agenda is shaped not only by his desire to address ethnic tensions but also by his personal ambition and the need to secure his legacy. His shift away from the traditional, rural life of his father, who was a farmer in the small town of Beshasha, toward a more modern, progressive vision of Ethiopia reflects a deep personal transformation. Abiy's desire to be a leader who leaves a lasting mark on Ethiopia is evident in his push for modernization, technological advancement, and national unity. However, his focus on creating a modern Ethiopia is not purely ideological; it is also deeply tied to his own ego and desire for power. His approach to leadership has sometimes been described as top-down and authoritarian, with a strong emphasis on centralizing control and diminishing dissent.

This centralization of power and focus on personal legacy has often been in tension with his image as a reconciler of ethnic divisions. Abiy's leadership style is heavily influenced by his personal ambition, which often supersedes the collective aspirations of the people he governs. His public statements, policies, and political maneuvers suggest that Abiy is not only interested in uniting Ethiopia but in doing so under a vision that is unmistakably tied to his own personal image and influence. His emphasis on technology, the modernization of infrastructure, and a vision of economic growth are closely linked to his desire to be seen as a transformative leader, akin to historical figures who have left their mark on the country's future.

Despite the rhetoric of inclusivity and unity, Abiy's leadership has faced significant pushback from those who feel that his political agenda favors his personal ambitions over the needs of specific ethnic groups, particularly the Oromo. While Abiy has sought to present himself as a leader for all Ethiopians, many Oromo people have criticized him for not adequately addressing their unique concerns. Some argue that his policies, particularly around the decentralization of power and the management of regional autonomy, have fallen short in addressing the specific socio-political needs of the Oromo community. The complex dynamics of Abiy's leadership reveal that while he may have helped to elevate the Oromo into the national spotlight, his ability to translate this empowerment into tangible political benefits has been inconsistent.

In balancing his Oromo identity with his broader national vision, Abiy faces the dual challenge of maintaining the support of his Oromo base while also unifying Ethiopia's diverse ethnic and religious groups. On the one hand, his desire to integrate the Oromo identity into the fabric of the nation is a powerful part of his political appeal, especially among younger Oromos who view his rise as a victory for their community. On the other hand, his push for a unified, modern Ethiopia, one that seeks to overcome the divisions of ethnicity and religion, sometimes clashes with the reality of governance, where the specific grievances of various ethnic groups, including the Oromo, remain unresolved.

***

The Roots of Identity: Religion and Cultural Tensions

Abiy Ahmed's religious identity is shaped by his upbringing in a family marked by religious plurality. Born to a Muslim father and a Christian mother, Abiy grew up in a household where both Islam and Christianity were practiced. This dual religious heritage has had a profound impact on Abiy's worldview, yet his personal religious journey appears to diverge significantly from traditional Christian teachings, especially in the context of his leadership and policies.

Abiy identifies as a Pentecostal Christian, a denomination characterized by an emphasis on personal spiritual experiences, the active presence of the Holy Spirit, and a strong focus on evangelism, prophecy, and healing. Pentecostalism, like many other Christian traditions, encourages believers to care for the poor, practice compassion, and work towards social justice. However, Abiy's actions in leadership appear to be at odds with these fundamental Christian values, especially as he faces increasing criticism for the stark contrasts between his religious proclamations and his policies.

In his leadership, Abiy has espoused a vision of a modern, unified Ethiopia, yet this vision has often been marked by paradoxes. On one hand, Abiy has sought to project himself as a leader who values religious tolerance and inclusivity. He has emphasized the need for unity and national pride, often invoking Christian values to guide his leadership. He is an active member of the Ethiopian Full Gospel Believers' Church, where he occasionally preaches and teaches the Gospel, and his wife, Zinash Tayachew, is also a Christian who ministers as a gospel singer.

Yet, in his public and policy decisions, Abiy's actions have raised serious questions about the alignment of his leadership with the compassion and humility espoused by Christianity. One glaring example of this paradox is his approach to Ethiopia's growing poverty and inequality. While Abiy has claimed that the country has an agricultural surplus, particularly in wheat, many Ethiopians, especially in Addis Ababa, continue to struggle with hunger and deprivation. Instead of addressing these pressing needs, Abiy has made statements that seem to reflect a callous disregard for the suffering of his people, such as his suggestion to "eat bread, but don't eat too much," while billions of dollars are being spent on beautifying the capital city. At the same time, millions of young and old Ethiopians continue to die from poverty, hunger, and neglect.

This stark contrast between Abiy's rhetoric and his policies suggests a paradox at the heart of his leadership. As a Pentecostal Christian, he is expected to embody the teachings of Jesus Christ, which emphasize love for the poor, care for the marginalized, and the call to "feed the hungry" (Matthew 25:35). However, his leadership style has often been characterized by an authoritarian streak, with a focus on grandiose projects such as city beautification and infrastructure development, rather than addressing the urgent needs of Ethiopia's impoverished population. The destruction of poor people's homes to make way for luxurious developments, while millions live in dire conditions, further highlights the contradiction between his Christian identity and his political actions.

The Bible teaches believers to care for the poor and to avoid selfishness and excess. In the Old Testament, the prophet Isaiah condemned the oppression of the poor and the indulgence of the wealthy, stating: *"Is this not the fast that I choose: to lose the bonds of injustice, to undo the thongs of the yoke, to let the oppressed go free, and to break every yoke?"* (Isaiah 58:6). This teaching seems to stand in stark contrast to Abiy's focus on beautifying the city at the expense of those who are struggling to survive.

In addition, the Christian call for empathy and humility seems to clash with Abiy's more ego-driven leadership style, which prioritizes personal legacy, grandeur, and power. His policies and public statements often reflect a strong desire for recognition and a drive to build a legacy that is largely centered on his personal vision of Ethiopia's future, rather than the welfare of its people. This has raised questions about his sincerity in applying Christian values of humility and service to the poor, particularly when his actions often seem to prioritize his political image over the lives of Ethiopians who continue to suffer.

The Quran, which Abiy also grew up exposed to due to his father's Muslim heritage, speaks strongly about the value of charity and justice. In Surah Al-Baqara (2:177), it states: *"It is not righteousness that you turn your faces towards the East or the West, but righteousness is in one who believes in Allah, the Last Day, the Angels, the Book, and the Prophets, and gives of their wealth, in spite of their love for it, to relatives, orphans, the needy, the traveler, those who ask [for help], and for freeing slaves."* This verse underscores the importance of caring for the needy and those who are less fortunate, a value that should resonate with Abiy given his own exposure to Islamic teachings. Yet, his policies often appear to ignore the urgent need for such charitable actions, focusing instead on creating a highly visual, modernized image of Ethiopia that overlooks the suffering of the people.

The paradox is further compounded by Abiy's public persona, which combines elements of religious fervor with a focus on political power and legacy-building. He promotes an image of religious piety, yet his leadership practices often reveal a more pragmatic, authoritarian approach. Abiy's actions as a leader seem to reflect a complex tension between his religious identity and the demands of his political ambitions. While he claims to be motivated by Christian ideals, such as love and reconciliation, his policies, especially those that prioritize infrastructure projects over addressing the basic needs of Ethiopia's most vulnerable citizens, appear to betray the very principles of compassion and justice that lie at the heart of both Christianity and Islam.

In general, Abiy Ahmed's religious identity is intricately shaped by his Pentecostal Christian faith, his exposure to Islam through his father, and his complex leadership style. However, the paradoxes in his actions, especially in regard to poverty, inequality, and the marginalization of the poor, raise serious questions about the alignment of his policies with the core values of both Christianity and Islam. His focus on personal legacy, combined with his reluctance to directly address Ethiopia's deepest social issues, suggests a leadership style that, while steeped in religious rhetoric, is often at odds with the teachings of compassion, justice, and service to the poor that lie at the heart of both religions.

***

Beshasha, Jimma: A Small Town with Big Significance

Beshasha, though a small and relatively obscure town in the Jimma Zone of the Oromia region, holds great cultural significance. The region is known for its agricultural richness, particularly the cultivation of coffee, which plays a vital role in both Ethiopia's economy and its cultural heritage. The Oromo people, who make up the majority of the population in this region, have a deep connection to the land and a strong sense of cultural identity. Abiy's upbringing in such a setting exposed him to the realities of rural Ethiopia, where the struggles of everyday people often go unnoticed by the country's political elite.

The town of Beshasha, and the broader Jimma Zone, have been integral to the cultural and political developments of Ethiopia. The Oromo people have long been a significant force in Ethiopia's history, though they have often been marginalized by successive regimes. Abiy's rise to power as Ethiopia's first Oromo prime minister was a watershed moment in the country's history, but it was also a reflection of the shifting political currents in a nation on the verge of transformation.

***

Education and Early Development: Shaped by Change

Abiy Ahmed's early life was marked by ambition and imagination. As a young boy, he was known for dreaming big, often envisioning himself in luxurious situations far removed from the reality he experienced. When his mother would send him to the local market, Abiy would run, but in his mind, he imagined driving a beautiful car. He would sleep on a mattress-less bed, but in his imagination, he was living in a grand palace. These early dreams of success and grandeur would later become central to Abiy's personal narrative, especially as he rose to prominence in Ethiopian politics.

However, little is known about the specifics of Abiy's educational journey, especially during his secondary school and early college years. It is widely reported that he stopped formal schooling after grade 7. Some sources suggest that his education trajectory was significantly influenced by the Ethiopian People's Revolutionary Democratic Front (EPRDF). Through the intervention of the EPRDF, he was reportedly able to obtain recognition for his educational achievements, which included military service. These gaps in his education have led to skepticism surrounding his academic credentials. Many critics have accused Abiy of embellishing his education and even of plagiarism in his speeches. There have been allegations that his doctoral dissertation may have been copied from existing works, raising questions about the authenticity of his academic credentials.

Despite his limited formal education, Abiy's rise to political power is deeply intertwined with the societal changes occurring in Ethiopia during his formative years. The collapse of the Derg regime in the early 1990s and the subsequent establishment of the EPRDF set the stage for a new political order, but the country remained deeply scarred by its history of violence, division, and inequality. Abiy, who was coming of age during this transition, witnessed the political upheaval firsthand. These experiences profoundly shaped his worldview, instilling in him a sense of urgency to address Ethiopia's deep-rooted challenges. He was determined to contribute to the transformation of his country, and this desire for change pushed him toward political involvement.

During his tenure as Prime Minister, Abiy made several controversial statements regarding the state of Ethiopia's education system. In one instance, he openly told parliament that he wasn't focused on building universities, which led some critics to accuse him of not valuing higher education. Some claim that his own academic credentials are questionable, and this sentiment has fueled skepticism about his leadership and academic integrity. Abiy's speeches, at times, have only added fuel to this fire. For example, he once made a remark about the financial status of doctors, questioning why they were poor despite their intellectual pursuits, and comparing them unfavorably to wealthy merchants. This statement led many to see him as disparaging the value of intellectual achievement, reinforcing the idea that his approach to leadership and education was not grounded in the values of knowledge and intellectual rigor.

Abiy's speeches have at times been riddled with contradictions, further complicating the public's perception of his authenticity. Recently, there were claims that some of his speeches were word-for-word copies of those made by other famous figures, adding to the growing accusations of plagiarism. These controversies regarding his educational background and the authenticity of his words have led some to question whether Abiy's self-made image, one that projects power, intellect, and authority, is, in fact, a façade.

In general, while Abiy Ahmed's early life was filled with ambition and dreams of success, his educational background remains a contentious issue. From his limited formal education to the allegations of plagiarism, there are many questions surrounding the authenticity of Abiy's credentials. His statements about education and intellectualism have only compounded the doubts about his commitment to knowledge and the value of higher learning. These controversies are part of a broader narrative in which Abiy's personal ambitions and political leadership often seem at odds with the reality of Ethiopia's complex social and educational landscape.

***

A Military Career and a Path Toward Leadership

Abiy Ahmed's formative years in national service began in the early 1990s, when he joined the Oromo People's Democratic Organization (OPDO), the Oromo wing of the EPRDF coalition, during the final struggle against the Derg regime. In 1993, he officially enlisted in the Ethiopian National Defense Force (ENDF), specializing in intelligence and communications. His entry into the military was less a selfless act of national duty than a calculated choice to secure influence and upward mobility within the newly established order. In a force dominated by Tigrayan commanders, Abiy distinguished himself by quickly learning Tigrinya, not out of solidarity, but as a strategic move to integrate into the power structure and advance his career. His training in intelligence sharpened his understanding of strategy and control, tools he would later employ not for collective peace but for consolidating personal authority.

In 1995, Abiy served with the United Nations Assistance Mission for Rwanda (UNAMIR), a peacekeeping mission created after the genocide. His assignment in communications exposed him to international networks and the rhetoric of reconciliation, but these experiences did not cultivate in him a genuine conviction for peace. Instead, they provided exposure and credentials he would later leverage for political capital. His outlook remained fundamentally self-serving: he interpreted the lessons of Rwanda not as a call for healing but as evidence of how narratives of peace could be instrumentalized for legitimacy.

The turning point of his military career came during the 1998–2000 Eritrean–Ethiopian War. As a military intelligence officer, Abiy led operations mapping Eritrean positions and feeding critical intelligence to the Ethiopian command. This period solidified his reputation as ambitious and calculating. Rather than emerging from the war with humility about the cost of violence, he absorbed the lesson that war and diplomacy alike could be manipulated for personal gain. His later use of the peace agreement with Eritrea in 2018 reflected the same pragmatism, framing himself as a peacemaker on the international stage while leveraging the Nobel Peace Prize as a political shield at home, even as his government slid deeper into authoritarianism and civil war.

Within the ENDF, Abiy also met his future wife, Zinash Tayachew, an Amhara woman from Gondar who was serving as a fellow officer. Their marriage was a personal union but also carried symbolic weight, crossing Ethiopia's entrenched ethnic divides. While this was presented as a sign of unity, Abiy increasingly used such personal narratives as part of his political image-making. Together, they have four children, three daughters and one adopted son, whose presence humanized his public profile at the same time that he pursued divisive policies.

Through his years in uniform, Abiy did not emerge as a soldier committed to reconciliation, but as a political opportunist shaped by conflict and ambition. His service in intelligence and international missions gave him a unique skill set in manipulation, narrative construction, and the projection of authority. Rather than being molded into a statesman devoted to peace, these experiences became the foundation of his ego-driven pursuit of power.

***

Early Political Career and Contributions to Peacebuilding

Abiy Ahmed began his political journey as a member of the Oromo Democratic Party (ODP), which has been the ruling party in the Oromia Region since 1991. The ODP is also one of the four parties that form the Ethiopian People's Revolutionary Democratic Front (EPRDF), the ruling coalition in Ethiopia. Abiy quickly rose through the ranks, becoming a member of the ODP's central committee. His political influence expanded further when he was elected to the executive committee of the EPRDF, a body that oversees the coalition's policy direction.

In the 2010 national elections, Abiy was elected as a representative of the Agaro district to the House of Peoples' Representatives, the lower chamber of the Ethiopian Federal Parliamentary Assembly. During his tenure in parliament, Abiy found himself at the forefront of efforts to address escalating religious conflicts between Muslims and Christians in the Jimma Zone of Oromia. These confrontations, often violent, resulted in loss of life, property, and strained interfaith relations. In response, Abiy took a proactive approach, collaborating with religious institutions and community elders to mediate and promote reconciliation in the region. His leadership led to the creation of the "Religious Forum for Peace," a platform aimed at developing long-term solutions for fostering harmonious relations between the Muslim and Christian communities.

In 2014, Abiy's influence in the political and academic spheres grew as he was appointed the director-general of the Science and Technology Information Center (STIC), a government research institute established in 2011. In this role, he focused on fostering innovation and research in Ethiopia's science and technology sectors. The following year, Abiy's political career advanced further as he was appointed an executive member of the ODP. In the same year, he was re-elected to the House of Peoples' Representatives, this time representing his home district of Gomma.

***

Language, Identity, and Religion

Abiy Ahmed's leadership, as seen through the lens of his public speeches, actions, and political strategies, presents a paradox when examined from a Christian ethical standpoint. His leadership is marked by inconsistencies, manipulation of ethnic divisions, and an apparent lack of accountability, which seem to be at odds with the values of truthfulness, integrity, and unity that are central to Christian teachings.

One of Abiy's most significant assets is his multilingualism. Fluent in Oromo, Amharic, and Tigrinya, Abiy has been able to speak directly to Ethiopia's diverse ethnic groups, which has allowed him to build a powerful image as a leader who can bridge divides. However, this linguistic versatility has also allowed him to engage in what some critics describe as deceptive political maneuvers. By speaking different languages to different ethnic groups, he has been accused of telling people what they want to hear rather than upholding a consistent and honest position. Abiy's ability to appeal to each ethnic group in their native tongue, while avoiding meaningful follow-through on promises, has made him appear manipulative. For example, Abiy's promises regarding the GERD and his interactions with Egypt demonstrate this strategic duplicity. While publicly reassuring Egyptian President Abdel Fattah el-Sisi that Ethiopia would not harm Egypt's interests concerning the Nile River, Abiy's government later found itself at odds with Egypt over the dam's construction and water usage. His rhetoric, seemingly aimed at placating the Egyptians, contrasted sharply with the realities of Ethiopian domestic policy, where the GERD is a symbol of national pride and economic progress. This contradiction between his statements and actions reflects a leader who is willing to say whatever is necessary in the moment to maintain support, even if it means abandoning previous commitments.

Furthermore, Abiy's shifting positions on issues of Ethiopian identity and regional autonomy further highlight the inconsistencies in his leadership. On the one hand, he has promoted the idea of a unified Ethiopia, dismissing the notion of a "plural Ethiopian identity" and instead emphasizing the singular identity of an "Ethiopian citizen." On the other hand, he has also made statements supporting regional autonomy, as seen in his controversial comments about the future status of Welkait and the Amhara-Tigray conflict. These conflicting messages to various groups, where he promises the Oromo community that his government represents their interests, while also pushing for a unified Ethiopian identity to the Amhara, have led many to question his authenticity and long-term commitment to national unity.

From a Christian perspective, Abiy's leadership style raises concerns about his adherence to the moral and ethical principles emphasized in the Bible. Scripture teaches that leaders should be truthful, consistent, and accountable. In Proverbs 12:22, the Bible clearly states, "The Lord detests lying lips, but he delights in people who are trustworthy." Ephesians 4:25 echoes this sentiment, calling for Christians to "speak truthfully to your neighbor," reinforcing the Christian imperative to uphold honesty in all interactions. However, Abiy's rhetoric often seems to serve his personal political agenda rather than a higher moral purpose, as he adapts his words to suit different audiences without regard for consistency or truthfulness.

In James 1:8, the Bible warns that "A double-minded man is unstable in all his ways." Abiy's double-speak on issues like ethnicity, governance, and national identity paints him as unstable and lacking in the consistency that Christian leadership demands. A true Christian leader is called to lead with integrity, not to manipulate and deceive for personal gain. Abiy's apparent use of language to placate different ethnic groups while making contradictory statements behind closed doors undermines this biblical expectation.

Moreover, Christian teachings emphasize the importance of fulfilling one's promises and being accountable for one's words. Matthew 5:37 instructs, "Let your 'Yes' be 'Yes,' and your 'No,' 'No.'" This call for consistency and honesty in speech is a stark contrast to Abiy's leadership style, which appears to bend with political convenience.

Abiy's leadership is also in tension with the Christian calling to serve the people selflessly. In Mark 9:35, Jesus teaches, "Anyone who wants to be first must be the very last, and the servant of all." Christian leadership involves self-sacrifice and putting the needs of others above one's own ambitions. However, Abiy's behavior often suggests that his focus is on preserving and consolidating his own power, sometimes at the expense of the country's stability and the well-being of its people. His disregard for the suffering of Ethiopians, such as the ongoing humanitarian crisis exacerbated by internal conflict, the starvation in parts of the country, and the displacement of millions, indicates a leader who prioritizes his image and political legacy over the welfare of his people.

Finally, the Bible calls for leaders to be agents of unity rather than division. Romans 12:10 speaks to this ideal: "Be devoted to one another in love. Honor one another above yourselves." Abiy's contradictory approach to ethnic and regional issues, where he plays different ethnic groups against one another for political gain, stands in stark contrast to the Christian value of promoting unity and peace. His promises to the Oromo community, his efforts to please the Amhara, and his shifting stance on national unity indicate a lack of a coherent vision for a truly united Ethiopia. Instead, it seems he is more concerned with maintaining his power and satisfying short-term political interests, rather than working for the long-term peace and harmony that Christian teachings advocate for.

Abiy Ahmed's leadership reveals a profound disconnect between his political strategies and the Christian principles of honesty, integrity, and unity. While his multilingualism and political agility have allowed him to gain influence, they also serve to mask the contradictions and inconsistencies in his leadership. By prioritizing personal ambition and political maneuvering over truthfulness, accountability, and selfless service, Abiy's actions appear to diverge from the biblical values that should guide a Christian leader. His leadership may serve his political goals in the short term, but it falls short of the ethical standards set by scripture.

***

From Hope to Controversy: The Rise, Deception, and Challenges

In 2018, Abiy Ahmed's appointment as Prime Minister of Ethiopia marked a dramatic turning point in the country's political landscape. The resignation of Hailemariam Desalegn, following increasing political unrest and protests, left a power vacuum that Abiy, with the strategic assistance of several key political figures, was able to fill. The rise of Abiy to power was not solely the result of his personal efforts, but also due to the support of prominent leaders within the ruling coalition, particularly Lemma Megersa, Degu Andargachew, Demeke Mekonnen, and others. It was Lemma, the then-leader of the Oromo People's Democratic Organization (OPDO), who played a pivotal role in Abiy's ascension. As the head of OPDO, Lemma held the keys to the prime ministership within Ethiopia's ruling coalition, the Ethiopian People's Revolutionary Democratic Front

(EPRDF), as it was customary for the chairperson of the largest party to be nominated as prime minister. In an unexpected move, Lemma handed over the chairmanship of OPDO to Abiy just before the election, positioning him as the prime ministerial candidate.

This maneuver, while seen as strategic, was not without opposition. Jawar Mohammed, a powerful figure in the Oromo political landscape and a critic of the political establishment, publicly expressed his frustration over Lemma's decision. Jawar, who had significant influence among the Oromo diaspora and the youth movement, believed that Lemma's choice of Abiy as the OPDO's candidate was a political betrayal. Jawar had envisioned Lemma himself becoming the prime minister, not Abiy, and he became one of the most vocal critics of Abiy's rise to power. Despite this, the alliance between Lemma, Degu Andargachew, and other key figures within the ruling party facilitated Abiy's smooth ascension to the prime ministership. This alliance, however, would later unravel as Abiy consolidated his power, eventually turning against many of those who helped him achieve his political position.

Abiy's appointment as prime minister marked a historic moment for Ethiopia. For the first time in the country's history, an Oromo, a group that had been politically marginalized for much of Ethiopia's history, assumed the highest office in the land. This was seen as a moment of great hope for millions of Ethiopians, particularly for the Oromo people, who had long been excluded from political power and were often subjected to systemic oppression. Abiy's rise to power symbolized the possibility of a new era of inclusivity and equity, offering a sense of justice and acknowledgment to a community that had historically been sidelined. Many believed that Abiy would finally give voice to the Oromo people and their longstanding grievances.

However, Abiy's leadership also marked the beginning of a period of intense political maneuvering and personal glorification. Even though he was hailed as a symbol of hope and change, Abiy's rise to power was not entirely without controversy. His leadership style quickly became charracterized by contradictions, and his promises of reform seemed to clash with the political realities unfolding under his watch. Abiy, while initially presenting himself as a leader committed to inclusivity and reconciliation, began to make moves that would eventually alienate many of his early supporters and collaborators.

One of the most significant shifts in Abiy's leadership came with his dramatic political reforms. Within months of taking office, Abiy took steps that were seen as groundbreaking in Ethiopia's political landscape. He released several political prisoners, including high-profile figures like Andargachew Tsige, who had been imprisoned under the previous government. Abiy also welcomed opposition groups back into the political fold, lifting media restrictions and pushing for a more open political environment. These reforms were viewed as a major break from the authoritarian tendencies of Ethiopia's past and were welcomed by many as signs of a new era of political freedom and democracy. For a time, Abiy's leadership seemed to promise a more inclusive and peaceful future for Ethiopia.

Abiy's political reforms, however, were not without their challenges and contradictions. While he made strides in creating a more open political system, the changes also led to growing tensions within the ruling coalition and the broader Ethiopian political establishment. Abiy's moves to release prisoners, dismantle the former party structure, and promote a more centralized vision of governance quickly alienated key figures within the EPRDF and other regional parties. His push for national unity, while appealing to many, seemed to be built more on Abiy's personal vision of Ethiopia's future rather than a consensus-driven political process. The power dynamics shifted rapidly, and those who had supported Abiy's rise to power, particularly Lemma Megersa, Degu Andargachew, and other leaders , found themselves marginalized or at odds with Abiy's increasingly authoritarian leadership.

The same year that Abiy was awarded the Nobel Peace Prize, Ethiopia's internal political situation began to unravel. While Abiy had presented himself as a unifying figure, the country's ethnic tensions escalated. The Oromo, Amhara, and Tigray communities, among others, were increasingly at odds over issues of identity, autonomy, and governance. Abiy's centralization of power, his dismantling of the EPRDF, and his failure to adequately address the deep-seated grievances of Ethiopia's various ethnic groups contributed to growing divisions. The tensions ultimately erupted into violent conflicts, particularly in the Tigray region, where the Tigray People's Liberation Front (TPLF) was engaged in armed opposition against Abiy's government.

Abiy's political journey, while marked by early promises of peace and reform, has been deeply complicated by his authoritarian tendencies, his betrayal of former allies, and his failure to navigate the complex ethnic and political landscape of Ethiopia. While his rise to power represented a hopeful moment for many, the years that followed would reveal a leader who was willing to use political manipulation and deception to consolidate his authority. The Nobel Peace Prize he received was perhaps the peak of his international acclaim, but it did little to address the underlying issues of governance, ethnic division, and political instability that have plagued Ethiopia under his leadership. Ultimately, Abiy's tenure as prime minister has become a story of broken promises, betrayal, and the difficult balance between power and reconciliation in a deeply divided country.

***

Physical Fitness, Public Image, and Leadership: A Closer Look at Abiy Ahmed's Persona

Abiy Ahmed's public persona, which balances fitness, personal values, and political leadership, presents an image carefully constructed to appeal to a diverse range of domestic and international audiences. At first glance, his emphasis on physical health and family values, combined with his high-profile political achievements, paints the picture of a well-rounded, energetic, and relatable leader. However, a closer examination of Abiy's actions, both in the realm of fitness and his personal life, reveals a complex and at times inconsistent narrative that challenges the authenticity of the image he strives to project.

Abiy Ahmed has frequently positioned himself as an advocate for physical well-being, aligning with the long-held belief that a healthy body is essential for a healthy mind. His advocacy for fitness serves multiple purposes, but more than a genuine commitment to physical health, it often appears to be a carefully curated element of his public relations strategy. Abiy has been photographed at various public sports events, particularly soccer games, where his presence has been highlighted in the national media. These events, while reinforcing his image as a physically active leader, seem less about personal fitness and more about crafting an image of youthfulness, vigor, and relatability.

For instance, one such event in which he was seen scoring a goal in a friendly soccer match became a significant talking point in the Ethiopian media. This moment, accompanied by media celebrations of his goal, added to the political narrative that Abiy is not only politically astute but also youthful and energetic. His involvement in sports has been interpreted by critics as strategically timed to reinforce the perception of a leader who is deeply connected to Ethiopia's youth. However, such spectacles often leave doubts about the authenticity of his engagement in these activities, with many questioning whether they reflect a genuine passion for sports or whether they are simply a form of staged publicity.

Furthermore, Abiy's close relationships with prominent athletes further contribute to the image-building process. He often poses for photographs with famous sports figures, highlighting his connection to Ethiopia's sports culture. These moments, carefully crafted for media consumption, contribute to the broader narrative that Abiy is a man of the people, youthful, dynamic, and forward-thinking. However, this aspect of his leadership has been criticized for resembling more of an ego-driven attempt to craft a specific image rather than a true representation of his leadership style. Abiy's sporadic appearances at these events, and the way they are publicly staged, suggest that his fitness persona may be less about personal commitment to health and more about enhancing his public image.

***

The Family-Oriented Leader: A Deliberate Public Persona?

Abiy's public image as a family-oriented leader is another area where his political strategy meets public relations. Family values are central to Ethiopian society, and Abiy has skillfully utilized this to present himself as a caring and compassionate leader who balances the demands of national governance with the priorities of family life. His wife, Zinash, and their children are frequently featured in media outlets, and Abiy often speaks about the importance of maintaining strong familial bonds. This portrayal of Abiy as a family man, dedicated to his loved ones, aligns with traditional Ethiopian values, making him a relatable figure for the masses.

However, like his fitness narrative, his family-oriented image has not gone without scrutiny. Critics argue that Abiy's political decisions have sometimes conflicted with the very family values he champions. For example, while he presents himself as a protector of families, many of his policies have disproportionately affected the poorest segments of Ethiopian society. His administration has been involved in large-scale displacement projects that have forced families to relocate, often under harsh circumstances. The contradiction between his portrayal of caring leadership and the impact of his policies on vulnerable families has raised questions about the sincerity of his personal values.

Abiy's speeches on family life often come across as attempts to project stability and normalcy during a time of political turmoil. His family values rhetoric serves as a tool for humanizing him in the eyes of the public, presenting him as a stable and nurturing figure. However, given the upheaval caused by his government's policies, particularly in marginalized communities, the portrayal of Abiy as a devoted family man has started to lose credibility among some segments of the population. This tension between his public persona and his political actions reinforces the perception that Abiy's focus on family is a part of a broader strategy to cultivate an image that appeals to Ethiopian traditionalism rather than a reflection of his personal life.

At the heart of the critique against Abiy Ahmed is the growing discrepancy between the image he crafts and the reality of his leadership. His portrayal as a leader deeply committed to Ethiopia's well-being often contrasts sharply with his policies, which have been criticized for failing to address the structural issues facing the country's poorest and most vulnerable populations. Abiy's frequent public appearances, where he distributes food to the needy or engages in other philanthropic activities, have been framed as demonstrations of his commitment to Ethiopia's poorest citizens. However, reports have surfaced that reveal a starkly different picture, one in which Abiy's leadership has been linked to decisions that exacerbate poverty, displace communities, and increase instability.

For example, his government's involvement in large-scale urban development projects, which have led to the forced displacement of thousands of families, highlights a troubling contradiction between his rhetoric and his actions. In some cases, the communities affected by these projects are left without adequate compensation or resettlement plans, further contributing to the vulnerability of the very people he claims to support. The media portrayal of Abiy as a leader who prioritizes the well-being of the poor clashes with the reality on the ground, where his policies seem to prioritize development and modernization over the basic rights of Ethiopia's marginalized groups.

In addition, Abiy's leadership has faced criticism for its authoritarian tendencies. While he initially presented himself as a reformist leader, opening up political space and promoting national unity, his subsequent actions have indicated a shift toward more centralized control. These contradictions have further fueled skepticism about his true motivations and the effectiveness of his governance. Abiy's narrative of progressive leadership, rooted in a vision of reconciliation and peace, is increasingly at odds with the more authoritarian aspects of his administration, including the targeting of opposition groups and the use of military force to suppress dissent.

***

A Complex Legacy: Abiy Ahmed's Image and Ethiopia's Future

Abiy Ahmed's legacy is already emerging as one of the most troubling in Ethiopia's modern history, shaped less by genuine reform than by ignorance, deception, and a relentless obsession with image-making. While his name is often associated with the 2019 Nobel Peace Prize, awarded for his role in brokering a peace agreement with Eritrea, this achievement has since come under scrutiny as symbolic rather than substantive. The award elevated his international profile, granting him a reputation as a peacemaker, yet the reality inside Ethiopia told a far different story. His reforms, initially hailed as historic steps toward opening the political space and reconciling with opposition groups, quickly dissolved into authoritarian patterns, violent crackdowns, and the silencing of critics. What began as promises of transformation soon revealed themselves as hollow performances designed to impress external audiences while neglecting the deeper crises of the Ethiopian state.

The contradictions between Abiy's cultivated persona and his policies are glaring. He has projected himself as a modern, youthful leader, often photographed jogging, lifting weights, or surrounded by family seeking to embody a narrative of vitality, compassion, and unity. Yet this carefully managed image has masked a government plagued by heavy-handed tactics, widespread corruption, ethnic violence, and the brutal suppression of dissent. His ignorance of Ethiopia's complex historical and cultural balances has been matched by a tendency to substitute rhetoric for strategy, leaving the country fractured along deeper ethnic and political lines. In place of serious structural reform, Abiy has relied on grand speeches, symbolic gestures, and empty promises that conceal more than they reveal.

What makes his legacy particularly alarming is the depth of deception that underpins it. Abiy's claim to be a reformer contrasts sharply with his government's record: mass displacement, famine in conflict zones, internet blackouts, imprisonment of journalists, and unchecked violence by state and paramilitary forces. His rhetoric of unity has been accompanied by divisive governance, in which selective alliances and targeted repression perpetuate Ethiopia's instability. In this sense, his leadership reflects a dangerous pattern where public image and propaganda eclipse meaningful action, and where the leader's personal ego overshadows the real needs of his people.

The most frightening element of Abiy's legacy lies in how his ignorance and deception have fueled one of the gravest humanitarian crises in Ethiopia's modern era. The Tigray War (2020–2022) left hundreds of thousands dead, millions displaced, and entire regions devastated by famine and atrocity. Instead of acknowledging responsibility or seeking genuine reconciliation, Abiy's government doubled down on secrecy, disinformation campaigns, and relentless denial of abuses. His strategy of silencing independent media, controlling narratives through state propaganda, and portraying himself as both victim and savior demonstrates a calculated manipulation of truth. International recognition, such as the Nobel Prize, was quickly repurposed as a shield against accountability, while inside Ethiopia, voices of dissent were crushed under the weight of military force. The war not only shattered the country's fragile trust in its institutions but also exposed Abiy's legacy as one defined by cruelty masked in rhetoric, a legacy where national suffering is exploited for personal and political survival.

Even in his broader political trajectory, Abiy's emphasis on self-promotion over substance has left the country more vulnerable. He has succeeded in reshaping Ethiopia's political discourse, but often in ways that deepen suspicion and polarize communities. His obsession with projecting a multifaceted identity, fitness enthusiast, devout believer, family man, compassionate visionary, has created a veneer of authenticity that distracts from the failures of his governance. The result is a legacy not of reform but of deception, where the appearance of leadership overshadows the absence of genuine solutions.

Ultimately, Abiy Ahmed's legacy may be remembered not for the peace prize or the rhetoric of renewal, but for the widening gap between what he claimed to represent and what he delivered. His reliance on ignorance of Ethiopia's deeper social complexities, combined with his mastery of image-based politics, risks leaving behind a country more fractured, impoverished, and distrustful than when he rose to power. Far from being the unifier and reformer he once appeared to be, Abiy stands as a cautionary figure: a leader whose deception and self-serving vision turned hope into disillusion, and whose legacy continues to haunt the future of Ethiopia.

***

Psychological Perspective: A Leader Caught Between Image and Reality

From a psychological perspective, Abiy Ahmed's leadership and persona can be understood as the manifestation of deep psychological contradictions, driven by a complex interplay of personal ambition, insecurity, and the pressures of power. Leaders who engage in deception, manipulation, and performative behaviors often do so as a way to construct a persona that shields them from their own vulnerabilities. In Abiy's case, his public image, one of fitness, family values, and compassion may be a strategic construction aimed at projecting an idealized self, masking the underlying insecurities or fears that influence his governance.

Psychologically, such behaviors can stem from a deep need for control, especially in individuals who face significant internal conflict. Abiy's childhood, spent in poverty and surrounded by socio-political instability, may have contributed to a desire to redefine himself and his circumstances. This could manifest in the public display of power, wealth, and fitness, as well as a carefully curated narrative of leadership. In this sense, Abiy may be seeking validation and a sense of mastery over his environment, using his position of power to construct an image of success and competence. These performances might also be a way to cope with the overwhelming challenges and contradictions inherent in his role, creating a psychological shield from the stresses of leadership.

From an expert point of view, Abiy Ahmed's approach to governance also reflects the psychological mechanisms of narcissism and authoritarianism. Narcissistic tendencies are often characterized by a desire for admiration, grandiosity, and a lack of empathy for others. Abiy's frequent contradictions, including his promises of inclusivity followed by divisive policies, suggest a disconnect between his words and actions, which is often a hallmark of narcissistic behavior. Such leaders seek adulation and control, often presenting themselves as benevolent and capable while failing to address the deeper structural issues they face. This discrepancy can create a sense of disillusionment among those who initially supported them, as the leaders' inability to match their public image with their policies erodes trust.

Abiy's authoritarian tendencies are also evident in his governance. Authoritarian leaders typically view dissent as a threat to their control and often resort to manipulation, repression, and deceit to maintain power. His approach to dealing with opposition, whether it be through political suppression or manipulation of ethnic groups, indicates a need to suppress challenges to his authority. Such leaders often employ deception and cruelty as tools to maintain control, believing that these strategies ensure stability and dominance. Abiy's actions, such as the political repression of various groups and the use of state power to silence critics, align with the psychological traits of authoritarianism, where loyalty is demanded, and opposition is treated as a personal betrayal.

Additionally, psychiatric theory suggests that leaders who engage in such deception may suffer from a dissonance between their public persona and their private psyche. This dissonance can lead to cognitive distortions and a false sense of invulnerability. For Abiy, this might explain his willingness to promise one thing to different audiences, creating a series of contradictions that he believes he can manipulate without facing long-term consequences. Such behavior may be driven by a profound need to maintain an image of control and omnipotence, masking feelings of inadequacy or vulnerability.

The psychological toll of holding power in such a manner is often significant. Abiy's personal brand, built on charisma and idealized portrayals of strength, beauty, and family values, requires constant maintenance. This relentless performance can lead to burnout, psychological strain, and a greater willingness to engage in increasingly deceptive behaviors to protect that image. Leaders who rely on the "cult of personality" often find themselves trapped in a cycle of self-promotion, where every decision and action is weighed against the need to sustain their public persona.

Abiy's leadership style exemplifies the profound psychological complexities of power. His external projection of unity, peace, and reform contrasts sharply with the internal contradictions of his governance, where control, manipulation, and deception play central roles. These inconsistencies are not merely political strategies; they are psychological mechanisms that allow Abiy to navigate the pressures of leadership while simultaneously grappling with his own insecurities and desires for control.

In conclusion, from both a psychological and psychiatric standpoint, Abiy Ahmed's leadership reflects a deep-seated need for validation, control, and personal legacy. His tendency to deceive, manipulate, and create contradictory narratives can be seen as coping mechanisms for the psychological stress and insecurity associated with holding such immense power. The ultimate challenge for Abiy, both as a leader and as a person, will be whether he can reconcile the image he has constructed with the deep, systemic reforms Ethiopia needs to heal and move forward. Without addressing the psychological factors driving his behavior, his leadership risks becoming increasingly detached from the realities of governance, further alienating those he aims to serve.

***

CHAPTER 2

Behind the Spotlight: The Life of Abiy Ahmed's Family

The Beginning

Zinash Tayachew was born on January 13, 1978, in the historic city of Gondar, located in the Amhara region of Ethiopia. Gondar, often called the "Camelot of Ethiopia," was where she developed a deep connection to her country's history and culture. She was raised in a family that valued education and community, and it was these values that would later influence her choices. However, Gondar also represents a region that, over time, has experienced significant political and social struggles, particularly within the context of ethnic identity and power dynamics in Ethiopia.

Growing up in Gondar, Zinash witnessed firsthand the challenges faced by the Amhara people, a region historically significant but often overshadowed by other ethnic groups, especially as Ethiopia's political landscape evolved over the years. Despite the turbulent history, she found a path that led her to military service, something relatively uncommon for women in her community at the time.

***

First Lady: Meeting Abiy Ahmed

While serving in the Ethiopian military, Zinash met Abiy Ahmed, a young officer with a vision to bring Ethiopia together. At the time, Abiy was seen as someone who could transcend ethnic boundaries, as he was of mixed Oromo and Amhara heritage. Despite coming from different ethnic backgrounds, their relationship blossomed as they both shared a commitment to Ethiopia's future. Their bond was strengthened by their shared values of service and leadership.

However, what was often overlooked was the context of their relationship: Abiy's rise in the political landscape coincided with shifting power dynamics in Ethiopia. His rise to prominence, particularly as Prime Minister, involved a controversial approach to federalism and ethnic politics, including the handling of the relationship between the Amhara and Tigray regions. These issues would soon spill over into the public sphere and deeply affect the lives of the Ahmed family.

***

The Silent First Lady

After Abiy Ahmed became Prime Minister in 2018, the life of Zinash Tayachew shifted dramatically as she assumed the role of First Lady of Ethiopia, a position laden with both prestige and public responsibility. She quickly moved into areas expected of her office, advocating for women's empowerment, promoting children's education, and highlighting health care initiatives. These efforts earned her recognition in some circles, yet they were overshadowed by her striking silence in the face of Ethiopia's intensifying ethnic turmoil, particularly in her home region of Amhara. For many Ethiopians, and especially for the Amhara community, her muted response to the violence and marginalization of her people was jarring. Where others expected a voice of advocacy, they instead saw absence. This silence was interpreted by some as a betrayal, by others as ignorance of the depth of the suffering, and by still others as tacit agreement with her husband's agenda, even as atrocities mounted in the region she came from.

As Abiy pressed forward with his political reforms, policies that many viewed as advancing Oromo nationalist ambitions, Amhara voices grew increasingly uneasy. The Amhara, who had historically occupied a central and sometimes dominant place in Ethiopia's political hierarchy, felt increasingly excluded from national decision-making under Abiy's administration. Zinash, by virtue of her identity as an Amhara woman from Gondar, was uniquely positioned to acknowledge this growing alienation and lend her voice to the plight of her people. Yet her public persona remained carefully aligned with her husband's, avoiding any open criticism or even acknowledgment of the fear, displacement, and violence that consumed Amhara towns and villages. The contrast between her advocacy for children's schooling and health programs, and her refusal to address the killing of children and families in her own region, made her silence appear not merely passive but complicit.

Abiy's move to weaken ethnic federalism, a system designed under the 1995 FDRE Constitution to grant autonomy and recognition to Ethiopia's diverse nationalities, fueled this perception of betrayal. For the Amhara, the dismantling of ethnic protections was not a technical reform but a direct threat to their political and cultural security. Zinash's unwillingness to stand publicly with her community gave the impression that she prioritized the preservation of her husband's carefully constructed image of authority over the defense of her people's dignity and safety. In the eyes of many Amhara, her silence was not neutrality but a moral failure, a choice to ignore suffering rather than confront the contradictions within the government she represented.

Her role as First Lady, therefore, cannot be separated from the broader political trajectory of Abiy's administration. To some, Zinash's silence signaled a calculated survival strategy, an unwillingness to challenge power structures even when they inflicted devastation on her homeland. To others, it revealed a deeper alignment with her husband's ambitions, even at the expense of the Amhara people. Either way, her silence became a symbol of abandonment, reinforcing the sense that Ethiopia's ruling elite had turned their backs on the very communities they claimed to protect. In this context, Zinash Tayachew's legacy risks being remembered not for her social programs but for her refusal to speak when her people needed her most.

The divide between the Amhara community and Zinash's actions, or lack thereof, has been particularly pronounced during times of violence and ethnic conflict. As the political situation deteriorated in Ethiopia, with violence erupting between ethnic groups, some critics questioned why the First Lady, a woman with such an influential position, was not more vocal in calling for peace and justice for her people. Many Amhara people, who had been proud of Zinash's achievements before her rise to First Lady, found it increasingly difficult to reconcile her silence with the struggles their community faced.

***

A Complex and Troubled Legacy

Zinash Tayachew's legacy, much like that of her husband, cannot be told without reckoning with the shadow it casts. Though she has been credited with certain contributions in education, health, and women's rights, these achievements often appear pale and distant when weighed against her silence during the darkest hours of Ethiopia's turmoil. For the Amhara people in particular, her absence in moments of unspeakable suffering is not viewed as neutrality, but as betrayal. To them, she is not merely a bystander, but a symbol of complicity in a regime that has overseen their marginalization, violence, and displacement. Her legacy, instead of being remembered as one of courage and moral leadership, is etched in the memory of silence, a silence that deepened wounds rather than healing them.

The Amhara see in Zinash an emblem of the ruling order that stands aloof from their struggles. Their reality has been shaped by massacres, forced evictions, and an erosion of political rights, while she has spoken only in broad and carefully measured terms about peace and unity. To those whose families have been broken, whose lands have been seized, and whose children have been buried, her silence feels like a refusal to acknowledge their pain. It is not the absence of words alone, but the absence of solidarity in the very hour when solidarity mattered most. Her legacy among the Amhara is therefore not that of a defender, but of an absentee voice in a time of fire and blood.

Her defenders argue that her broader vision transcends ethnic boundaries—that her devotion to education, her advocacy for women's empowerment, and her support for national peace initiatives ought to be remembered as noble. Yet such praise rings hollow when placed beside the suffering of her own people, who expected not only symbolic gestures but a clear stand against injustice. The truth is that her silence has come to outweigh her accomplishments, and her reluctance to confront the violence visited upon her community has created an unbridgeable gulf between her and those she was expected to represent. What could have been remembered as a legacy of courage has instead hardened into a narrative of distance, timidity, and complicity.

The paradox of Zinash's story lies in her dual role: as First Lady of the nation and as a daughter of a people under siege. In choosing to lean toward the rhetoric of unity promoted by her husband's administration, she distanced herself from the Amhara cause, effectively aligning with power rather than conscience. This choice has stained her image with the perception that personal ambition and political convenience mattered more than ethnic solidarity and justice. In the court of public opinion, her silence has been as loud as the cries of her people, and history will likely remember her more for what she did not say than for what she accomplished.

Her tenure as First Lady, therefore, is not merely defined by programs or campaigns but by the chasm between rhetoric and reality. Addis Ababa may celebrate her for dignity and grace, but in the villages and towns scarred by violence, her name evokes disappointment, anger, and disillusionment. Zinash's legacy is not simply "complex"—it is one marred by a failure to rise to the moral challenges of her time. In a nation where ethnic politics defines survival, her reluctance to speak for the Amhara has come to symbolize abandonment.

In the end, Zinash Tayachew's story is less about personal achievement and more about the haunting power of silence. It is a cautionary tale of how proximity to power can strip away authenticity and tether a leader's identity to complicity. Her silence during Ethiopia's most turbulent years has not preserved her dignity—it has eroded it. For many, her legacy will not be a tapestry woven with achievements in education or women's rights, but rather a reminder of the bitter truth: when her people cried out, she turned away.

Thus, her story mirrors the painful realities of Ethiopia's fractured identity, where national duty is often wielded as a shield for political silence, and where the cost of inaction is measured not in policy failures but in lives lost. Zinash's legacy is therefore less a beacon of inspiration than a warning about the corrosive effects of silence in the face of oppression.

***

CHAPTER 3

The "Stabbing" of Allies

The Relationship Between Abiy Ahmed and Lemma Megersa

The political trajectories of Abiy Ahmed and Lemma Megersa are intricately linked, particularly within the context of the Oromo protests and the subsequent political reforms that ushered Abiy into the role of Prime Minister. Both men rose as symbols of hope for Ethiopia's Oromo people, promising to address their grievances, unify the country, and pave the way for significant political change. Their partnership, however, would ultimately unravel, revealing deeper tensions within Ethiopia's shifting political landscape.

Born in 1970 in Welega Province, Oromia, Lemma Megersa's path to political prominence was shaped by his education and deep understanding of governance. After completing his schooling in Oromia, he earned a degree in political science and international relations from Addis Ababa University, later obtaining his graduate degrees in a similar field. His academic background equipped him with the skills to navigate Ethiopia's complex political environment, where regional autonomy and national unity often clashed.

Lemma's political ascent began in Oromia, where he served as the speaker of the regional parliament before becoming the President of Oromia in October 2016. At a time when Ethiopia was facing mounting ethnic and political tensions, particularly surrounding the Oromo people's historical grievances, Lemma emerged as a leader who could address those issues. His presidency in Oromia marked a shift toward a leadership that sought to curtail federal interference, strengthen regional autonomy, and protect the rights of the Oromo people.

During his tenure, Lemma advocated for a balance of power that respected the constitutional rights of regions while ensuring that they operated within a legal framework. His government closed illegal mining operations and regulated investments, ensuring they benefited local communities. His efforts to rein in federal powers, particularly the military and federal police in Oromia, earned him a reputation as a reformist, positioning him as a central figure in Ethiopia's broader push for political change.

Abiy Ahmed's rise to power in 2018 was shaped by Ethiopia's political upheavals, particularly the Oromo protests of 2015–2018. These protests had exposed the deep-seated issues of ethnic marginalization, with the Oromo community at the forefront of the demands for political reform. Abiy, a member of the Oromo ethnic group, was seen as the leader capable of bridging the ethnic divides that had long plagued the nation. Lemma Megersa, as the President of Oromia, played a pivotal role in supporting Abiy's ascension, providing much-needed legitimacy and political backing to the new Prime Minister.

Their partnership was seen as a political marriage of convenience: Abiy, a charismatic figure, paired with Lemma, a seasoned regional leader, was expected to bring about a new era of reform, inclusivity, and peace. Initially, their alliance was powerful, with Lemma's support instrumental in securing Abiy's leadership. Together, they appeared to be the political duo capable of breaking the chains of Ethiopia's deeply ingrained ethnic divisions.

As Abiy implemented his reform agenda, which included liberalizing the political space, making peace with Eritrea, and curbing the influence of ethnic federalism, the fractures in his relationship with Lemma began to show. Lemma, a staunch advocate for ethnic federalism, grew increasingly wary of Abiy's push for a more centralized government. While Abiy envisioned a unified Ethiopia with less regional autonomy, Lemma remained committed to the notion of greater self-rule for regions like Oromia, which had long struggled with political marginalization.

Their differing views on the future of Ethiopia came to a head in 2019, when Abiy initiated the formation of the Prosperity Party, a move that many saw as an effort to consolidate power under a single political banner. Lemma's refusal to join the party was seen as a sign of his discontent with Abiy's increasing centralization. This ideological divergence marked the beginning of a gradual yet bitter political estrangement between the two men.

As Abiy's popularity soared, particularly after his peace deal with Eritrea, Lemma found himself sidelined in the new political order. His influence waned, and he increasingly felt marginalized. His position on ethnic federalism, once a cornerstone of his leadership, now set him at odds with the Prime Minister, whose reforms appeared to undermine the very autonomy Lemma had championed.

In 2019, Abiy removed Lemma from his position as President of Oromia. This move was seen as a betrayal of the very man who had been instrumental in Abiy's rise to power. Lemma's ousting was a stark reminder that, in Abiy's political calculus, loyalty was conditional. As Abiy consolidated his authority, he began to distance himself from those who had helped him, including Lemma. This marked the first of many political betrayals that would come to define Abiy's leadership.

For Lemma, the removal was a painful blow. He had supported Abiy not only for political expedience but also in the hope of delivering lasting reforms for the Oromo people. As Abiy's vision for Ethiopia shifted away from regional autonomy, Lemma found himself increasingly disillusioned. What had once been an alliance based on shared goals and values became a symbol of betrayal. Abiy's actions, including his treatment of former allies like Lemma, were seen by many as a strategic move to consolidate power at the expense of those who had once been his most trusted partners.

Lemma Megersa's political career stands as a testament to the complexities of Ethiopian politics, where issues of ethnicity, regional autonomy, and national unity collide. His rise and fall, from a celebrated reformer to a symbol of political betrayal, reflects the challenges of navigating a system marked by competing visions of governance. His refusal to submit to Abiy's centralization, his advocacy for regional rights, and his eventual removal from power underscore the difficulties of balancing national reform with the protection of regional autonomy.

Though Lemma's political influence has waned, his impact on Ethiopia's political landscape, especially in Oromia, remains significant. His commitment to regional autonomy and his opposition to the erosion of federalism will continue to resonate with those who believe that Ethiopia's future lies in embracing diversity and decentralization rather than centralization and control. In the end, Lemma's journey is one of political disillusionment, but it also serves as a reminder of the complexities that define Ethiopian politics.

***

Abiy Ahmed and Gedu Andargachew

Gedu Andargachew Alene was born on 13 August 1963 in Wollo Province, Ethiopia. His career has spanned key political roles in the country, with a particular focus on regional governance and national security affairs. Gedu's political journey reflects both his personal commitment to Ethiopia's governance and the broader challenges the nation has faced during his tenure.

Gedu's educational journey began in his home region of Amhara. From 1979 to 1985, he attended Chet Primary and Junior Secondary School before continuing his studies at Wogel-Tena Secondary Comprehensive School between 1987 and 1989. In 1998, Gedu furthered his education by earning a bachelor's degree in development administration from the Ethiopian Civil Service University in Addis Ababa, a foundation that equipped him with the skills necessary for a career in public service.

Gedu pursued further studies in organizational leadership, obtaining a Master of Arts degree from Azusa Pacific University in 2007. His advanced education allowed him to develop the leadership and organizational skills that would become crucial in his political career.

Gedu Andargachew's political rise began in the Amhara Region, where he became a key figure within the regional and national political landscape. He was appointed President of the Amhara Region in 2013, following the tenure of Ayalew Gobeze. During his presidency, Gedu focused on improving the region's socio-economic policies, contributing to the growth and influence of the Amhara Democratic Party (ANDM) at the regional level and the Ethiopian People's Revolutionary Democratic Front (EPRDF) at the national level. His leadership was marked by efforts to strengthen the region's governance and address local challenges, making him a prominent political figure within the Amhara community.

Gedu was reelected as President of the Amhara Region in 2015 and again in 2018. However, his tenure came to an unexpected end in March 2019 when he resigned, citing reasons that were never fully disclosed. In his farewell address, Gedu warned of rising ethnic tensions, particularly between the Amhara and Tigray regions, a prediction that would later become significant as political tensions escalated in Ethiopia.

In 2019, Gedu's political career took a new turn when Prime Minister Abiy Ahmed appointed him as the Minister of Foreign Affairs of Ethiopia. Serving in this capacity until November 2020, Gedu played a critical role in representing Ethiopia's foreign policy interests, particularly during a period of intense internal and external challenges. His leadership in foreign affairs was part of Abiy's broader effort to reshape Ethiopia's political and diplomatic landscape, which included efforts to enhance regional relationships and promote peace initiatives, particularly in relation to Eritrea.

In November 2020, Gedu Andargachew was appointed by Prime Minister Abiy Ahmed as the National Security Affairs Advisor to the Prime Minister. This role placed him at the heart of Ethiopia's national security strategy during a tumultuous period in the country's history, which included ongoing conflict in the Tigray Region. Gedu served in this position until June 2022 when he was succeeded by Redwan Hussein. His appointment to this role underscored his importance within the Abiy administration and his continued influence in Ethiopian politics.

Gedu was one of the prominent figures in the political transformation that helped topple the Tigray People's Liberation Front (TPLF) and ultimately bring Prime Minister Abiy Ahmed to power. Alongside Lemma Megersa, Gedu played a pivotal role in the Oromo-Amhara movement, which united two of Ethiopia's most influential ethnic groups to challenge the dominance of the TPLF and the Ethiopian People's Revolutionary Democratic Front (EPRDF). This political collaboration culminated in Abiy's rise to power in April 2018. Their efforts were particularly crucial in shifting the balance of power, as both the Amhara and Oromo regions were key players in this dramatic change.

One of the most notable moments in this movement occurred at a summit in Bahir Dar, a few weeks or months before the TPLF was overthrown. Gedu, who was serving as the president of the Amhara region at the time, stood at the forefront of these discussions. His influence, along with that of Lemma Megersa, was essential in the formation of the political alliances that would lead to Abiy Ahmed's ascension to the premiership. This moment marked a turning point in Ethiopian history, as it represented a coordinated challenge to the old political order, largely dominated by the TPLF.

However, Gedu's contributions to Ethiopian politics, especially his role in Abiy's rise to power, are often viewed with complexity. Despite his political achievements and the support he had built within the Amhara region, Gedu's later years in office were marked by rising tensions and increasing uncertainty. In March 2019, Gedu resigned from his position as president of Amhara, citing reasons that were never fully explained. In his farewell speech, he warned about the escalating ethnic tensions, particularly between the Amhara and Tigray regions, and the potential for further instability. His departure from the presidency marked the beginning of a more uncertain chapter in Ethiopian politics, as the country's political landscape began to shift even further.

The relationship between Gedu and Abiy Ahmed is a key element in understanding the turbulence of Ethiopian politics during this period. Many argue that Gedu, like Lemma Megersa, was ultimately betrayed by Abiy. Once Abiy secured his grip on power, he systematically marginalized the very individuals who had helped him rise to the position of Prime Minister. In doing so, Abiy effectively cleared the path for his own increasingly autocratic rule, sidelining his former allies in favor of consolidating his personal power.

This sense of betrayal is central to the political narrative surrounding Abiy's leadership. Abiy's consolidation of power has often been described as a personal quest, driven by a desire to shape Ethiopia's future in his image. Critics suggest that Abiy's actions are not merely about governing Ethiopia but are rooted in a deeper, ego-driven need to rewrite the country's history. Some even suggest that Abiy is motivated by a psychological insecurity, driven by jealousy of historical figures like Menelik II, the emperor who is often credited with unifying modern Ethiopia. Abiy's political maneuvers, including his treatment of former allies like Gedu and Lemma, have led some observers to claim that he is attempting to position himself as the central figure in the new Ethiopian narrative, replacing the legacy of Menelik II with his own.

Abiy's political style has been marked by a willingness to betray those who helped him rise to power, dismissing them as he seeks to maintain his own dominance. His decision to discard figures like Gedu and Lemma, individuals who were instrumental in his ascent, is seen by many as a sign of Abiy's ruthless pursuit of power and his apparent disregard for the people who helped him achieve it. This behavior has fueled criticisms that Abiy is driven by an unhealthy obsession with consolidating power and rewriting Ethiopia's history in his own image.

Furthermore, some argue that Abiy's tendency to isolate and abandon his former allies reflects a deeper psychological weakness. The criticism is that Abiy's need to control the narrative of Ethiopia's future is not just a political strategy, but a manifestation of insecurity and an inability to share power. This is often interpreted as a desire to erase any potential threats to his authority, including the historical figures who contributed to Ethiopia's identity, and replace them with his own self-serving vision of what Ethiopia should be.

In this context, Gedu Andargachew's political trajectory becomes a tragic story of betrayal and personal sacrifice. Despite his significant contributions to Ethiopia's political landscape and his role in the movement that brought Abiy to power, Gedu's legacy is now seen through the lens of Abiy's authoritarian consolidation. His once-promising political career has been overshadowed by Abiy's actions, and his story serves as a cautionary tale of the dangers of political ambition, betrayal, and the fragile nature of alliances in Ethiopia's volatile political environment.

Ultimately, the trajectory of Gedu's career, and the betrayal he experienced, illustrates the complexities and challenges of Ethiopian governance, where alliances are often fragile, and political fortunes can change rapidly. It also underscores the personal sacrifices that leaders like Gedu and Lemma made in the pursuit of a better Ethiopia, only to see their efforts turned against them by a leader who seemed willing to do anything to secure his own power.

***

CHAPTER 4

Prosperity Gospel and Its Impact on Abiy Ahmed, His Family, and Administration

The rise of Abiy Ahmed to the role of Prime Minister of Ethiopia in 2018 came with an unprecedented wave of political and social reforms aimed at transforming the country. Yet, alongside his political career, Abiy's personal life, particularly his religious beliefs, has played a pivotal role in shaping his leadership style and public persona. One of the most notable aspects of Abiy's spirituality is his connection to the Prosperity Gospel, a form of Christian faith that emphasizes success, wealth, and health as signs of divine favor. This belief has had a notable impact on his political leadership, his family, and the broader national discourse in Ethiopia.

***

The Rise of Prosperity Gospel in Ethiopia

Ethiopia, a country with a rich history rooted in Ethiopian Orthodox Christianity and a significant Muslim population, has long been a place where religion and politics intersect. However, unlike Western evangelical movements, the relationship between religion and politics in Ethiopia has historically been more nuanced. Over the past few decades, particularly in urban areas and among certain Protestant communities, the Prosperity Gospel has found fertile ground. This doctrine, which emphasizes that God rewards faithful Christians with material wealth, health, and success, has been embraced by some as a guiding principle for both individual and national prosperity.

As the Bible teaches in Proverbs 3:9-10, *"Honor the Lord with your wealth, with the firstfruits of all your crops; then your barns will be filled to overflowing, and your vats will brim over with new wine."* This scripture illustrates the belief that honoring God through one's faith and actions leads to material blessings. In line with this thinking, Prosperity Gospel proponents often link spiritual devotion with tangible rewards in life. Proverbs 10:22 further echoes this belief, stating, *"The blessing of the Lord brings wealth, without painful toil for it."*

The movement's influence has been particularly evident through the rapid expansion of Pentecostal and Evangelical churches in Ethiopia, especially in the capital, Addis Ababa, and the South. These churches have actively promoted the notion that divine favor manifests not only in spiritual well-being but also in financial and material success. This idea aligns with passages in the Bible, such as Isaiah 61:6, which says, *"But you will be called priests of the Lord, you will be named ministers of our God. You will feed on the wealth of nations, and in their riches you will boast."* The Prosperity Gospel encourages believers to view material wealth as a reflection of God's favor, and this idea has been widely embraced by many Ethiopians as they navigate a rapidly changing socio-political landscape.

Abiy Ahmed, who identifies as a Protestant Christian, has often expressed his deep faith in public forums, and his leadership style frequently incorporates spiritual and moral elements aligned with Prosperity Gospel teachings. While Abiy is not overtly connected to any specific Prosperity Gospel preacher or movement, his approach to governance and national development reflects a belief that divine favor manifests in national prosperity. As Luke 6:38 highlights, *"Give, and it will be given to you. A good measure, pressed down, shaken together and running over, will be poured into your lap. For with the measure you use, it will be measured to you."* This verse encapsulates the notion that the blessings of God are directly tied to one's actions and generosity, a sentiment that resonates with Abiy's leadership, which emphasizes national growth through moral and spiritual guidance.

In Ethiopia, the Prosperity Gospel has become an influential force in the intersection of religion and politics. While Abiy's leadership is not explicitly rooted in Prosperity Gospel doctrine, the tenets of this faith are reflected in his policies and public discourse. By integrating spiritual beliefs with national governance, Abiy's leadership exemplifies the complex relationship between religion and politics in

Ethiopia today, where the pursuit of national prosperity is often seen as a reflection of divine will.

Abiy Ahmed presents himself as a devout Christian who prays regularly and seeks divine guidance for his leadership. However, his actions suggest that his faith is not aligned with the core teachings of Christ but instead reflects the tenets of the Prosperity Gospel, where material wealth and success are equated with spiritual righteousness. Prosperity Gospel preachers often emphasize that "God rewards the faithful with wealth, health, and success," a view that resonates with Abiy's public persona as a leader who claims to be blessed with divine favor. Yet, such a belief is in stark contrast to the message of humility, sacrifice, and service to others that Jesus Christ embodied.

There are millions who, under the guise of deep faith, use the Bible and religious teachings to serve their own psychological needs and personal egos. This manipulation of spirituality is especially prevalent among those who adhere to the Prosperity Gospel, a doctrine that teaches material success, wealth, and health as signs of God's favor. While it is presented as a message of hope, in reality, this distorted interpretation of Christianity often masks deeper psychological issues and serves as a tool for self-serving motives, leaving behind a trail of ethical contradictions and betrayal. A prime example of this can be seen in the case of Abiy Ahmed, the Prime Minister of Ethiopia.

The Prosperity Gospel, which has gained significant traction in various parts of the world, particularly among Pentecostal and Evangelical communities, holds that financial prosperity is a sign of divine blessing. However, the teachings of Jesus Christ present an entirely different approach to wealth and success. Jesus warned against the dangers of greed and materialism, emphasizing humility and service to others. In Matthew 6:19-21, Jesus says: *"Do not store up for yourselves treasures on earth, where moths and vermin destroy, and where thieves break in and steal. But store up for yourselves treasures in heaven, where moths and vermin do not destroy, and where thieves do not break in and steal. For where your treasure is, there your heart will be also.".*

Here, Christ teaches that true wealth is not found in material possessions but in spiritual richness. Those who seek to use the faith as a means of gaining wealth are essentially missing the point of Christian discipleship. Jesus also condemned the pursuit of power and material success as ends in themselves, as seen in his confrontation with the rich young ruler in Mark 10:21-25: *"Jesus looked at him and loved him. 'One thing you lack,' he said. 'Go, sell everything you have and give to the poor, and you will have treasure in heaven. Then come, follow me.' At this the man's face fell. He went away sad, because he had great wealth. Jesus looked around and said to his disciples, 'How hard it is for the rich to enter the kingdom of God!'"*.

In contrast to the Prosperity Gospel's emphasis on acquiring wealth, Christ's message was clear: material riches can be a hindrance to spiritual growth. True prosperity, in the Christian sense, is not financial but spiritual.

At the heart of the Prosperity Gospel movement is often a self-serving mentality, an ego-driven desire for power, recognition, and success. Abiy Ahmed's political actions reflect this psychology of self-interest. While publicly presenting himself as a devout Christian, Abiy has betrayed many of his former allies. These betrayals raise questions about the integrity of his leadership. How can someone who claims to be a faithful follower of Christ, a teacher of humility, love, and forgiveness, engage in such actions? This hypocrisy speaks to the psychological sickness of those who, like Abiy, hide behind their faith to promote their personal agendas. Their reliance on the Prosperity Gospel is not rooted in true spirituality but rather in a deep-seated need for validation and power. James 4:3 states: *"When you ask, you do not receive, because you ask with wrong motives, that you may spend what you get on your pleasures."* (James 4:3)

This verse warns against the dangers of using faith for selfish desires. Those who manipulate religion for personal gain are asking for blessings not to glorify God but to satisfy their own egos. Their focus is on personal advancement rather than the service of others, contradicting the example of Christ, who came "not to be served, but to serve" (Mark 10:45).

The distortion of religion for personal gain is not unique to Christianity. In Islam, the pursuit of wealth is acknowledged but cautioned against. The Quran states in Surah Al-Tawbah 9:34: *"O you who have believed, indeed, many of the scholars and the monks devour the wealth of people unjustly and avert them from the way of Allah. And those who hoard gold and silver and spend it not in the way of Allah, give them tidings of a painful punishment."*

This warning emphasizes that wealth should not be hoarded for personal gain but should be used for the service of others. Similarly, in Buddhism, attachment to wealth is seen as a source of suffering. Buddha taught in the Dhammapada: *"Those who are attached to worldly things suffer in this world and the next. Those who have freed themselves from attachment will find peace."* (Dhammapada, 180)

These teachings align with the broader idea that the pursuit of material wealth for its own sake can lead to spiritual emptiness and personal corruption.

As Jesus said in Matthew 7:15-20, *"Watch out for false prophets. They come to you in sheep's clothing, but inwardly they are ferocious wolves. By their fruit you will recognize them."* Abiy's actions speak louder than his words, revealing the true nature of his leadership. His approach to religion and politics is a cautionary tale of how religious teachings can be distorted to serve personal desires, causing harm to both individuals and nations. True Christian leadership, as taught by Christ, is not about personal wealth or status but about loving and serving others, especially the poor and oppressed.

Abiy's public image is that of a charismatic leader who came to power with promises of political reform, unity, and reconciliation in Ethiopia. However, his leadership has taken a darker turn, with critics accusing him of cruelty, authoritarianism, and a disregard for human rights. In stark contrast to the humble, self-sacrificial nature of Christianity, Abiy's government has been marked by severe human rights violations, including mass detentions, extrajudicial killings, and a heavy-handed crackdown on opposition groups and the media.

The Tigray conflict, which erupted in November 2020, stands as one of the most glaring examples of Abiy Ahmed's authoritarianism and disregard for human life. Thousands of civilians, including women and children, have been killed, while millions have been displaced. The region, once vibrant with culture and heritage, now lies in ruins. Despite the immense devastation and suffering, Abiy continues to frame the situation as a national security issue and as an effort to preserve Ethiopia's unity. His relentless pursuit of military victory has drawn sharp criticism from international organizations, human rights groups, and religious communities, questioning whether his actions align with the Christian principles of love, forgiveness, and peace that he claims to uphold.

However, the impact of this conflict has been devastating not only in Tigray but also in the Amhara region. The suffering in Amhara is equally dire, with families torn apart, homes destroyed, and an entire generation of children and mothers enduring unimaginable hardship. The violence inflicted on innocent civilians in Amhara, particularly through aerial bombings by drones and helicopters, has caused horrific casualties. Many have witnessed the destruction of their homes and communities, with no place to run or hide. The indiscriminate killing of innocent people, the targeting of civilians in the fight between government forces and regional militias like Fano, and the destruction of churches, monasteries, and mosques leave a clear message of disregard for human life and dignity.

The cries of mothers who have lost their children and the anguish of children who have lost their families echo through the region. These cries for justice and peace fall on deaf ears as the Ethiopian government continues its military campaign, seemingly with little regard for the sanctity of human life or the values of compassion, peace, and love that Christianity teaches.

The continued suffering in both the Amhara and Tigray regions is a painful reminder of the need for leaders who seek peace and reconciliation, not power and destruction. Abiy's actions do not reflect the life of Christ but instead embody a version of power and ego that stands in direct opposition to the Christian call to love one's neighbor, seek justice, and live in peace with all people. Since late 2020, Ethiopia has endured overlapping armed conflicts centered first in Tigray, then diffusing into Amhara and other regions. Independent investigations and rights reporting bodies have documented large scale violations of international humanitarian and human rights law, including unlawful killings, starvation crimes, sexual violence, obstruction of medical care, and air and drone strikes that hit civilians and health facilities. Credible estimates place the toll of the Tigray war in the hundreds of thousands, and serious abuses have continued amid renewed fighting in Amhara. Multiple open source and expert analyses indicate that the Ethiopian government acquired and used armed drones from foreign suppliers, including systems of Turkish, Iranian, and Chinese origin, with cargo airlifts from the United Arab Emirates frequently reported by open source flight trackers in late 2021. Responsibility attaches to all parties that committed violations; as head of government and commander in chief, Prime Minister Abiy Ahmed bears political and chain of command responsibility to prevent, punish, and remedy these crimes

International law binding on Ethiopia prohibits attacks on civilians, starvation of civilians as a method of warfare, sexual violence, collective punishments, and attacks on medical services. In November 2021, the Office of the United Nations High Commissioner for Human Rights and the Ethiopian Human Rights Commission released a joint investigation that found reasonable grounds to believe that all parties committed violations which may amount to war crimes and crimes against humanity. The report described extrajudicial executions, sexual violence, torture, and widespread arbitrary detention, and urged credible accountability mechanisms.

The exact death toll remains contested because independent access was restricted for long periods and communications blackouts impeded data collection. Nevertheless, several converging estimates place the number of war related deaths in the hundreds of thousands. Syntheses of academic and media analyses frequently cite figures from researchers associated with Ghent University, who estimated between about 162,000 and 378,000 deaths by mid 2023, while other assessments and mediators cited numbers as high as six hundred thousand total deaths from violence, starvation, and lack of medical care. The scale led major outlets to describe Tigray as one of the world's deadliest contemporary conflicts of that period.

Patterns of violations were grave. The joint UN–EHRC report documented killings, torture, and widespread sexual violence against women and girls, including gang rape, often accompanied by ethnic slurs and extreme brutality. In 2025, a large medical legal study by Physicians for Human Rights and the Organization for Justice and Accountability in the Horn of Africa, drawing on hundreds of clinical records and interviews with health workers, concluded that systematic sexual violence, forced pregnancy, and sexual torture were committed primarily by Ethiopian and Eritrean forces and amounted to crimes against humanity, with some patterns possibly constituting genocidal acts. Survivors included children and the elderly, and many victims were held in captivity for extended periods.

Starvation and denial of services compounded the toll. Analysts and human rights groups described restrictions on aid and services during key phases of the conflict, contributing to excess mortality due to hunger and treatable disease. The same bodies reported obstruction of medical care and attacks on health infrastructure, in breach of international humanitarian law.

Beginning in 2021, the federal military increasingly relied on air power including drones. A humanitarian security analysis published in December 2022 identified three drone families in Ethiopian use during the war: Turkish Bayraktar TB2, Chinese Wing Loong II, and Iranian Mohajer series, and it cataloged the humanitarian risks posed by air delivered munitions, particularly when used in populated areas or near medical and aid sites. Parallel open source investigations and think tank analysis described a surge of suspicious cargo flights into

Ethiopia during September to November 2021, with one tracker logging about fifty one such flights in September and October alone, forty five from the United Arab Emirates and six from Iran, and a cumulative total near ninety from the Emirates by November, coinciding with the appearance of new drone types in satellite imagery. While early media commentary in late 2020 cautioned that there was no definitive proof that Emirati drones based in Eritrea had been used in Ethiopia at that time, subsequent analyses point to later procurement channels and growing reliance on drones through 2021 and 2022.

The humanitarian consequences were severe. Peer reviewed and rights reporting linked air and drone strikes to civilian deaths in multiple incidents across northern Ethiopia. Although comprehensive nationwide strike counts remain incomplete, the pattern of harm documented in medical data and case investigations includes mass casualty events, injuries to children, and damage to civilian objects, which require independent criminal inquiry into targeting decisions and weapons use rules.

Following the November 2022 Pretoria accord which silenced the front lines in Tigray, tensions escalated in Amhara. The government sought to integrate or dismantle regional armed structures and arrested suspected supporters of the Fano militia, triggering clashes across towns and rural districts. In August 2023 the federal government declared a nationwide state of emergency focused on Amhara. The United Nations human rights office reported at least one hundred eighty three people killed in the Amhara region between July and mid August 2023 amid fighting and alleged abuses, including an airstrike in Finote Selam that killed twenty six civilians. Rights monitors also documented mass arrests during that period.

In July 2024, Human Rights Watch issued a detailed investigation into attacks on medical care in northwestern Amhara, concluding that Ethiopian security forces engaged in patterns of assault, killing, intimidation, and obstruction against health workers and patients, and that strikes damaged or destroyed health facilities. HRW assessed that these actions amount to war crimes and called for accountability and protection of medical neutrality. The report contains case studies, dates, and locations that meet evidentiary standards used in previous conflict monitoring.

Fighting again intensified in 2025. International news agencies reported that Fano elements claimed control of parts of the region, schools were shuttered in large numbers, and new allegations of extrajudicial executions by security forces surfaced, as did reports of killings by armed groups. The United States Department of State's 2024 Human Rights report for Ethiopia also recorded conflict related abuses in Amhara and Oromia, including extrajudicial killings and arbitrary detentions, signaling entrenched impunity and a continuing crisis of protection for civilians.

The government in Addis Ababa deepened security and commercial ties with several external partners during the conflict. The most visible link to new capabilities was the rapid fielding of armed drones. Open source air logistics data and satellite imagery analysis summarized by a leading European think tank reported substantial cargo flights from the United Arab Emirates into Ethiopia during Autumn 2021, overlapping with the first appearance of Mohajer and Wing Loong drones in the Ethiopian theater. These findings are consistent with a broader pattern in which states procure turnkey drone platforms and munitions via third country logistics, rather than through public defense contracts. While an early 2020 media report noted that analysts had not yet verified the use of Emirati operated drones from Eritrea in the first weeks of the Tigray war, the later cargo flight surge and imagery evidence indicate that external supply, including via Emirati channels, materially enabled Ethiopia's drone war by late 2021.

Beyond platforms, civil society investigators traced European and Western manufactured components within drones operated by Ethiopia, underscoring the global nature of the supply chain and the importance of export control enforcement and end use monitoring. These components included engines, avionics, altimeters, and fuel systems, which can be lawfully exported for civilian use but later diverted into armed platforms. The presence of such parts does not in itself prove unlawful end use by governments, yet it highlights the need for rigorous due diligence when there is a substantial risk of serious violations.

Under international law, individual criminal liability attaches to those who commit, order, aid, or abet war crimes and crimes against humanity. Commanders and political leaders can bear responsibility when they knew or should have known that subordinates were committing crimes and did not take necessary and reasonable measures to prevent them or to punish perpetrators. The UN–EHRC joint investigation concluded that violations were widespread and committed by all major parties. As head of government and commander in chief during the conflicts in Tigray and Amhara, Prime Minister Abiy Ahmed holds an obligation to ensure impartial investigations, to cooperate with credible international and regional inquiries, and to remove and prosecute officials responsible for crimes, regardless of rank. The persistence of abuses in Amhara, including documented attacks on health care by federal forces, underscores the urgency of such measures. Until such values are upheld, the cries of those suffering will continue to echo, and the legacy of this conflict will serve as a tragic reminder of the failure to embrace the true teachings of Christ in leadership.

While Abiy professes to follow Christian teachings, particularly as a Pentecostal believer, his leadership suggests a greater commitment to political power and economic growth than to the spiritual ideals of humility, justice, and care for the poor. Instead of seeking reconciliation, peace, and humility, his government has been accused of ruthlessness, exemplifying what some critics believe is a form of Christianity that prioritizes power and wealth over compassion and empathy for the suffering of others.

***

The King Who Crowned Himself

Once upon a time in the small town of Beshasha, a mother told her son that he would be a king. Most children hear such words and later discover the world has other plans. But Abiy Ahmed clung to this bedtime prophecy as if it were a coronation decree waiting for its hour. By his own retelling, he was never meant to be an ordinary public servant, a mere reformer, or a cautious politician, he was destined for the throne. And when opportunity knocked, he did not hesitate. He seized the crown with both hands, never mind the trail of blood, betrayal, and broken promises left behind him.

His supposed destiny was neatly paired with the prosperity gospel, that convenient theology which insists wealth and power are signs of divine favor. What luck for a man who longed for both. Skyscrapers could be spun as proof of God's blessing, highways as evidence of heaven's applause. And when opponents vanished into prisons or villages were scorched by drones, perhaps the angels were still clapping, only louder. Prophecy and prosperity together formed a perfect shield, a gospel not of salvation but of self-preservation, where every victory was God's plan and every atrocity a necessary sacrifice.

Thus was born the kingdom of contradictions. Abiy styled himself as a unifier, yet his reign fractured the nation more deeply than ever. Tigray starved under siege while its towns burned. Amhara villages were shelled, their civilians buried in hurried graves. Even his own Oromo kin felt the sting of betrayal, as crackdowns and arrests spread like wildfire. This was leadership by double-speak: peace announced from the podium while bombs fell from the sky, democracy promised in speeches while critics filled the prisons, unity declared in public while division was sown in blood. To love Ethiopia in such a manner required a strange arithmetic, one that measured devotion by the number of its dead.

Supporters point to new roads, glass towers, and shining projects as evidence of progress. But progress photographs well, while famine and mass graves do not. For critics, these developments are mere decorations, shiny ornaments covering rot. In Abiy's gospel, prosperity is proof of divine blessing, while dissent is nothing less than demonic interference. It is a theology of deception, almost poetic in its cruelty: every ribbon-cutting hailed as triumph, every atrocity dismissed as regrettable necessity. Ethiopians are told to clap for their king even as they bury their children.

At the heart of it all lies a peculiar love story. Abiy Ahmed surely loves Ethiopia, but he loves himself a little more. The two loves are so entangled they cannot be separated. Ethiopia becomes his mirror, reflecting his prophecy, his gospel, his vision. To love the nation means to love the man who claims to embody it. To oppose him is to betray the land itself. Contradiction is not a flaw in this worldview, it is the very principle of its logic. And even in this theater, the First Lady, Zinash Tayachew, plays her part. A gospel singer by calling, she lends spiritual harmony to the royal script. While she sings of heaven's glory, her husband commands drone strikes. Together they form a duet of faith and firepower, a household sanctified in rhetoric while steeped in blood.

And so Abiy Ahmed stands: the child foretold as king, the reformer turned autocrat, the preacher of peace who wages war, the builder who destroys, the lover of Ethiopia who scars it. His mother's prophecy has become the script of his rule, each contradiction recast as destiny. Yet history is not easily deceived. It has a sharp memory and a cruel sense of humor. Kings who crown themselves on prophecy often find that posterity remembers less about their visions and more about their victims. And Abiy may learn, in time, that he is not remembered as Ethiopia's chosen king, but as the ruler who believed his own legend far too much.

***

CHAPTER 5

The Demise of the TPLF

The Tigray People's Liberation Front (TPLF) traces its roots to the late 1970s, a period marked by intense political and military turmoil in Ethiopia. The country, under the Emperor Haile Selassie, had experienced several decades of relative stability, but by the mid-1970s, discontent and opposition to the monarchy had grown. In 1974, a Marxist military junta known as the Derg overthrew Haile Selassie, establishing a socialist government that would go on to implement radical land reforms and nationalize key sectors of the economy.

However, the Dregs' rule was marked by political repression, brutal purges, and military conflict, which would eventually lead to the rise of various armed rebel groups, including the TPLF. The rebellion against the Derg was fueled by widespread poverty, ethnic tensions, and dissatisfaction with the regime's centralization of power, particularly in regions like Tigray.

The TPLF was founded in 1975, in the midst of this volatile political climate, by a group of young intellectuals and activists from the Tigray region, located in the northern part of Ethiopia. The Tigray region had long felt marginalized and excluded from political power, with the central government often dominated by Amhara and Oromo elites. The social, economic, and political marginalization of Tigrayans by the central government, combined with the overall discontentment with the Derg's rule, served as the driving force behind the TPLF's establishment.

The group was born out of a desire to assert the rights and autonomy of the Tigray people, seeking to address the historical injustices and oppression faced by the region. The founders of the TPLF were influenced by Marxist-Leninist ideologies, and initially, the movement espoused a socialist, revolutionary platform aimed at overthrowing the Derg regime and creating a more equitable and just political system. This socialist ideology was also in line with the larger trends in many African liberation movements at the time, which sought to address economic inequality and colonial legacies.

One of the key features of the TPLF's founding ideology was its ethnic nationalism. Unlike other Ethiopian rebel movements, such as the Ethiopian People's Revolutionary Party (EPRP) or the All-Ethiopia Socialist Movement (MEISON), which sought to establish a more centralized, pan-Ethiopian state, the TPLF focused specifically on the plight of the Tigray people. This ethnic nationalist approach became a cornerstone of the TPLF's identity and later played a significant role in Ethiopia's political trajectory, especially with the introduction of ethnic federalism in the 1990s.

***

The Early Struggles: Armed Resistance and Growth

In the early years of its existence, the TPLF faced significant challenges. The Derg's military forces were formidable, and the TPLF had limited resources. However, the group relied heavily on guerrilla tactics, using the rugged terrain of Tigray to their advantage. Over time, the TPLF built up a network of supporters and fighters, gaining momentum in the fight against the Derg.

The TPLF quickly became one of the most prominent and successful of the various rebel movements operating against the Derg, which also included the Ethiopian People's Revolutionary Democratic Front (EPRDF), the Oromo Liberation Front (OLF), and the Southern Ethiopian People's Democratic Movement (SEPDM). The TPLF's ability to effectively mobilize the Tigray people, both in terms of military support and ideological backing, contributed to its growing strength. By the mid-1980s, the TPLF had established strongholds in northern Ethiopia, especially in Tigray, and had developed close ties with the Eritrean People's Liberation Front (EPLF), another armed group fighting against the Derg in Eritrea.

This alliance between the TPLF and the EPLF would prove crucial in the downfall of the Derg regime. In 1991, after years of sustained military pressure, the Derg finally collapsed. The TPLF, alongside the EPLF and other rebel groups, took control of Ethiopia's capital, Addis Ababa. The TPLF's military victory marked the end of the Derg regime and the beginning of a new political era in Ethiopia.

Following the Derg's fall, the TPLF emerged as the dominant political force in the new government. However, it did not establish a Tigrayan-only government. Instead, the TPLF formed a coalition known as the Ethiopian People's Revolutionary Democratic Front (EPRDF), which included various ethnic-based parties, such as the Amhara National Democratic Movement (ANDM), the Oromo People's Democratic Organization (OPDO), and the Southern Ethiopian People's Democratic Movement (SEPDM). Despite this apparent inclusivity, the TPLF remained the dominant party within the coalition, and its leadership held key positions in the government and military.

The TPLF's dominance in the EPRDF and Ethiopia's political system was solidified through the establishment of the ethnic federalism system in the early 1990s. This system was designed to grant a significant degree of autonomy to Ethiopia's various ethnic groups by creating regional states based on ethnic identity. Each ethnic group was supposed to have the right to govern itself, including control over its own resources and political institutions.

***

The Rise of Abiy Ahmed and the Fall of the TPLF

The fall of the Derg regime in 1991 marked the beginning of a new era in Ethiopia, led by the Tigray People's Liberation Front (TPLF) through the Ethiopian People's Revolutionary Democratic Front (EPRDF). This political shift promised to bring an end to the brutal repression of the Derg, which had been responsible for widespread human rights abuses and a devastating famine in the 1980s. However, the TPLF-led government, despite its economic successes, became a source of significant suffering for millions of Ethiopians, particularly the Amhara and Oromo ethnic groups, under its rule.

Ethnic federalism was introduced as a way to address the grievances of Ethiopia's various ethnic groups, many of whom had long felt marginalized and oppressed by previous governments. For the TPLF, ethnic federalism was an effective way to ensure Tigray's political and cultural autonomy while maintaining the TPLF's control over the central government.

Under the leadership of Meles Zenawi, a highly strategic and intelligent figure, Ethiopia experienced notable economic growth. His government emphasized rapid infrastructural development, growth in GDP, and modernization in sectors like education and health. However, this economic growth came at a cost. The TPLF, having a stronghold in Ethiopia's ruling party, remained an ethnically driven movement that crafted an ethnic-based constitution in 1995. The new constitution granted regional autonomy, ostensibly to address the historical marginalization of Ethiopia's ethnic groups, yet it deeply entrenched ethnic divisions and ultimately led to increased tensions between various groups.

While the TPLF claimed to be fighting for equality and recognition of oppressed peoples, its policies and actions resulted in the marginalization of certain groups, most notably the Amhara and Oromo populations. The TPLF's policies favored its ethnic base in Tigray, leading to disproportionate representation of Tigrayans in military and government leadership positions. Tigrayans dominated key military ranks and administrative posts, and the TPLF became entrenched in Ethiopia's political system, exacerbating resentment among the Amhara, Oromo, and other ethnic groups. This centralization of power among Tigrayans created a growing sense of alienation and frustration among Ethiopians from other regions, particularly the Amhara, who felt that their political influence had been eroded and that they were victims of systemic discrimination.

The TPLF's response to dissent and protests was often violent, further deepening ethnic divisions. Human rights violations, including extrajudicial killings, torture, forced disappearances, and arbitrary arrests, were widespread during the TPLF-led government. These violations were most apparent in the treatment of the Amhara and Oromo people, who began to organize mass movements calling for justice and political reform. The Oromo, the largest ethnic group in Ethiopia, faced brutal repression from the state for years, while the Amhara felt that they were being scapegoated for Ethiopia's historical problems. Ethnic-based violence, such as the 2005 election massacre and crackdowns on peaceful protests, became routine under the TPLF, fueling the discontent that would later contribute to its fall.

Tensions reached a boiling point in 2016 when widespread protests broke out in the Amhara and Oromia regions. What started as localized demonstrations over issues like land rights and political exclusion evolved into a national movement that questioned the very structure of Ethiopia's political system. In response, the TPLF regime resorted to violent repression, including the use of military force to crush these uprisings, but the resistance only grew stronger. The government's inability to listen to the grievances of the Ethiopian people, particularly the Amhara and Oromo populations, led to the eventual collapse of the TPLF's control over the nation.

Abiy Ahmed's rise to power in 2018 marked a pivotal moment in Ethiopia's history. Abiy, who hailed from the Oromo ethnic group, was seen as a reformist leader with the potential to heal the divisions that had been exacerbated by the TPLF's policies. His promises of national reconciliation, political reforms, and inclusivity struck a chord with many Ethiopians who had been marginalized by the TPLF's ethno-centric policies. Abiy's appointment as Prime Minister and his subsequent dissolution of the EPRDF, replacing it with the Prosperity Party in 2019, further alienated the TPLF, which saw its dominance in the ruling coalition end. The TPLF's refusal to join the new party and Abiy's push for a more unified Ethiopia set the stage for the ongoing conflict.

***

Human Rights Violations under TPLF

The human rights abuses committed under the TPLF regime were not limited to physical violence. The Ethiopian government, under TPLF leadership, used systematic suppression and coercion to silence opposition and control ethnic groups that were deemed "problematic" for the regime. Organizations like Human Rights Watch and Amnesty International documented numerous violations, such as arbitrary detentions, extrajudicial killings, and forced displacement, particularly in the Oromo and Amhara regions. Additionally, the TPLF's manipulation of ethnic identities and political power had a significant role in deepening divisions within Ethiopia, contributing to the rise of ethnic nationalism.

The system of ethnic federalism introduced by the TPLF in the 1990s has been one of the most contentious issues in modern Ethiopia. While the constitution provided the right to self-determination for various ethnic groups, it also entrenched ethnic identity as a political tool, dividing the country into ethnically based regions. This system created an environment where political power was fragmented along ethnic lines, often at the expense of national unity. The Amhara, in particular, felt their identity and historical significance were being erased in favor of the Tigray-led system, which led to growing resentment. The Oromo people, who had long been marginalized, initially saw the TPLF's federalist policies as a step toward recognition, but they too were subjected to severe repression as they sought greater political autonomy.

The TPLF's refusal to adapt to the changing political landscape, coupled with its brutal treatment of dissidents and its domination of Ethiopia's political system, ultimately led to its downfall. The anger of the Amhara and Oromo, and the resentment of the broader Ethiopian populace toward the TPLF's continued hegemony, provided the foundation for the anti-TPLF movements that emerged in the 2010s. Abiy Ahmed's rise to power in 2018, with his promises of reform and unity, sparked a seismic shift. Despite his efforts to implement reforms, including the release of political prisoners, the TPLF's refusal to abandon its grip on power, and its unyielding pursuit of autonomy, set the stage for the Tigray conflict that erupted in 2020. The war in Tigray not only revealed the violent suppression of ethnic movements but also exposed the deep divisions within Ethiopia that had been exacerbated by the TPLF's policies.

The rise of Abiy Ahmed and the demise of the TPLF are deeply intertwined with the political and ethnic divisions that have plagued Ethiopia for decades. The TPLF's use of ethnic federalism, its marginalization of various groups, and its authoritarian tactics sowed the seeds of its own demise. While Meles Zenawi's leadership achieved significant economic progress, it was ultimately the TPLF's inability to address the grievances of the Amhara, Oromo, and other ethnic groups that led to its downfall.

***

Legacy of the TPLF

The legacy of the Tigrayan People's Liberation Front (TPLF) is etched into Ethiopia's modern history with both moments of triumph and a long shadow of destruction. On one hand, the TPLF played a central role in overthrowing the brutal Derg regime in 1991, an act that was initially celebrated as the dawn of freedom and a new era of governance. Yet on the other hand, its rule entrenched a system that planted the seeds of division and instability for decades to come. The most defining aspect of the TPLF's governance was the introduction of ethnic federalism through the 1995 FDRE Constitution. While this framework was presented as a progressive attempt to grant Ethiopia's many nationalities recognition, equality, and the right to self-determination, it quickly became clear that the structure functioned less as a foundation for unity and more as a fault line that deepened ethnic fractures across the country. By embedding ethnicity at the heart of political identity and territorial administration, the TPLF institutionalized division, making national solidarity increasingly fragile.

Few wounds in modern Ethiopian history cut as deeply as the loss of Assab, the small Red Sea port that once anchored Ethiopia to the world's oceans. The separation of Eritrea and Ethiopia in the early 1990s was hailed by some as the resolution of a long and bloody war, but the way it was carried out, particularly the 1993 referendum, left enduring scars. For Ethiopia, a nation of more than 130 million people, the verdict was not simply about Eritrea's independence; it was also about the permanent cutting away of its only coastline. Assab, historically and geographically part of the Afar homeland, was handed over without due consideration of history, demography, or Ethiopia's right to access the sea.

Historically, Assab was never merely "Eritrean." In the nineteenth century, the area was sparsely populated by the Afar, who have always been part of the Ethiopian cultural and political fabric. When the Italian colonial project expanded in the 1880s, Italy purchased Assab from local chiefs of the Afar and later folded it into the colony of Eritrea. This colonial boundary, drawn by European hands, ignored the deeper ties between the Afar people and Ethiopia. For centuries, the Afar had been linked by blood, trade, and political allegiance to the Ethiopian highlands, serving as a bridge between the inland Christian kingdom and the Red Sea coast. Their identity was never confined by colonial maps, nor were they consulted when the question of Eritrea's future was put to a vote.

The 1993 referendum that granted Eritrea independence was celebrated by the global community as an act of self-determination. Yet it was far from fair. Ethiopia itself, still fragile after the fall of the Derg, was in no position to negotiate. The process, managed under the shadow of the Tigray People's Liberation Front (TPLF), left Ethiopia with no seat at the table to secure its historic rights to the sea. The TPLF leadership, desperate to consolidate power, accepted Eritrea's full separation and in doing so abandoned Assab, a decision that has haunted Ethiopia ever since. The Afar, who were denied a chance to voice their position, were effectively uprooted from their own heritage. In any genuine act of self-determination, their voices should have mattered. A new referendum among the Afar, free from the distortions of the past, would at least begin to right this historical injustice.

Beyond the question of history lies the matter of law and equity. International law recognizes that landlocked states are entitled to access the sea for trade and economic survival. The United Nations Convention on the Law of the Sea (UNCLOS) guarantees the right of transit to and from the sea for landlocked countries. Yet Ethiopia, one of Africa's largest nations, with the second-largest population on the continent, is confined to a precarious dependence on Djibouti, paying enormous costs for port access. This situation is neither sustainable nor just. No modern state of Ethiopia's size should remain deliberately locked away from its natural coastline only sixty miles away. To deny Ethiopia its rightful maritime outlet is to enforce a structural handicap on its economy, its security, and its people's future.

Eritrea, with a population of barely four million, commands over 1,000 kilometers of Red Sea coastline, while Ethiopia, with 130 million citizens, has none. This imbalance mocks the very principles of fairness and international cooperation. If the global order truly believes in justice and stability, it must address this glaring contradiction. The case for Ethiopia's return to Assab, or at the very least for a shared arrangement, is not one of conquest, but of survival and historic restoration. Ethiopia is not asking to erase Eritrea, but it cannot accept to be permanently strangled by decisions made in haste, under the shadow of post-Derg chaos, and reinforced by TPLF shortsightedness.

The legacy of Assab's loss is a dark one. It is the mark of a political elite that abandoned Ethiopia's long-term interests for short-term power. It is the story of colonial borders triumphing over indigenous history. And it is the ongoing tragedy of a great nation left without a coast while its people struggle to lift themselves out of poverty. To remain silent is to accept that Ethiopia—a civilization that has endured for millennia—should exist as an inland island, cut off from the waters that have always been part of its story.

Assab must be reconsidered. Whether through a renewed referendum for the Afar people, an international arbitration that restores Ethiopia's access to the sea, or a bilateral agreement grounded in justice rather than colonial precedent, the question cannot be left buried. Ethiopia's future prosperity and stability are bound to the sea, and the world cannot afford to ignore it. The case of Assab is not merely a territorial dispute; it is a test of whether history, law, and fairness can converge to correct one of the most glaring injustices of modern African statehood.

Over the years of its dominance within the Ethiopian People's Revolutionary Democratic Front (EPRDF), the TPLF wielded disproportionate influence over the military, the intelligence services, and the economy, despite Tigray representing only a small fraction of the country's population. This concentration of power fueled resentment among other ethnic groups, particularly the Oromo and the Amhara, who saw their political space constrained and their voices muted under an authoritarian order cloaked in the language of federalism. Ethnic nationalism was not diminished under TPLF leadership; rather, it was sharpened, weaponized, and often used to suppress dissent. The very system designed to provide autonomy became a tool for control and punishment, creating cycles of distrust and hostility between Ethiopia's diverse peoples. The human cost of this legacy is staggering. Under TPLF dominance, thousands of Ethiopians were imprisoned, silenced, or exiled for opposing the system. Periodic protests, such as the widespread demonstrations in 2005 following contested elections, were met with brutal crackdowns that left hundreds dead and many more injured. Entire generations came of age under a climate of fear, where authoritarianism was justified in the name of stability, and ethnic identity became the prism through which all politics were conducted. This model, rather than creating a cohesive federation, fractured Ethiopia into competing enclaves of suspicion and grievance. When the TPLF eventually fell from power and later clashed with the federal government during the devastating Tigray War (2020–2022), the cycle of violence it had helped to normalize returned with catastrophic consequences, plunging the country into mass death, famine, and displacement.

Today, the TPLF's legacy is remembered less for liberation than for the suffering it left behind, a fractured country where ethnic violence has become endemic, and where trust in national institutions remains shattered. The system it championed proved unsustainable, producing instability rather than equality, and civil war rather than coexistence. Its rise and fall reveal not only the perils of embedding ethnic identity as the organizing principle of statehood but also the dangers of authoritarian governance masked as federal reform. What remains is a landscape scarred by conflict, division, and disillusionment, a legacy of death and destruction that Ethiopia continues to struggle to overcome.

***

CHAPTER 6

The Fall of The Ethiopian People's Revolutionary Democratic Front (EPRDF)

The Ethiopian People's Revolutionary Democratic Front (EPRDF), an ethnic federalist political coalition, played a pivotal role in shaping the modern history of Ethiopia. The coalition, which existed from 1988 to 2019, consisted of four key political parties: the Tigray People's Liberation Front (TPLF), Amhara Democratic Party (ADP), Oromo Democratic Party (ODP), and Southern Ethiopian People's Democratic Movement (SEPDM). These parties were united under the EPRDF banner after successfully overthrowing the military regime of the People's Democratic Republic of Ethiopia (PDRE) in 1991. The EPRDF controlled Ethiopian politics for nearly three decades, until the coalition was dissolved in 2019, marking a significant shift in the country's political landscape.

The roots of the EPRDF trace back to the Ethiopian Civil War (1974–1991), a brutal conflict that saw the fall of the imperial regime of Haile Selassie and the rise of the Derg, a Marxist military junta led by Mengistu Haile Mariam. The Derg's rule, marked by extreme repression, widespread human rights violations, and the deaths of tens of thousands of Ethiopians, generated significant opposition. Throughout the 1980s, various insurgent groups fought against the Derg, including the TPLF and the Ethiopian People's Democratic Movement (EPDM). These groups came to be known as the rebel fronts.

The EPRDF itself was formally created in 1989 from the alliance of the TPLF and the EPDM. The new coalition was primarily formed to challenge the Derg's military dominance and, eventually, to seize power in Ethiopia. The Oromo People's Democratic Organization (OPDO), which represented the Oromo ethnic group, and the Ethiopian Democratic Officers' Revolutionary Movement (EDORM), consisting of former Derg officers captured by the TPLF, joined the EPRDF shortly afterward.

The Ethiopian civil war was not only a political conflict but also a clash of ideologies. The EPRDF and its member parties came from diverse political backgrounds, but their unity was rooted in a shared desire to overthrow the oppressive Derg regime and create a new, more inclusive political order. Their victory in 1991, which led to the collapse of the Derg, marked a transformative moment in Ethiopia's political history.

The fall of the People's Democratic Republic of Ethiopia (PDRE) in 1991 marked the end of the Derg regime and the beginning of a new political era under the EPRDF. With the support of Western powers, especially the United States, the EPRDF managed to consolidate its position and assume leadership over the transitional government that was established after the PDRE's collapse.

One of the critical aspects of the EPRDF's rise to power was the alliance between its core parties, which represented different ethnic and regional groups in Ethiopia. The TPLF, which dominated the new coalition, was initially the most influential member of the EPRDF. The TPLF's leadership, led by Meles Zenawi, played a central role in shaping the political trajectory of the country during the 1990s and early 2000s. While the coalition allowed for ethnic representation in the political system, it was widely criticized for fostering a centralized and highly controlled political environment that was dominated by the TPLF.

The EPRDF's official ideology, Revolutionary Democracy, evolved over time. Originally influenced by Marxist–Leninist thought, the EPRDF adjusted its ideology following the collapse of the Soviet Union. The core idea behind Revolutionary Democracy was the belief that a vanguard party should govern Ethiopia because it possessed superior knowledge of social development. In this regard, the EPRDF considered itself the true representative of the people, particularly the rural peasantry, which formed the majority of Ethiopia's population.

Despite the adoption of Revolutionary Democracy, the EPRDF's policies remained rooted in its Marxist origins. The party viewed imperialism, particularly capitalist free-market systems, as the primary adversary, while also adhering to the idea that economic growth should be based on export-driven industrialization. However, the EPRDF also recognized the need for liberal economic policies in certain areas, such as privatization and market liberalization, even as it maintained its ideological stance.

The EPRDF's relationship to liberal democracy was ambivalent. While it officially rejected liberal democratic practices, its economic policies and reforms demonstrated a pragmatic acceptance of some aspects of market capitalism, albeit under strict state control.

The EPRDF promised to establish an inclusive political order, and this was reflected in the 1991 Constitution of Ethiopia, which introduced an ethnic federalism system. This system allowed for greater autonomy for Ethiopia's diverse ethnic groups, while also emphasizing the importance of unity within the country. However, despite the promises of federalism, the centralized control of the EPRDF, especially under Meles Zenawi's leadership, created a tense relationship with some ethnic groups, particularly those that were not well-represented in the government structure.

The leadership of the EPRDF was marked by significant political figures who influenced not only the course of the coalition but also the broader trajectory of Ethiopian politics. The three key leaders of the EPRDF were Meles Zenawi, Hailemariam Desalegn, and Abiy Ahmed.

***

Meles Zenawi: Architect of Ethiopia's Ethnic Federalism and the TPLF's Decline

Meles Zenawi, born Legesse Zenawi Asres on May 9, 1955, in Adwa, Ethiopia, was a prominent political figure whose legacy remains both contentious and influential. Initially involved in student activism, Meles adopted the name "Meles" following the execution of his peer Meles Takele during the Derg regime in 1975. He joined the Tigray People's Liberation Front (TPLF) in the same year, becoming a pivotal figure in the resistance against the Mengistu Haile Mariam-led dictatorship. By 1989, Meles had risen to the chairmanship of the TPLF and assumed leadership of the Ethiopian People's Revolutionary Democratic Front (EPRDF) upon its formation in 1988. Under his leadership, the EPRDF played a crucial role in the overthrow of the Derg regime, ultimately bringing Meles to power.

Meles Zenawi served as the president of Ethiopia from 1991 to 1995, and as prime minister from 1995 until his death in 2012. During his tenure, he transformed Ethiopia's political landscape, introducing ethnic federalism as the core structure of the state. This system allowed ethnic groups within Ethiopia to maintain their languages, cultures, and lands, which Meles believed was necessary for national unity. However, ethnic federalism, a policy championed by Meles and the TPLF, is seen by many as the root cause of the subsequent fragmentation and ethnic tensions that plague the country today.

Meles's administration was marked by economic growth, with Ethiopia becoming one of Africa's fastest-growing economies during his time in office. He implemented ambitious reforms, particularly in the fields of agriculture, education, and land management, aimed at tackling Ethiopia's recurring droughts and poverty. His tenure, however, was also marred by widespread human rights abuses. The 2005 general election, in which Meles's party was accused of electoral fraud, triggered violent protests in Addis Ababa, resulting in the deaths of 193 people at the hands of the police. The brutal crackdown led to widespread criticism of Meles's government, but he remained firmly in control of the country's political apparatus.

Despite the economic achievements, Meles's policies of ethnic federalism led to deepening divisions within Ethiopian society. The TPLF, under his guidance, held a monopoly on power, and many Ethiopians, particularly from the Amhara and Oromo ethnic groups, felt marginalized and excluded from the political process. This alienation would later contribute to mass protests, particularly during the later years of Meles's rule, as ethnic-based movements gained traction.

Meles's death in 2012 was seen as a turning point for the TPLF and Ethiopia. His leadership had been the driving force behind the TPLF's dominance in Ethiopian politics. After his passing, the TPLF began to face increasing internal and external challenges, culminating in the rise of Abiy Ahmed and the eventual fall of the TPLF. Despite Meles's brilliance in shaping Ethiopia's modern political structure, his firm belief in ethnic federalism and the policies implemented by the TPLF would leave a legacy of division and conflict that continues to shape Ethiopia's present-day struggles.

***

TPLF's Role in Losing the Coastal Advantage

Ethiopia's history of competing for access to the sea dates back centuries, but the current dilemma of being a landlocked nation stems from the complex political developments of the 20th century. After the dissolution of the Ethiopia-Eritrean federation, the late 20th century saw a prolonged and bitter struggle for the Red Sea coastline between Ethiopia and Eritrea, which would ultimately culminate in Ethiopia losing access to its Eritrean coastline.

The TPLF's decision to allow Eritrea's independence and Ethiopia's subsequent landlocked status has been the subject of much debate and criticism. While the formal process of granting Eritrea independence came through a referendum in 1993, it was the TPLF-led government under Meles Zenawi that effectively gave its blessing to this decision. Many argue that this move was not in the best interest of Ethiopia and its people, but rather part of a long-term strategic plan to weaken the country politically and economically.

One of the most damning critiques of the TPLF's decision is that Ethiopia, despite being one of the main parties involved in the Eritrean struggle for independence, was not given a fair seat at the negotiating table. In fact, many Ethiopians contend that the TPLF made a calculated, perhaps even "evil," decision to allow Eritrea to become an independent nation, which would later result in Ethiopia losing access to its coastline and, ultimately, becoming landlocked.

This was seen by many as a deliberate act to weaken Ethiopia, since a landlocked country would have to depend heavily on its neighbors, giving the TPLF leverage and control over national affairs.

Some critics further argue that the TPLF's true intent was not to build a stronger Ethiopia, but rather to create a fragmented and weakened nation that could not stand in the way of the TPLF's future ambitions. These critics suggest that one of the long-term motivations for TPLF's approach was a desire to later push for the independence of Tigray itself. By undermining Ethiopia's national unity and sovereignty, the TPLF leadership may have been laying the groundwork for their own eventual ambitions to secede and form an independent Tigray state.

This theory has gained traction in light of subsequent events, particularly the rise of ethnic federalism and the growing ethnic divisions under TPLF rule. While it's difficult to say definitively whether the TPLF intended to use Eritrea's independence as a steppingstone toward a weakened Ethiopia or as part of a broader plan to eventually push for Tigray's independence, many view it as a deeply shortsighted and self-serving political decision.

The decision to give Eritrea its independence not only left Ethiopia without a direct route to the sea but also intensified the ethnic tensions between Ethiopia's various groups, particularly between the Tigrayans, Amharas, and Oromos. It also set the stage for years of conflict and instability, particularly after the outbreak of the 1998-2000 Eritrean Ethiopian War, where the dispute over the border and access to strategic ports became one of the main points of contention.

In hindsight, it's clear that TPLF's approach to Eritrean independence and the subsequent loss of Ethiopia's coastline has had a lasting and profound impact on the country's economic and geopolitical standing. The political and economic repercussions of this decision are still being felt today, particularly as Ethiopia seeks new ways to access the sea through neighboring Djibouti and other routes.

Ultimately, the TPLF's handling of the Eritrean question remains one of the most controversial and consequential chapters in Ethiopia's modern history. Whether this decision was driven by a long-term vision of weakening Ethiopia for the benefit of Tigray, or simply a result of political miscalculation, the loss of Eritrean ports was a major blow to Ethiopia's national interests and its economic future.

***

Hailemariam Desalegn: A Transitional Leader in the Shadow of the TPLF

Hailemariam Desalegn Boshe, born on July 19, 1965, in the Wolayta region of Ethiopia, served as the Prime Minister of Ethiopia from 2012 to 2018, following the death of the long-standing leader Meles Zenawi. Initially, Hailemariam assumed the role of Prime Minister in an acting capacity, before being formally elected as the chair of the ruling Ethiopian People's Revolutionary Democratic Front (EPRDF) in September 2012. Prior to becoming Prime Minister, he had served as the Deputy Prime Minister and Minister of Foreign Affairs under Meles from 2010 to 2012, which positioned him within the inner workings of the TPLF-led government.

Despite his formal rise to power, Hailemariam's tenure as Prime Minister was often seen as one marked by a lack of authority and decisiveness. Many Ethiopians viewed him as a figurehead, a leader who was installed by the TPLF but lacked the political clout and influence to enact meaningful change on his own. His leadership was overshadowed by the legacy of Meles Zenawi, the mastermind behind the ethnic federalism system that had deeply divided the country. The TPLF, which had controlled the political landscape since the fall of the Derg, continued to exert substantial influence over Ethiopia's political and military spheres, even as Hailemariam took on the role of Prime Minister.

Throughout his time in office, Hailemariam struggled to address the mounting unrest and popular discontent that was spreading across Ethiopia. In 2016, mass protests erupted, particularly in the Oromo and Amhara regions, against the government's policies, economic inequality, and perceived TPLF dominance. These protests, which began as grassroots movements for greater political freedom and economic justice, were met with heavy-handed security responses, further escalating tensions.

Despite his public statements of support for reforms, many Ethiopians saw Hailemariam as little more than a puppet of the TPLF. His speeches often came across as ineffective, lacking the conviction and authority expected from a head of state. Rather than leading the country with a clear vision, he was perceived by many as someone who was more concerned with maintaining the status quo than with addressing the grievances of the people. His leadership style was seen as passive, and he was often accused of acting as a mere administrator rather than a proactive leader. His attempts to engage in dialogue with opposition groups and initiate reforms were often stymied by the entrenched TPLF leadership, which still controlled much of the government apparatus.

In February 2018, after years of unrest and pressure from both domestic and international actors, Hailemariam took the unprecedented step of resigning from both his position as Prime Minister and as the chair of the EPRDF. His resignation marked a rare moment in Ethiopia's political history, as previous leaders had either died in office or been overthrown. Hailemariam cited his desire to pave the way for political reforms and a peaceful resolution to the crisis in the country, but his departure was seen by many as an acknowledgment of the TPLF's inability to maintain control and manage the growing crisis.

Though Hailemariam's resignation was seen as a necessary step in the face of widespread discontent, his legacy remains one of missed opportunities. Many Ethiopians never truly believed he had the power to lead the country on his own, with some critics describing him as a "puppet" of the TPLF. His leadership was often mocked for its perceived lack of decisiveness, as he failed to address the growing ethnic and political divisions that ultimately contributed to the erosion of the TPLF's dominance. While Hailemariam may have been a transitional figure in Ethiopian politics, his time in power was marked by a struggle for agency, and his resignation opened the door for new leadership under Abiy Ahmed, which would usher in a period of significant political change.

In hindsight, Hailemariam's time in office is often viewed as a period of stagnation, where the hopes for genuine reform and change were undermined by the lingering influence of the TPLF. Despite his outwardly calm and diplomatic demeanor, his leadership was unable to overcome the deep-rooted divisions within Ethiopian society, particularly the tensions created by ethnic federalism. His decision to step down, however, created the opportunity for a new generation of leadership, symbolized by Abiy Ahmed, to emerge and take the country in a new direction, one that would eventually see the dismantling of the TPLF's grip on power and the beginning of a new political era, the Prosperity Party, in Ethiopia.

***

The Silent Death of the EPRDF and the Birth of the Prosperity Party: A Funeral Without Mourning

The Ethiopian People's Revolutionary Democratic Front (EPRDF), once the mighty architect of Ethiopia's political order, did not collapse with thunder or spectacle. It died quietly, almost like an old monarch suffocating in his own palace, ignored even by those who once swore loyalty at his feet. By 2018, the coalition that Meles Zenawi and his TPLF-led circle had built had rotted from within, its promises of revolutionary democracy turned into an edifice of repression, corruption, and ethnic division. The death of the EPRDF was not sudden, it was a long, suffocating decline marked by betrayal, bloodshed, and growing contempt from the very people it claimed to serve.

The signs of decay had been visible for years. The so-called developmental state suffocated political freedoms, ethnic federalism deepened divides rather than healing them, and a ruling party that once marched under the banner of liberation had become indistinguishable from the autocracy it overthrew. By 2016, the eruption of massive protests led by Oromo youth, the Qeerroo and by Amhara communities revealed the brittle skeleton of a regime that relied more on bullets than legitimacy. The streets filled with chants of defiance, met with live rounds and repression, yet the EPRDF could not extinguish the fire. Its silence in the face of people's demands for justice was not the silence of dignity but the silence of death. The party was still standing, but its soul had already departed.

The ascension of Abiy Ahmed in April 2018 was the moment the corpse was finally recognized. To a population weary of blood and stagnation, Abiy appeared like a new dawn, the first Oromo prime minister, a leader who promised forgiveness, openness, and reconciliation. Yet even his earliest reforms, the release of prisoners, the return of exiles, the opening of political space, were less a rebirth than a burial. The old order had lost the will to fight for its own survival. Abiy's announcement in November 2019 that the EPRDF would be dissolved and replaced by the Prosperity Party was, in truth, less an act of creation than the reading of a death certificate. The EPRDF had already been dead, abandoned by its people, cursed by its history, and hollowed by its contradictions.

But death does not always cleanse. The Prosperity Party rose not as a phoenix from the ashes, but as a ghost draped in the illusion of renewal. Its claim to transcend ethnic divisions was a carefully woven myth. In reality, it sought to centralize power under Abiy, tightening the grip of one man where once a coalition had ruled. To the Oromo who bled for justice, and to the Amhara who demanded recognition, Prosperity's promises rang empty. The TPLF, stripped of the dominance it enjoyed under the EPRDF, rejected the new order outright. Its refusal to join was not a quarrel within the family but a declaration of war. The wound between Mekelle and Addis widened into a chasm, and by 2020, that rift ignited the Tigray War, a war that turned the burial of the EPRDF into the birth of an era even darker, bloodier, and more uncertain.

The symbolism is stark: the EPRDF, once hailed as Ethiopia's pathway to modernization, died without honor, its legacy stained by authoritarianism and ethnic fragmentation. The Prosperity Party, instead of healing the fractures, inherited the corpse's disease and spread it further. The "silent death" of the EPRDF did not usher in peace, but silence of another kind, the silence of villages bombed, of voices imprisoned, of millions displaced with no one to mourn them. Abiy's rhetoric of unity masked the same cycle of deception and coercion. The new party promised national prosperity, but its birth was baptized in blood and betrayal.

History may one day write that Ethiopia's transition from the EPRDF to the Prosperity Party was not a transformation but a mutation, where the decay of one regime merely gave rise to another with sharper teeth. The death of the EPRDF was a death without mourning because the people had already turned away from it in disgust. The birth of the Prosperity Party was a birth without joy, a child delivered into a cradle of division and violence.

Thus, Ethiopia entered a new era not through rebirth but through funeral procession. The EPRDF's corpse lies unburied, its sins still haunting the land, while the Prosperity Party carries forward a legacy of control dressed as reform. This is not progress but repetition, a cycle where death masquerades as birth and silence conceals the sound of suffering. Ethiopia, once promised renewal, finds itself instead trapped in the mausoleum of its politics, where the ghosts of the dead still rule the living.

***

CHAPTER 7

The Shattered Historic Peace Agreement with Eritrea under Abiy Ahmed

One of Abiy's most defining accomplishments in his early tenure was the signing of a peace agreement with Eritrea in 2018. The peace deal, which ended a two-decade-long conflict between the two nations, brought Abiy widespread international acclaim, culminating in his receipt of the Nobel Peace Prize in 2019. The war between Ethiopia and Eritrea, which began in 1998, had been a major source of tension in the Horn of Africa. Despite a ceasefire in 2000, the two countries remained in a state of no-war, no-peace for nearly two decades.

Abiy's decision to engage in peace talks with Eritrean President Isaias Afwerki was seen as a bold and unprecedented move. The agreement involved the normalization of diplomatic ties, the reopening of borders, and the resumption of trade and transportation links. It was a significant step toward stability in the Horn of Africa and marked a high point in Abiy's early tenure as Prime Minister.

The signing of the peace agreement was celebrated as a victory for diplomacy, and Abiy's efforts were lauded globally. The Nobel Peace Prize committee praised his "decisive initiative" in resolving the long-standing conflict and his commitment to fostering peace in the region. This achievement was a major boost to Abiy's reputation both within Ethiopia and on the international stage.

However, the peace deal with Eritrea also exposed Abiy to criticism at home, particularly from those who believed the agreement undermined Ethiopia's national security or that it was signed too hastily. The opposition, particularly from the Tigray region, expressed concern about the terms of the peace deal, and some questioned Abiy's ability to maintain the country's sovereignty while pursuing regional peace.

***

Nobel Peace Prize

Abiy Ahmed received the Nobel Peace Prize in 2019 for his role in resolving the 20-year conflict with Eritrea, initiating broad political reforms in Ethiopia, and promoting regional cooperation in the Horn of Africa. His award came amidst ongoing challenges in Ethiopia, including internal ethnic tensions and the early stages of the Tigray conflict. Thus, the speech holds dual significance: it reflects his achievements, but also his ongoing commitment to overcoming the hurdles of his leadership. In his acceptance speech, Abiy begins reflecting on the idea of peace. For him, peace is not merely the absence of conflict but a dynamic process that requires work, dialogue, and empathy. Abiy's framing of peace as a process rather than a mere state of being indicates his recognition of the complexity of achieving lasting peace.

Abiy's emphasis on peace aligns with his political journey and his efforts to reconcile with Eritrea. By stating that peace is a "process," Abiy acknowledges the challenges of maintaining it, especially in a region as historically volatile as the Horn of Africa. The focus on dialogue reflects his commitment to diplomacy and negotiation over military confrontation. This has been a hallmark of his approach, particularly in his handling of the long-standing conflict with Eritrea.

However, the reality of peacebuilding is more complicated, and Abiy's speech, in hindsight, must be read with the understanding that Ethiopia was already beginning to experience significant internal challenges, particularly with ethnic violence and political instability. The Tigray conflict, which erupted months after his speech, raised questions about the practicality of his peace-building efforts, both internally and regionally.

Abiy emphasizes Ethiopia's unity throughout his speech. He speaks of the "nation" as an evolving entity that must be inclusive and respect its diversity. A recurring motif in the speech is the idea of "oneness" and the need for unity across Ethiopia's ethnic groups. Abiy calls for a collective effort to overcome the divisions that have long characterized Ethiopian politics, especially under the ethnic federalism system.

Abiy Ahmed's call for unity was indeed timely, especially considering Ethiopia's complex ethnic composition and the divisive legacy of the ethnic federalism system implemented by the TPLF-led EPRDF. Ethnic federalism, which was designed to give each ethnic group autonomy over their region, was widely criticized for fostering divisions and inflaming tensions between Ethiopia's diverse ethnic groups. Abiy's vision of a unified Ethiopia that transcended these ethnic lines seemed like a beacon of hope, promising national healing and a fresh start for the country.

However, in hindsight, many believe that Abiy's calls for unity may have been more aspirational than genuine. Many argue that Abiy's approach was more about consolidating his power and securing his own political future than genuinely fostering unity and democracy. While he initially spoke of reconciliation and cooperation, his government's heavy-handed approach to dealing with opposition and ethnic groups, as well as his military intervention in Tigray in late 2020, raised doubts about his commitment to the principles of peace and unity. The brutal war in Tigray and Amhara, along with reports of human rights violations, further fueled criticism of Abiy's leadership and revealed a significant gap between his words and actions.

Furthermore, Abiy's leadership has increasingly appeared to prioritize his own ego and ambitions. His efforts to centralize power and eliminate rivals, even within his own party, have undermined his claims of promoting dialogue and democratic governance. Some believe that Abiy manipulated the international community's perception of him, using his reformist rhetoric as a tool to gain support and further his own agenda.

Abiy's vision of unity in Ethiopia has proven to be extraordinarily difficult to achieve. Ethiopia's deep ethnic divisions, combined with a legacy of political manipulation and distrust, make any attempt to unite the country a monumental challenge. His administration's policies have often exacerbated these divisions, further polarizing Ethiopian society. While Abiy may have started with aspirations of unity and peace, his methods and actions have raised questions about whether he was genuinely committed to these ideals or if he was simply using them as a means to secure his own power.

Abiy's message of unity can also be interpreted as a response to growing political fragmentation and ethnic violence in Ethiopia during his tenure. While his rhetoric about national unity was seen as a powerful ideal, its practical implementation has faced severe challenges, particularly with the outbreak of conflict in Tigray and the proliferation of ethnic-based violence.

In his Nobel Peace Prize acceptance speech, Abiy Ahmed presented a vision of Ethiopia as a nation undergoing profound transformation. He emphasized his commitment to liberalizing Ethiopia's economy, fostering a more open political environment, and expanding democratic freedoms. He talked about privatizing state-owned enterprises, improving governance, and creating a society where there was greater access to information, free expression, and a reduction in corruption. Abiy framed himself as a reformer, keen on reshaping Ethiopia's political and economic landscape and positioning the country as a model of democratic progress.

However, over time, his promises have begun to unravel, and the reality of his administration has become increasingly contradictory. While Abiy's rhetoric of reform and anti-corruption has earned him accolades, including the Nobel Peace Prize, the country's current reality paints a far different picture. Despite Abiy's personal claims of fighting corruption, Ethiopia is grappling with deeply entrenched corruption, particularly within the public sector.

Abiy himself has openly acknowledged the rampant corruption in his government, criticizing officials within his administration and calling for greater accountability. In several of his speeches to parliament, he has complained about the state of corruption, even stating that it is one of the greatest threats to his reform agenda. However, despite his warnings and acknowledgment, the situation has only worsened. While Abiy may not personally be seen as corrupt, many argue that his failure to effectively address the systemic issues of corruption within the government points to a deeper problem, one that stems from the very structure of the political system he inherited.

Some critics claim that Abiy's efforts to fight corruption have been selective and ineffective. While he has dismissed or prosecuted certain high-profile individuals, many argue that he has failed to address the root causes of corruption that have taken hold across Ethiopia's public sector. The patronage system, nepotism, and cronyism that were rife under the TPLF and EPRDF regimes have not disappeared under Abiy. Rather, some claim that they have been reinforced, and the same patterns of corruption persist in his government.

One major issue is that, despite Abiy's promises of good governance, his administration has struggled to implement meaningful reforms. Government officials, both at the local and national levels, continue to operate with impunity, abusing power and indulging in acts of bribery, embezzlement, and favoritism. Public sector services, which are often vital to citizens' well-being, continue to be plagued by inefficiency and corruption. Many Ethiopians report that, in order to receive basic services, they must pay bribes or navigate a complex network of nepotism and favoritism.

Moreover, Abiy's push for economic liberalization has been marred by the same issues. While privatization and the opening up of markets were intended to foster competition and spur growth, they have often been accompanied by opportunities for elite groups to profit from the process. As a result, there is widespread perception that the benefits of these reforms have disproportionately favored those with political connections, rather than the general public.

In essence, Abiy's promises of a transparent and accountable government have been overshadowed by the continued prevalence of corruption. His administration, despite its initial wave of reforms, has been unable to break free from the deep-seated political and economic practices that hinder progress. Ethiopia's public sector continues to function, in many cases, as a system of patronage where personal connections and financial incentives outweigh merit and efficiency. Even if Abiy is not personally corrupt, his inability to tackle these systemic issues has left Ethiopia in a precarious position.

The failure to address corruption is one of the key reasons why Abiy's government, despite its reformist rhetoric, has failed to meet the expectations of both the Ethiopian people and the international community. In order for Abiy to prove that his reforms are genuine and sustainable, he will need to confront the corruption that remains entrenched at every level of government and society. Until then, his calls for unity and democratic governance will ring hollow, and Ethiopia will continue to struggle with the same issues that have plagued it for decades.

In his acceptance speech, Abiy Ahmed made it clear that his efforts to bring peace and unity were accompanied by significant domestic reforms. He emphasized his commitment to liberalizing Ethiopia's economy, improving governance, and expanding democratic freedoms. These reforms included the privatization of state-owned enterprises, fostering a more open political environment, and increasing access to information and free expression. Abiy also spoke about his efforts to address corruption and make Ethiopia a more transparent and accountable state. His vision for a more democratic and market-oriented Ethiopia was central to his narrative.

Abiy's reforms were indeed seen as a bold move in a country with a highly centralized political structure and a state-controlled economy. His leadership marked a shift towards reducing the role of the state in business, allowing greater political participation, and improving civil liberties. These actions were positioned as a genuine attempt to transform Ethiopia's political and economic landscape, reflecting his aspiration for a modernized, democratic nation.

However, the ambitious nature of these reforms has also led to significant backlash, both domestically and internationally. While some political liberalization has occurred, critics argue that Abiy has not implemented enough institutional change to support these reforms in a meaningful way. The rise in political violence, escalating ethnic conflicts, and the devastating Tigray war raised serious concerns about the effectiveness of Abiy's reforms. His political reforms have been overshadowed by an inability to quell growing violence, foster national unity, or prevent regional and ethnic tensions from spiraling out of control.

Abiy also underscored the importance of regional peace and cooperation, specifically with Eritrea. His peace agreement with Eritrea, signed in 2018, ended two decades of tension and military conflict between the two nations. The agreement was hailed as a breakthrough, and Abiy highlighted it as one of the cornerstones of his leadership, earning him the Nobel Peace Prize in the process. However, some critics argue that the peace agreement with Eritrea was not entirely genuine. Rather than being a purely selfless act for peace, Abiy's motivations have been questioned. His approach to Eritrea can be seen as a strategic move to bolster his image and achieve greater personal power, rather than a sincere desire for reconciliation between the two nations.

Some suggest that Abiy's actions towards Eritrea were driven by his personal ambitions, specifically his desire to construct a greater Ethiopia in the image of his own leadership. The peace deal, in this view, was not motivated by genuine concern for peace, but rather by Abiy's ego and psychological need for recognition and power. The Nobel Peace Prize, awarded prematurely in some eyes, became a symbol of Abiy's desire to shape his legacy and secure a prominent place in history. The reality, according to these critics, is that the agreement served his political goals more than it served the people of Ethiopia or Eritrea.

Indeed, it's been argued that Abiy's true motivations behind the peace deal with Eritrea were tied to his own personal image-building and ambition for national consolidation. His focus was on securing power and prestige, not necessarily peace. Abiy's leadership style and the diplomatic steps he took with Eritrea reflect a larger narrative of his pursuit of greatness at the expense of genuine diplomatic efforts and regional stability. This self-centered approach may have blinded the Nobel Peace Prize committee, who awarded him the prize without fully understanding the complexities and underlying motivations behind his actions.

In hindsight, it can be argued that the Nobel Committee's decision to award Abiy the prize was premature. They failed to anticipate the fallout from his political and military decisions, particularly the escalation of violence and conflict that would erupt later on. His leadership, once seen as a harbinger of peace and progress, now faces scrutiny, as Ethiopia plunges deeper into internal conflict. The promised reforms have faltered, and the international community is left questioning whether the man they once hailed as a beacon of peace truly had the country's long-term interests at heart or if he was simply building a monument to his own power.

The Tigray war, which began as a conflict between the federal government and the Tigray People's Liberation Front (TPLF), has complicated Abiy's relationships both within Ethiopia and with neighboring countries, including Eritrea. Eritrean forces became involved in the conflict, ostensibly to help Abiy's government against the TPLF, which had been an adversary of Eritrea during the period of the border war. The Ethiopian government's alignment with Eritrea in the Tigray war marked a dramatic shift from Abiy's earlier position of diplomacy and cooperation.

When the Tigray conflict erupted, Eritrean troops were quickly deployed to support Abiy's government against the TPLF. This military cooperation between Ethiopia and Eritrea has exposed the fragility of the 2018 peace agreement, as it was originally framed as a political and diplomatic rapprochement rather than a military alliance. The involvement of Eritrean forces in Tigray has led to accusations of human rights violations and atrocities committed by both sides, further souring relations between the populations of Ethiopia and Eritrea.

Moreover, the Tigray conflict has shifted the balance of power in the Horn of Africa, complicating regional dynamics. As Ethiopia's internal strife continues, neighboring countries like Sudan and Egypt have become increasingly concerned about the stability of the region, especially with the Grand Ethiopian Renaissance Dam (GERD) dispute still unresolved. Eritrea's role in supporting Abiy's government in the Tigray war has only added to the tensions, especially as the conflict spills over into neighboring areas, threatening broader regional stability.

Eritrea's position in the evolving Ethiopia-Eritrea relationship is also shaped by its own interests. While the peace agreement with Ethiopia initially benefited Eritrea by providing economic opportunities and political legitimacy, Eritrea has its own strategic priorities that often conflict with those of Ethiopia. Isaias Afwerki, who has ruled Eritrea with an iron fist for decades, has a history of prioritizing security concerns and regional influence over diplomatic engagement.

One of Eritrea's primary concerns has been ensuring its sovereignty and security. The Tigray conflict provided Eritrea with an opportunity to weaken a regional adversary, the TPLF, which had played a leading role in Ethiopia's previous government and was considered a threat to Eritrean stability. From Eritrea's perspective, Abiy's reforms and the shift toward ethnic federalism may have been seen as a destabilizing force, further justifying their involvement in the conflict. Eritrea's commitment to supporting Abiy has been primarily driven by security interests, rather than any long-term vision of peace or cooperation.

Moreover, Eritrea's economic situation remains precarious, and its leadership may view the evolving political landscape in Ethiopia as an opportunity to expand its influence in the region. However, the continued instability in Ethiopia, particularly in the aftermath of the Tigray war, has made it clear that Eritrea's self-interest may be at odds with the long-term peace envisioned by Abiy. Eritrea's leadership, which has been historically resistant to outside influence, may see Abiy's shifting political stance as a challenge to its own power and regional ambitions.

The war in Tigray has undeniably complicated Ethiopia's internal political landscape, with the Amhara region playing a critical role in shaping the conflict and its broader implications for the country's future. Historically, the Amhara region has long had territorial disputes with Tigray, especially concerning areas such as Welkite and Tegedi, which Amhara believe rightfully belong to them. These territorial claims, combined with the broader ethnic-nationalist sentiments that have been rising in the Amhara region, have deepened the rift between the region and Tigray, further complicating the overall situation.

In the early stages of the Tigray conflict, Abiy Ahmed's government sought support from the Amhara region, particularly from Amhara militia groups such as Fano, which played a pivotal role in the military offensives against Tigray forces. Abiy's government praised Fano for their contributions, hailing the Amhara region as the "backbone" of the Ethiopian military, as it helped to capture significant territories in Tigray, including the region's capital, Mekelle. For Abiy, the military assistance from Amhara fighters seemed crucial in the fight against the Tigray People's Liberation Front (TPLF), a key target in the conflict.

However, as the war progressed, Abiy's relationship with the Amhara forces began to deteriorate. The tensions between his central government and the growing ethnic nationalism in the Amhara region became more pronounced. Initially, the government embraced Fano and other Amhara militias as essential allies in the fight, but over time, Abiy's actions shifted, especially as he sought to consolidate his power and avoid giving the Amhara region too much influence or autonomy. The situation quickly took a dramatic turn, as Abiy now finds himself in direct conflict with Fano and some of the very forces that once supported him in his campaign against Tigray. In essence, Abiy's efforts to centralize power led him to clash with Amhara militias, as they continue to push for greater autonomy and the reclamation of lands, they consider rightfully theirs.

Meanwhile, Tigray, which had been seen as the enemy throughout the conflict, is now at the negotiation table with Abiy's government, underlining the shifting political dynamics. After a devastating war that resulted in thousands of deaths, widespread displacement, and destruction, the government has started negotiations with the Tigray People's Liberation Front (TPLF), and both parties are discussing the future of Tigray. This dramatic reversal has led to a complex political situation where Abiy, once opposed to the TPLF and its leadership, is now in talks with the group, while his previous allies, including Fano and other Amhara forces, are at odds with his government.

The broader implications of these developments are significant for Ethiopia's future. The conflict has not only deepened ethnic divisions but has also further strained Ethiopia's fragile national unity. The war has created a situation where political and ethnic allegiances are constantly shifting, making it difficult for Abiy to maintain a coherent strategy that balances the competing interests of Ethiopia's diverse ethnic groups. Abiy's shift from embracing the Amhara militias to engaging with the TPLF underscores the complexities of Ethiopian politics, where pragmatic considerations often trump long-standing ideological or territorial disputes.

***

Fano's Role in Ethiopia's Peace: Nationalism, Conflict, and the Struggle for Unit

The Amhara region's role in the conflict has raised concerns about regional stability. The Ethiopian government's peace process with Eritrea, initially hailed as a diplomatic breakthrough, is now being complicated by these internal power struggles. Eritrea's interests in the Tigray region, coupled with its longstanding grievances with Tigray, have made the relationship between Ethiopia and Eritrea more fragile. The broader regional stability of the Horn of Africa is at risk, as Ethiopia's internal conflicts are spilling over into its relations with neighboring countries.

The situation in Ethiopia, particularly within the Amhara and Tigray regions, has become a complex and volatile political landscape, one that could ultimately determine the future trajectory of Abiy Ahmed's leadership and his aspirations for a "Greater Ethiopia" built in his own image. The Amhara region, with its rising nationalist sentiment and the active involvement of Fano, the Amhara militia group, plays a pivotal role in this unfolding drama. Over the past two years, Fano has been embroiled in fierce fighting in the Amhara region, focusing on territorial disputes, particularly over areas such as Western Tigray, which both Amhara and Tigray claim as their own.

Abiy Ahmed faces an increasingly difficult challenge in balancing the competing forces within Ethiopia, especially as Fano pushes for greater autonomy and territorial control, often at odds with his centralized vision for the country. The Amhara region's growing sense of nationalism, fueled by territorial grievances and ethnic pride, has led to tensions with Abiy, who has previously relied on Amhara support in the conflict with Tigray. However, as his leadership evolves, Abiy's approach to managing this situation has become more authoritarian, and his willingness to accommodate the interests of Amhara nationalists has waned, leading to a deterioration of the relationship between the central government and Fano.

Some within the Amhara diaspora have called for a more radical shift in tactics, urging Fano to come to terms with the Tigray forces and even form alliances with external actors like Egypt and Somalia. The suggestion to collaborate with Egypt, which has its own geopolitical interests, especially related to the Nile River, and Somalia, which shares ethnic ties with some Amhara groups, points to the extent to which the conflict has become a regional power struggle with far-reaching consequences for the Horn of Africa. These calls reflect a growing sense of disillusionment with Abiy and his leadership, as well as the belief that a more pragmatic and strategically coordinated approach with Tigray could ultimately lead to the overthrow of Abiy's government.

On the other hand, the Tigray forces, after being involved in intense combat with the Ethiopian federal army, have adopted a more cautious approach. While they remain deeply distrustful of Abiy and his government, they seem to be refraining from direct confrontations with the Amhara forces, at least for now, to avoid deepening internal divisions and weakening their own position. The Tigray forces have been careful to avoid exacerbating tensions with Abiy, likely in the hopes of preserving their own political standing and preparing for a potential negotiation process. Their relatively low-profile stance at the moment could be part of a longer-term strategy aimed at influencing the political future of Ethiopia, especially as negotiations and peace talks continue to evolve.

This delicate balance of power between the Amhara and Tigray forces is critical in shaping the future of Abiy's government. His dream of consolidating power is at risk of unraveling as both regions assert their own claims and ambitions. Abiy's leadership, which has been marked by both bold reforms and authoritarian tendencies, now faces the challenge of managing these ethnic factions that are increasingly willing to challenge his authority. His earlier attempts at bringing unity and peace, including his peace agreement with Eritrea, seem increasingly hollow as internal ethnic divisions and territorial disputes take center stage.

As the conflict between the Amhara and Tigray regions continues to simmer, the political landscape in Ethiopia appears to be on the brink of a new phase. Whether Abiy can maintain his grip on power or whether regional forces, particularly those from Amhara and Tigray, will ultimately shape the future of the country remains uncertain. The path to national unity seems increasingly elusive, and the risks of further fragmentation and violence loom large.

Ultimately, the future of Ethiopia may hinge on the actions of the Amhara and Tigray forces, as well as the ability of Abiy to navigate these complex dynamics. If the situation continues to escalate, it could lead to further destabilization not only within Ethiopia but also in the broader Horn of Africa region. Abiy's leadership, characterized by ambition and a desire to leave a lasting legacy, may be tested by the very forces he once relied on, making it increasingly unclear whether his vision of power and national unity will come to fruition or be overtaken by the competing nationalist ambitions of Ethiopia's diverse ethnic groups.

***

The Perils of Leadership: Psychopathic Tendencies in Power

The story of Abiy Ahmed has become one of the most startling paradoxes in modern political history. Initially hailed as a symbol of hope for a new era in Ethiopia, Abiy's leadership has since transformed into a narrative of conflict, instability, and human suffering.

In politics, the line between benevolent leadership and the abuse of power can often blur, especially when it comes to individuals exhibiting traits of narcissism and psychopathy. These psychological conditions are commonly found in some of history's most destructive leaders—individuals whose manipulation, lack of empathy, and insatiable desire for control can have devastating impacts on their countries.

At the core of narcissism and psychopathy lies a dangerous cocktail of arrogance, deceit, and a profound lack of empathy. Leaders exhibiting these traits often manipulate their followers with charm and rhetoric, presenting themselves as invincible and beyond reproach. However, beneath this carefully constructed façade lies a web of destructive behaviors that can lead to national collapse.

Narcissistic leaders, such as Abiy Ahmed, thrive on attention and admiration, and this need often shapes their political decisions. For Abiy, this craving for validation has led him to prioritize his image over the well-being of his country. A grandiose sense of self-importance, driven by the need for validation, causes leaders to make reckless decisions that endanger their citizens in the name of self-preservation.

Abiy's ambitious rhetoric, his constant presentation of himself as a visionary for Ethiopia's future, and his attempts to project an image of a peace broker all feed into a narrative of inflated ego and disregard for the real consequences of his actions. His leadership, at its core, seems less about the people of Ethiopia and more about the accumulation and maintenance of personal power.

Psychopathy, characterized by a lack of empathy, can lead to horrifying outcomes when it takes root in a leadership position. A psychopathic leader exhibits a chilling willingness to manipulate, deceive, and discard those who do not serve his interests.

The absence of empathy means that such leaders can make decisions that result in widespread human suffering without feeling remorse. In Abiy's case, the escalation of ethnic tensions, the war in Tigray and Amhara, and the subsequent humanitarian crisis are stark examples of how a leader's psychopathic traits have led to unthinkable destruction, leaving civilians to bear the brunt of his unchecked actions.

The consequences of Abiy Ahmed's narcissism and psychopathy are evident in every corner of Ethiopian society. As his behavior has increasingly destabilized the country, it is clear that these psychological tendencies do not just affect the leader but also ripple through the entire nation, affecting millions of lives.

Abiy's willingness to instigate and escalate conflict, notably the war in Tigray and Amhara, exemplifies the dangerous outcomes of psychopathic leadership. In the pursuit of maintaining political control and bolstering his image as a strong leader, Abiy has embraced war as a tool for cementing power. His actions have caused untold suffering and displacement, turning peaceful communities into war zones and deepening ethnic divisions.

This manipulation of conflict serves a dual purpose: it distracts the public from his failures and provides an opportunity for him to consolidate power by framing himself as a commander-in-chief defending Ethiopia's sovereignty. In the process, he alienates opposition forces, undermines peace efforts, and creates an environment ripe for chaos.

The economic and social implications of Abiy Ahmed's leadership have been dire. His policies, particularly his approach to ethnic federalism and political exclusion, have contributed to the deterioration of Ethiopia's economy. Under his rule, inflation has soared, unemployment has increased, and social services have been disrupted. The war has further ravaged Ethiopia's economy, depleting resources that could have been better used to lift millions out of poverty.

Citizens now face an ever-worsening standard of living, with basic needs becoming more difficult to meet. Access to healthcare, education, and clean water has become scarcer, further exacerbating the already dire situation in Ethiopia. The social fabric of the country is unraveling, as citizens are left to fend for themselves in a state of constant turmoil.

One of the most insidious tactics employed by narcissistic and psychopathic leaders is the deliberate creation of chaos. By fomenting instability, these leaders create a sense of uncertainty that makes their subjects more dependent on their authority. Abiy's exacerbation of ethnic tensions and the fragmentation of the political landscape in Ethiopia serve to keep the populace in a constant state of fear and vulnerability.

Through propaganda, divisive rhetoric, and the suppression of dissent, Abiy ensures that his power remains uncontested. This manipulation of public perception is particularly dangerous, as it fosters an environment where truth is obscured, and the suffering of the people is overlooked in favor of a distorted narrative of nationalism and triumph.

The human cost of Abiy's actions is staggering. In Ethiopia, civilians bear the brunt of his psychopathic and narcissistic tendencies, enduring the devastating consequences of war, economic collapse, and social upheaval. Forced displacement, starvation, and the destruction of families are all common outcomes of his policies. This devastation, exacerbated by the government's failure to provide adequate relief, underscores the disconnect between Abiy's public persona and the suffering he has inflicted upon the people he is meant to serve.

The toll of this conflict is not just physical. The psychological scars left on Ethiopia's citizens will last for generations. Children grow up in a world defined by violence, fear, and uncertainty. Families are torn apart, and entire communities are left to pick up the pieces of their shattered lives.

Given the devastating impact of Abiy Ahmed's rule, it is crucial to explore ways in which such destructive leadership can be mitigated or prevented. The first step in countering narcissistic and psychopathic tendencies in leadership is fostering a culture of emotional intelligence and mental health awareness. Promoting empathy, self-awareness, and community engagement can help to create a political environment where leaders are held accountable for their actions and not allowed to exploit their positions for personal gain.

One of the most effective ways to mitigate the impact of dangerous leaders is to strengthen democratic institutions and ensure that leaders are held accountable for their actions. This can be achieved through transparent governance, robust checks and balances, and the involvement of civil society in decision-making processes. Such measures would help to prevent leaders from consolidating power in a way that harms the nation.

Empowering communities to participate in the political process and resist manipulative leadership is another key strategy. When people are informed, organized, and united, they become less susceptible to the divisive tactics of narcissistic and psychopathic leaders. Community resilience can be strengthened through education, access to resources, and support for grassroots movements that seek to promote peace and stability.

Abiy Ahmed's rise to power and subsequent reign in Ethiopia serves as a cautionary tale of the dangers of narcissistic and psychopathic leadership. His initial image as a peacemaker and reformer was quickly overshadowed by the destructive forces of war, chaos, and poverty that have defined his rule. The psychological characteristics of narcissism and psychopathy have manifested in his policies, leading to the suffering of millions and the destabilization of the country.

As Ethiopia continues to grapple with the aftermath of Abiy's leadership, it is crucial to learn from this painful chapter in the nation's history. The key to preventing such a devastating trajectory in the future lies in recognizing the signs of dangerous leadership, promoting emotional intelligence, and ensuring that leaders are held accountable for their actions. Only by fostering a political environment grounded in empathy, transparency, and community engagement can nations hope to break free from the cycle of chaos perpetuated by psychopathic and narcissistic leaders.

***

ABIY AHMED ALI

CHAPTER 8

Empty Promises: Ethiopia's Struggle with Food Security

The Ethiopian government under Prime Minister Abiy Ahmed has made significant claims about addressing the country's food insecurity. One of the more prominent promises was the widespread distribution of bread to the needy, with a particular focus on Addis Ababa. The initiative, framed around the surplus production of wheat in the country, was heralded as a solution to the hunger faced by many Ethiopians, especially in the capital city. The government even spoke of Shewa Bread—a company backed by billionaire Sheik Mohamed—playing a pivotal role in ensuring that bread, an essential food staple, would be abundant and accessible for all. However, as time has passed, these promises have failed to materialize in the lives of those most in need. The question remains: where is the bread? Why is it still so difficult for Ethiopians, particularly in Addis Ababa, to access basic food?

Despite the government's promises of a wheat surplus, food insecurity is worsening in Addis Ababa, with bread and other essential items becoming increasingly scarce and expensive. While officials assured the public that a surplus of wheat would translate into affordable and abundant bread, the reality is far different. Many residents are facing long queues at bakeries, where bread is either unavailable or priced beyond the reach of average workers. For many, a loaf of bread has become an unaffordable luxury, and it is not just bread. The cost of basic food items has skyrocketed, leaving families struggling to make ends meet. In some areas, a single meal costs the equivalent of a poor person's entire monthly salary. For the most vulnerable, especially mothers and children in low-income communities, hunger has become a daily struggle. The government's assurances of food abundance ring hollow as the public grapples with the painful reality of escalating food prices and widespread scarcity.

The situation in Addis Ababa underscores a wider systemic problem in Ethiopia: the gap between political promises and their on-the-ground realities. Despite the claims of an agricultural revolution and wheat production being at a historic high, much of the surplus wheat remains out of reach for those who need it most. The political rhetoric around this issue often portrays the country as being on the verge of solving its food insecurity problems, yet those living in poverty continue to struggle to access even the most basic food items. The discrepancy between the narrative and the reality has caused frustration and confusion among Ethiopians who are asking the same question: where is the bread?

Sheik Mohamed, a billionaire businessman, has been presented as a key player in the government's strategy to address food insecurity. His involvement with Shewa Bread, which was supposed to be a cornerstone in solving Ethiopia's bread shortage, has not lived up to expectations. Despite promises that Shewa Bread would supply enough bread for the entire city, it has failed. The issue isn't just limited to availability; it is also about affordability. Many Ethiopians simply cannot afford the bread that is available. For many in the lower-income brackets, the price of bread has risen beyond what they can pay, exacerbating food insecurity.

One of the reasons for the continued scarcity of bread is the broader challenges facing Ethiopia's economy. While wheat production has increased in some areas, issues such as poor distribution networks, lack of infrastructure, and corruption within supply chains have prevented the wheat surplus from reaching those who need it. The government's failure to address these structural issues has meant that even when there is enough wheat, it is not reaching the impoverished communities who struggle to access it. Additionally, inflation and economic instability have made staple goods like bread less affordable for the average Ethiopian family. As a result, the promises of an abundance of bread remain an illusion for many.

In a public relations attempt to address food insecurity, Abiy Ahmed's wife, Zinash, has also been presented as a key figure in the establishment of bread factories across the nation. While this initiative has been framed as a solution to the country's hunger crisis, many view it as little more than a public image strategy. The establishment of these factories, while it may sound promising on paper, has not been enough to alleviate the food shortages in many parts of Ethiopia. The factories that have been built have not produced enough bread to meet the needs of the population, and the bread that is produced is often not accessible to those who need it most. The focus on creating new bread factories, without addressing underlying issues such as distribution, affordability, and access, has done little to solve the pressing problem of hunger in Ethiopia.

The disconnect between public messaging and the lived experience of Ethiopians is stark. While government officials, including Abiy and Zinash, speak about the importance of food security and the establishment of bread factories, the reality on the ground is that many children are going to bed without food. The media often portrays these efforts as heroic and successful, but for many Ethiopians, these promises are empty words. In a country where hunger is a daily reality for millions, it is hard to take seriously the notion that Ethiopia is on the verge of solving its food insecurity problems when basic necessities like bread are still out of reach.

This growing frustration over unmet promises has left many questioning the sincerity of the government's actions. The recurring theme in these promises is the image-building efforts surrounding the government's leadership, often focused on individuals like Abiy and his family. The narrative of selflessness, devotion, and concern for the poor has become central to the government's public image. Yet, for many Ethiopians, these images are overshadowed by the harsh reality of scarcity and hunger. The ongoing bread shortages and the inability of the government to deliver on its promises of a wheat surplus have only deepened the skepticism surrounding Abiy's administration.

Ultimately, the question remains: where is the surplus wheat, and why is bread still so scarce in Ethiopia? The people of Addis Ababa and other regions are left with no answers. The promises of bread for all have proven to be just that, promises. For those struggling to feed their families, the image of a government that claims to be addressing food insecurity feels more like a carefully constructed illusion than a genuine effort to tackle the underlying issues of hunger and poverty. Until the government can effectively address the systemic problems of distribution, affordability, and access, the bread that was promised to Ethiopia will remain out of reach for many. The starving is still hungry, and the question remains unanswered: where is the bread?

Food security, as defined by the World Food Summit of 1996, exists when all people, at all times, have access to sufficient, safe, and nutritious food to maintain a healthy and active life. This definition emphasizes the need for both physical and economic access to food that satisfies people's nutritional requirements and preferences. Achieving food security is not merely about food availability but also about its accessibility, affordability, and stability, especially for vulnerable groups such as children, pregnant women, and the elderly.

In Ethiopia, food security has remained a persistent issue despite the country's agricultural potential. As of 2010, Ethiopia was one of the most food-insecure countries globally, with more than 5.2 million people requiring food assistance. The country's ranking in the Global Hunger Index (GHI), which measures the levels of hunger and undernutrition, further underlines the severity of the problem. Ethiopia's GHI score in 2020 ranked the country 92nd out of 107 nations, a reflection of the persistent hunger crisis.

Agriculture is the backbone of Ethiopia's economy, contributing significantly to the country's GDP and employing over 80% of the population, most of whom live in rural areas. The majority of Ethiopians depend on agriculture for their livelihoods. Ethiopia possesses abundant natural resources, such as fertile land, ample water sources, and a large labor force, which, in theory, should allow for substantial agricultural development. However, much of this potential remains untapped due to several structural and policy challenges.

The agricultural sector in Ethiopia is highly sensitive to climatic conditions. Frequent droughts and erratic rainfall patterns exacerbate food insecurity, as agricultural production is heavily dependent on these factors. For example, the 1984 famine, one of the most devastating events in Ethiopia's modern history, was largely caused by a severe drought, and it led to the deaths of over one million people. Unfortunately, similar events continue to occur, and Ethiopia remains vulnerable to the effects of climate change.

In addition to these figures, malnutrition remains a significant issue. In 2005, nearly 53.5% of children under the age of five and 30.6% of pregnant women were found to be anemic. Furthermore, 34.6% of children were underweight, and 50.7% suffered from growth retardation, which impairs both physical and mental development. These statistics reflect the deep-rooted nature of Ethiopia's food insecurity crisis and its far-reaching implications for the country's future.

The consequences of malnutrition in Ethiopia are severe, especially among children and pregnant women. Poor nutrition in early childhood leads to growth retardation, which not only stunts physical development but also impairs cognitive function. Malnourished children are more likely to suffer from illnesses and die at a young age, perpetuating the cycle of poverty and hunger. Furthermore, stunting in children has long-term effects, reducing their school performance and future economic productivity.

Additionally, malnutrition in women creates a vicious cycle that worsens food insecurity in the next generation. Women who are undernourished are more likely to give birth to low-birthweight babies, which increases the likelihood of infant mortality. Malnourished mothers also face a higher risk of complications during childbirth. This intergenerational cycle of malnutrition has a long-lasting impact on Ethiopia's development, and addressing this issue is crucial for improving the country's future.

By 2022, Ethiopia faced even greater food security challenges, with an estimated 50 million people in the eastern part of Africa suffering from food insecurity, including 10-15 million Ethiopians in need of food assistance. The low availability of fertilizers, coupled with ongoing conflict and political instability, particularly in northern Ethiopia, further exacerbated food insecurity. Despite Abiy Ahmed's promises to tackle the country's food security challenges, the reality for many Ethiopians has been one of growing hunger.

Abiy's administration has made several promises related to improving food security, such as increasing wheat production and ensuring that staple foods like bread would be widely available. However, these promises have not been translated into tangible results.

One of the critical issues under Abiy Ahmed's leadership is the continued inability to improve the food security situation. While he has promised various reforms, his administration has failed to address the root causes of hunger and malnutrition effectively. Despite claims of increased wheat production and better food distribution systems, many Ethiopian citizens find themselves struggling with hunger on a daily basis.

This failure is particularly apparent in urban areas like Addis Ababa, where the population expected significant improvements in food availability due to government initiatives. However, the reality is that access to food remains a challenge for the average citizen. In the public sector, workers such as teachers, healthcare workers, and students have all reported difficulty in obtaining sufficient food. Even when food is available, it is often too expensive for low-income families to afford, exacerbating inequality and hunger.

Abiy's approach to food security has been characterized by a series of promises that have yet to materialize into meaningful change. His administration has focused on public relations efforts to bolster its image, such as the symbolic feeding of the poor and the promotion of large-scale projects like Shewa Dabo bread factories. However, these initiatives have failed to address the fundamental issues that contribute to food insecurity in the country.

The government's reliance on external aid and its failure to deliver on promises of food self-sufficiency have made it clear that Abiy Ahmed's administration has not done anything substantially better than the previous government in terms of improving food security. In fact, the situation has worsened, with many Ethiopians now facing even more severe challenges in obtaining basic food staples. The rise of food insecurity under Abiy's leadership reflects a deeper failure to implement policies that directly address the structural issues of poverty, inequality, and underdevelopment that have long plagued the country.

***

Agriculture as the Backbone and Its Vulnerabilities

Agriculture remains the backbone of Ethiopia's economy, yet it is also the sector most vulnerable to the country's recurring food security crises. Despite efforts like the Agricultural Growth Program (AGP) focusing on increasing agricultural productivity, Ethiopia's agricultural sector faces numerous unresolved challenges, with climate vulnerability and limited technological innovation being the primary obstacles.

Ethiopia's agricultural sector is crucial to the livelihoods of over 80% of its population, with most people relying on rain-fed farming. This makes the country's agricultural productivity highly susceptible to the variability and unpredictability of the climate. With the majority of farmers dependent on two rainy seasons per year, any disruption in these patterns leads to severe consequences for food production. Climate change, through increasing instances of droughts, floods, and temperature extremes, poses an increasing threat to agricultural systems, making the sector vulnerable to frequent environmental shocks.

The Ethiopian government has undertaken initiatives, such as the AGP, to increase agricultural productivity and improve climate resilience. The program aims to enhance the capacity for climate adaptation, introduce better natural resource management practices, and increase agricultural productivity. However, despite these efforts, Ethiopia's agricultural system remains heavily reliant on traditional, rain-fed farming methods, leaving it exposed to climate-related disruptions. Large-scale irrigation systems and water management infrastructure are insufficient, hindering the sector's ability to adapt to these changing climatic conditions. Although small-scale irrigation systems and water conservation techniques have been explored, their reach remains limited.

Ethiopia's agricultural output is often dictated by the reliability of rainfall. Erratic or insufficient rainfall can drastically reduce crop production, leading to food shortages, which can trigger a cycle of food insecurity and even famine. For instance, the 2015-2016 El Niño event caused severe droughts, impacting crop yields and livestock production, and exposing the vulnerability of Ethiopia's food security systems. While the government's emergency relief efforts aimed to mitigate the crisis, the response was insufficient for addressing the scale of the environmental shock. Similarly, the country is facing increasingly unpredictable rainfall patterns, which often result in flooding that can wash away crops, exacerbate soil erosion, and displace communities.

The vulnerability of Ethiopia's agricultural sector is further compounded by temperature extremes, such as heatwaves and cold spells, which disrupt growing seasons, decrease crop yields, and strain water resources. Additionally, prolonged dry periods followed by intense rainfall create conditions that lead to crop failures due to waterlogging, a situation that exacerbates food insecurity.

To counteract these issues, Ethiopia has begun exploring alternative farming techniques, such as climate-smart agriculture practices, drought-resistant crops, and improved water management systems. However, these approaches face numerous obstacles, including limited resources, inadequate infrastructure, and a lack of technical knowledge among farmers. The country's agricultural policies also fail to provide comprehensive, long-term solutions to the climate change challenges facing the sector.

Despite these difficulties, there has been progress in promoting sustainable agricultural practices in partnership with international organizations. One key area of focus is small-scale irrigation systems, which could help farmers mitigate the risks of erratic rainfall. However, these systems remain costly to implement and maintain, and their coverage is still limited. Moreover, Ethiopia's agricultural policies, while focused on climate adaptation, face challenges in terms of slow implementation and insufficient resources to address the scale of the crisis.

Land degradation, deforestation, and soil erosion further complicate Ethiopia's agricultural challenges. Unsustainable land use practices, driven by population growth and limited land availability, exacerbate the impact of climate-related shocks. Deforestation not only reduces the availability of water resources but also accelerates soil erosion, further diminishing agricultural productivity. While efforts have been made to combat deforestation and promote sustainable land management practices, these efforts are hindered by limited implementation and funding.

As climate change continues to worsen, Ethiopia's agricultural sector faces greater pressures that will require urgent, long-term solutions to ensure food security and economic stability. A comprehensive, multi-faceted strategy, involving investments in irrigation infrastructure, access to climate-smart technologies, and improved farmer capacity, is essential to build resilience and secure sustainable food production.

***

Limited Technological Innovation in Ethiopian Agriculture under the Abiy Administration

Despite claims by the Abiy administration of prioritizing modernization in the agricultural sector, the reality is far from what is promised. With Ethiopia's vast natural resources, including abundant water and land, it remains a mystery why the country is still unable to feed itself. The government's approach to agriculture lacks genuine focus on empowering private farmers, and the situation continues to deteriorate due to systemic inefficiencies and barriers.

While the Agricultural Growth Program (AGP) has introduced improved agricultural practices, including quality seeds and fertilizers, the adoption of modern farming technologies remains limited and sluggish. The gap between traditional farming methods and modern techniques is one of the primary obstacles to improving productivity and food security. Many farmers are still using outdated, inefficient methods that not only limit agricultural output but also contribute significantly to ongoing food insecurity.

The most glaring issue in Ethiopia's agricultural modernization is the lack of mechanization. In contrast to other countries that have successfully integrated mechanized farming equipment, such as tractors and harvesters, Ethiopia's smallholder farmers, who are the backbone of the agricultural sector, still rely on labor-intensive, manual practices. The high costs of machinery make it inaccessible to most farmers, leaving them stuck in a cycle of low productivity and poverty. This lack of mechanization continues to be one of the greatest barriers to increasing agricultural efficiency.

Equally troubling is the underdeveloped irrigation infrastructure. With agriculture still largely rain-fed, Ethiopia's agricultural sector remains highly vulnerable to unpredictable rainfall patterns, exacerbated by climate change. Although the AGP advocates for irrigation, the country's large-scale irrigation systems are either non-existent, outdated, or poorly maintained. This lack of reliable irrigation systems places Ethiopia's food security in jeopardy, especially as climate change intensifies, bringing more unpredictable weather patterns.

Access to finance for smallholder farmers is another critical issue. Many farmers struggle to secure credit or loans, preventing them from investing in modern farming technologies, machinery, or necessary infrastructure. Without affordable access to capital, they are unable to purchase modern equipment, improve irrigation systems, or even buy high-quality seeds and fertilizers. This financial barrier severely limits their capacity to modernize their farms and improve productivity, keeping them locked in poverty.

In addition to financial barriers, Ethiopia's agricultural modernization is hindered by a lack of technical support and education for farmers. Many smallholder farmers are unaware of modern techniques or lack the knowledge and skills to effectively use new technologies. The agricultural extension services and local institutions that could provide crucial training and support are inadequate, limiting the ability of farmers to adopt best practices and modernize their operations.

These challenges are compounded by the government's focus on non-agricultural projects, including military investments and urban beautification projects in Addis Ababa, which siphon resources away from the agricultural sector. Instead of investing in the infrastructure and technological innovation necessary for a sustainable and productive agricultural system, much of the country's resources are spent on the city's development and military efforts, leaving the rural farmers with little support.

The potential to transform Ethiopia's agricultural sector remains, but only if these barriers, such as limited access to finance, lack of mechanization, inadequate infrastructure, and poor access to education and technology are addressed. The Abiy administration must prioritize investing in agricultural modernization by making technology, credit, and irrigation more accessible to farmers. This includes not only improving access to modern farming tools and techniques but also creating an environment where smallholder farmers can thrive without being suffocated by taxes and regulations that limit their potential.

If Ethiopia is to achieve agricultural self-sufficiency and reduce food insecurity, it requires a comprehensive approach that invests in sustainable agricultural practices, strengthens infrastructure, and provides farmers with the resources and support they need to succeed. Without this, Ethiopia's agricultural sector will remain stuck in a cycle of low productivity and poverty, and the country will continue to miss the opportunity to utilize its vast natural resources to their full potential.

***

Political Instability and Governance Issues Under Abiy Ahmed's Government

The administration of Abiy Ahmed was initially heralded as a new era for Ethiopia, with promises of peace, economic growth, and improved food security. However, the realities of governance have not lived up to the expectations set by the Prime Minister's early promises.

Internal Conflicts and Displacement
Since Abiy Ahmed came to power in 2018, Ethiopia has been mired in profound internal conflicts that have deeply affected various regions, especially Tigray, Oromia, and other parts of the country. The Tigray conflict, which erupted in late 2020, has been particularly devastating. The war has displaced millions of people, disrupted the lives of countless Ethiopians, and led to widespread human suffering. This conflict has had a catastrophic impact on agricultural production, a critical component of Ethiopia's economy, where a significant portion of the population relies on farming for their livelihoods.

In the war-torn regions, particularly Tigray, agricultural activities have been virtually halted. The destruction of farmlands, the looting of crops, and the displacement of farmers have left once-productive areas barren. Fields that were once used to grow essential crops like teff, maize, and sorghum are now left fallow, making it nearly impossible to sustain local food supplies. Farmers who were once able to feed their families and communities have been forced to flee their homes, leaving their land untended and their agricultural livelihoods destroyed.

Moreover, the conflict has caused extensive damage to vital infrastructure that supports agricultural production. Roads that connect rural areas to markets have been destroyed or rendered impassable, making it difficult for remaining farmers to transport goods to market or access necessary agricultural supplies, such as seeds, fertilizers, and tools. In many areas, irrigation systems, critical to farming in Ethiopia's semi-arid regions, have been damaged or completely wiped out. Without these systems, farmers face increased challenges in sustaining crop yields, especially as Ethiopia faces unpredictable and often extreme weather patterns due to climate change.

The war has also undermined the stability of the government and its ability to focus on long-term solutions to food security and agricultural development. Resources that would have been directed toward strengthening agricultural resilience, implementing irrigation projects, or improving market access have instead been diverted to the conflict. As a result, food security programs have faltered, unable to address the immediate and long-term needs of the population. This diversion of attention and resources has compounded the struggles faced by millions of Ethiopians who depend on agriculture not only for food but as their primary source of income.

The ongoing political instability has also made it difficult to implement effective agricultural policies. The lack of security, infrastructure, and governmental focus has created an environment where existing agricultural initiatives, such as the Agricultural Growth Program (AGP), cannot function effectively. Programs that could have helped farmers access modern technologies, improve productivity, and enhance food security have been sidelined due to the conflict, leaving rural areas increasingly vulnerable to hunger and poverty.

In conclusion, the internal conflicts under Abiy Ahmed's leadership have severely disrupted Ethiopia's agricultural sector. The destruction of infrastructure, displacement of farmers, and the diversion of government focus away from agricultural development have all exacerbated food insecurity and made it harder for farmers to rebuild and recover. This crisis not only threatens the livelihoods of millions of Ethiopians but also poses a significant challenge to the country's long-term food security and economic stability.

Weak Governance and Corruption
One of the key obstacles that has severely undermined food security initiatives under Abiy Ahmed's government is weak governance and rampant corruption. Despite efforts to address Ethiopia's food

insecurity through various programs, the lack of effective oversight and accountability has allowed these initiatives to fall short of their objectives. Corruption within local and regional governments has been a significant barrier, leading to the misallocation of resources meant for food aid and agricultural support. In many cases, essential assistance either never reaches the most vulnerable populations or is diverted for personal gain, leaving millions without the aid they desperately need.

The issue of corruption is compounded by bureaucratic inefficiencies and poor management within the government. These inefficiencies often hinder the timely distribution of food and agricultural inputs, delaying critical interventions that could mitigate hunger and food insecurity. At the same time, political infighting between regional administrations further exacerbates the problem. Regional leaders, each with their own political interests, have at times worked against one another, preventing coordinated action on food security. Instead of working toward a common national goal, the political fragmentation in Ethiopia has undermined the ability of the central government to respond swiftly and effectively to food security crises.

The lack of cohesion between different levels of government also creates confusion and delays in implementing food security programs. With conflicting priorities and territorial disputes, regions often face challenges in executing national policies. This results in fragmented efforts, where food aid and agricultural assistance programs are not aligned with the needs of the population, further deepening inequalities and worsening food insecurity in certain areas.

Ultimately, the combination of corruption, bureaucratic inefficiencies, and political instability has created a perfect storm that has hampered Ethiopia's ability to effectively address its food security challenges. These governance weaknesses have made it nearly impossible for the government to deliver on promises to ensure food access and security for all citizens. Until these issues are addressed, Ethiopia will continue to struggle in tackling its food insecurity crisis.

Excessive Focus on External Image Over Ground-Level Solutions
A major critique of Abiy Ahmed's leadership, especially in the realm of food security, is the emphasis on creating a favorable international image rather than confronting the underlying systemic issues that sustain hunger and malnutrition in Ethiopia. While there have been numerous publicized events, such as photo opportunities featuring government officials distributing food aid or showcasing agricultural projects, these acts often appear more designed to improve the government's image than to bring about meaningful, long-term solutions for the millions of Ethiopians grappling with food insecurity. These efforts frequently lack the substantial backing needed to address the structural causes of hunger, and the gap between public rhetoric and real-world impact is wide.

In Addis Ababa, the capital, the disconnect between the government's claims of food surplus and the actual food scarcity faced by many urban residents is particularly striking. Despite assertions of agricultural growth, food insecurity persists in many areas, with rising costs and insufficient access to nutritious food. The government's focus on publicizing its achievements in food aid often overlooks the larger, more systemic challenges, such as inflation, the disruption of supply chains, and inequality—that continue to hinder food access for the urban poor. In this context, the emphasis on image-building seems to prioritize international recognition over the urgent need for policies that directly address the country's food security challenges.

This pattern of performative gestures rather than substantive policy changes has eroded public trust in the government's ability to effect real progress. While the global community may view these events as signs of governmental responsibility, for many Ethiopians, particularly those in marginalized communities, the promised improvements never materialize in their daily lives. This disparity highlights the broader problem of governance in Ethiopia under Abiy's leadership, where political motives and media-driven narratives often overshadow the genuine needs of the population. Until the government shifts its focus toward addressing the root causes of food insecurity, the disconnect between rhetoric and reality will continue to plague Ethiopia's food security efforts.

In Ethiopia, social inequalities significantly affect access to food, exacerbating the country's food insecurity, particularly for vulnerable groups such as women, children, the elderly, and people with disabilities. These inequalities are deeply embedded in cultural norms, legal frameworks, and socio-economic structures, creating barriers that hinder access to resources necessary for food security and economic stability.

***

Gender Inequality and the Lack of Genuine Progress for Women under the Abiy Administration

The Abiy administration in Ethiopia has often positioned itself as a champion of women's rights, frequently boasting about its gender-inclusive initiatives. The appointment of a female president and the placement of women in almost half of the ministerial positions were initially applauded as signs of progress. However, beneath this surface-level image of female empowerment lies a reality that suggests these moves are more about public relations than a genuine commitment to addressing the systemic gender inequalities women face in Ethiopia.

Despite the government's claims, gender inequality remains deeply entrenched in Ethiopian society, particularly for women in rural areas. Women continue to struggle both at home and in the broader society. Thousands of Ethiopian women are still sent to Arab countries for work, where they endure what can only be described as modern-day slavery. These women are often forced into grueling labor in harsh conditions with little support or protection from the government. Rather than negotiating for better working conditions or advocating for their rights, the Abiy administration remains largely silent on this issue, turning a blind eye to the exploitation of Ethiopian women abroad.

In Ethiopia itself, even the small progress made for women in terms of property ownership is being undermined. There have been reports of properties, even those owned by women, being demolished under the guise of urbanization. Women's rights to property and land, although enshrined in law, are often disregarded in practice. Cultural norms and discriminatory laws continue to limit women's ability to fully exercise their rights, leaving them vulnerable to exploitation.

In rural areas, women face significant barriers to accessing land, credit, and agricultural resources, which remain key to their economic independence. While the law may offer equal land rights, traditional inheritance practices mean that land is often passed down through male family members, leaving women without control over agricultural resources. This lack of access to land, combined with limited access to credit and agricultural training, prevents women from improving productivity and increasing their income. Their reliance on seasonal farming deepens their vulnerability to food insecurity, making it harder for them to break free from poverty.

Efforts such as the Agricultural Growth Program (AGP) have been launched to address gender disparities in agriculture, but the progress has been minimal. Women are still largely excluded from training programs, which are often not tailored to their needs. Additionally, societal expectations regarding women's roles within the household further limit their ability to participate in agricultural training or to take on leadership roles in farming. Without access to the right tools, training, and financial support, women remain at a significant disadvantage.

Beyond these economic barriers, women in Ethiopia continue to face widespread social inequality. Despite their crucial roles in securing food and providing for their families, many women lack access to education, healthcare, and formal employment opportunities. These systemic barriers contribute to high rates of malnutrition and poor health outcomes for women and their families. The lack of education and healthcare leaves women with limited knowledge of nutrition and child health, which contributes to higher rates of food insecurity. The absence of stable employment opportunities leaves women economically vulnerable, especially when agricultural yields are poor, or food prices rise.

These persistent inequalities exacerbate food insecurity and malnutrition among women, placing them in a cycle of poverty and dependence. The Abiy administration's focus on image-building and gender equality in speeches and policies has not resulted in substantial change for the majority of Ethiopian women. The reality for many is that they continue to face violence, hunger, and marginalization in both urban and rural settings.

To truly address the gender inequality in Ethiopia, more than symbolic gestures are needed. Concrete actions, such as strengthening legal protections for women's land rights, ensuring access to credit and financial services, and implementing agricultural training programs that are inclusive and responsive to women's needs, are essential. Women must be empowered with the resources and opportunities to break free from the cycle of poverty, food insecurity, and gender-based violence. Until these systemic barriers are addressed, the Abiy administration's claims of gender equality will remain little more than a façade.

***

Child Malnutrition in Ethiopia: A Crisis Amidst Image-Building Priorities

Child malnutrition in Ethiopia continues to be a significant obstacle to the country's development, and Abiy Ahmed has failed to adequately address this pressing issue. While there are some efforts in place to combat malnutrition, these actions have not been enough, and millions of children, including in urban areas like Addis Ababa, are suffering from starvation. This crisis is not confined to the poor; the middle class is also feeling the effects, with many families unable to provide enough food for their children, leading to widespread malnutrition. Teachers, nurses, police officers, and other civil servants also struggle to feed their families, exacerbating the problem.

In Addis Ababa, for example, there were reports of public-school students collapsing due to lack of food, leading to the administration having to step in to provide meals at least once. Despite this, the overall situation remains dire. In the countryside, especially in regions like Amhara and Tigray, children are unable to go to school due to lack of safety, subsistence, and security, resulting in a deepening cycle of poverty and hunger.

The government's focus has been more on image-building initiatives such as constructing palaces, resorts, and paving city roads, rather than addressing these urgent humanitarian needs. In recent years, Prime Minister Abiy has made statements prioritizing Ethiopia's international image over the plight of starving children, even criticizing a popular song that highlighted the suffering caused by famine, arguing that it undermines Ethiopia's investment image. This disregard for the real issues faced by Ethiopians, particularly the children, is a stark reflection of the government's misplaced priorities.

According to the 2020 Global Hunger Index (GHI), Ethiopia remains one of the countries with high levels of child malnutrition. Stunting, which results from chronic undernutrition, affects nearly 38% of children under five, while 7.3% of children suffer from wasting, a sign of acute malnutrition that places them at immediate risk of death. The effects of malnutrition go far beyond physical health, affecting cognitive development, school performance, and future productivity. Children who experience stunting are more likely to struggle with learning and have lower IQs, which perpetuates cycles of poverty and limits their future opportunities.

Maternal malnutrition also plays a crucial role in child malnutrition. In rural areas, many women lack access to nutritious food, healthcare, and prenatal care, leading to underweight babies who are more vulnerable to health complications and malnutrition. This intergenerational cycle is a significant contributor to the country's high rates of malnutrition, further exacerbating the problem. Malnourished mothers are also less likely to produce enough breast milk, thus contributing to early childhood malnutrition.

The government's lack of focus on tackling malnutrition and improving food security is undermining Ethiopia's long-term development goals. Malnourished children are less likely to finish their education, secure stable employment, or contribute effectively to the economy as adults. This ongoing problem directly limits Ethiopia's ability to escape the cycle of poverty and achieve sustainable growth.

Ethiopia needs a comprehensive, coordinated approach to combat child malnutrition, focusing on the root causes of food insecurity. The first step is improving maternal and child nutrition during the critical first 1,000 days of life. Access to nutritious food, healthcare, and prenatal care for pregnant women is essential for breaking the cycle of malnutrition and improving the health of future generations.

Additionally, the government must prioritize investments in agricultural policies and practices that ensure food security and increase the availability of nutritious food. Rural infrastructure needs improvement, and smallholder farmers, especially women, must be empowered with the resources and training they need to enhance food production and access. Ethiopia must promote dietary diversity, fortify staple foods with essential micronutrients, and invest in nutrition education for both children and adults.

Abiy's failure to effectively address the growing child malnutrition crisis reflects a broader disregard for the immediate needs of the population. While focusing on infrastructure, international image-building, and superficial solutions, Prime Minister Abiy's administration has neglected the critical issue of food insecurity and malnutrition. A shift in priorities is necessary, focusing on improving the nutrition and wellbeing of Ethiopians, particularly children, if the country is to break free from the cycle of hunger and poverty and achieve sustainable development.

***

Addis Ababa's Urbanization and the Rising Crisis of Food Insecurity

Addis Ababa, Ethiopia's bustling capital, is undergoing rapid transformation. The city is being reshaped with new buildings, modern roads, and extensive urbanization efforts. While these changes promise to create a brighter, cleaner city, they come at the expense of the city's most vulnerable residents. Poor families, small businesses, and longtime citizens are being displaced, their homes and livelihoods dismantled for the sake of urban expansion. As the city grows, many residents are being forced to leave their old neighborhoods, and their social fabric is being torn apart in the process. For some, this urbanization is seen as necessary for progress, while others believe that there are less harmful ways to modernize the city without causing such disruption to its long-time citizens.

In fact, the urbanization process has become a major source of hardship for many of Addis Ababa's residents. Recently, a citizen's suicide sparked public outcry, drawing attention to the emotional and financial toll that forced relocation and displacement can have. Small businesses and families who have lived in the city for generations are now struggling to survive as their homes and workplaces are torn down to make way for new development. The government has made public efforts to promote its success in reshaping the city, with Prime Minister Abiy frequently seen bragging about the city's transformation. However, the suffering of the displaced and the struggles of countless vulnerable groups, including children, mothers, and low-income workers, remain largely hidden from the public view.

Food insecurity, once primarily associated with Ethiopia's rural areas, is increasingly becoming a pressing issue in Addis Ababa. As the city rapidly urbanizes, food insecurity is spreading among urban populations, particularly those in low-income groups. This shift is driven by several factors, including rising living costs, the growing demand for food, inflation, and disruptions in global food supply chains. Many urban residents, especially the poor, now find it difficult to access sufficient and nutritious food.

Food prices in Addis Ababa have skyrocketed in recent years, placing a heavy burden on low-income families. Global price increases for essential food items such as wheat, rice, and cooking oil, combined with Ethiopia's reliance on food imports, have contributed to these rising costs. The devaluation of the Ethiopian birr has further exacerbated the situation, making it even harder for many urban residents to afford basic staples. Items like injera, vegetables, fruits, and cereals, which were once affordable for most families, have now become out of reach for many in Addis Ababa.

For the urban poor, the issue is not just about the availability of food, but about its affordability. Even though food is available in markets, many low-income families cannot afford to buy enough to meet their nutritional needs. The rising costs make it increasingly difficult for families to buy food in bulk, forcing them to purchase smaller quantities at inflated prices. As a result, many households are forced to reduce the quality and quantity of their diets, leading to poor nutrition and its associated health impacts, especially for children, the elderly, and women.

Urban workers, including teachers, healthcare professionals, and other essential service providers, are also facing severe financial strain. Many of these workers are paid wages that do not keep pace with the rising costs of living. Public sector employees such as teachers and healthcare workers, who play critical roles in society, are among the hardest hit. Despite their vital work, their wages are insufficient to meet the increasing costs of food, rent, and transportation, leaving them with impossible choices between buying food and meeting other basic needs.

Students in Addis Ababa, particularly those attending universities away from home, are also struggling with food insecurity. With high living costs, including rent, utilities, and transportation, many students are left with little money for food, further exacerbating the crisis. The rise in food prices is not only affecting the poorest urban residents but also a significant portion of the middle class, who are finding it increasingly difficult to make ends meet.

The broader economic environment is compounding the problem of urban food insecurity. Ethiopia's reliance on imported food items such as wheat and cooking oil means that disruptions in global supply chains, such as those caused by the COVID-19 pandemic or geopolitical tensions, have a direct impact on food prices in the city. The vulnerability of Addis Ababa's urban population to global economic shifts highlights the city's dependence on international markets, further destabilizing local food prices and making nutritious food even more inaccessible.

The social consequences of urban food insecurity are wide-reaching. Malnutrition, particularly among children, has long-term impacts on physical and cognitive development, leading to stunted growth, weakened immune systems, and poor educational outcomes. These issues not only affect children's immediate health but also hinder their future opportunities. For adults, food insecurity contributes to chronic health problems such as anemia, cardiovascular diseases, and other diet-related illnesses, which strain the healthcare system and reduce workforce productivity.

Addressing the growing food insecurity crisis in Addis Ababa requires a multi-dimensional approach. First, targeted social safety nets and food assistance programs should be implemented to support the city's most vulnerable populations. These programs should not only provide immediate food relief but also focus on improving access to nutritious food through subsidies, food vouchers, and community-based food initiatives. Additionally, promoting urban agriculture, such as rooftop gardens or community farms, can help reduce dependency on expensive imported food and provide sustainable, local solutions.

Economic policies must also be adjusted to address the rising costs of living. Increasing wages to match inflation and promoting job creation in sectors that offer stable and fair incomes are essential steps to ensuring that urban residents can afford basic necessities. Urban planning should prioritize food security by ensuring that affordable food markets are accessible to low-income neighborhoods, while transportation infrastructure must be improved to ensure efficient food distribution throughout the city.

While Addis Ababa's rapid urbanization may bring certain benefits, the displacement of its most vulnerable citizens and the growing food insecurity in the city must not be overlooked. The government's focus on modernizing the city must be balanced with efforts to address the immediate needs of its residents, particularly those who are struggling to survive in the face of rising food prices and displacement. A coordinated approach that combines social safety nets, improved urban agriculture, and economic reforms is necessary to ensure that all of Addis Ababa's residents have access to the food and resources they need to thrive.

***

Balancing Survival and Sustainability

Ethiopia faces the dual challenges of a rapidly growing population and climate vulnerability, particularly in its heavily agriculture-dependent economy. With over 80% of the population relying on agriculture for their livelihood, the sector is highly susceptible to the impacts of climate change, including erratic weather patterns, droughts, and rising temperatures. These challenges demand that the government focus on climate-resilient agricultural practices to ensure food security and long-term economic stability. However, while investments in tree planting and environmental beautification are commendable, there needs to be a broader and more coordinated approach to both protecting these environmental assets and addressing the immediate survival needs of the people.

Abiy's administration has earned praise for its efforts in planting billions of trees, a step that aligns with global climate change mitigation goals. The scale of this initiative is impressive and should be acknowledged as a significant contribution to environmental sustainability. However, these efforts cannot stand alone. To ensure the long-term success of this initiative, the government must coordinate with regional authorities and local communities, fostering a sense of ownership and responsibility in nurturing these trees. At the same time, the focus should not only be on planting but also on educating the public about how to protect and care for these trees. People need to understand the importance of sustaining these resources in the face of climate change.

Unfortunately, Ethiopia is currently embroiled in internal conflicts, particularly in the Amhara and Oromia regions, where violence and instability have become widespread. Amid such a chaotic environment, survival and safety have taken precedence over environmental concerns. The people, enduring the trauma of violence and facing an uncertain future, are less likely to prioritize environmental initiatives when their basic survival is at stake. Abiy's statement that trees should be planted to provide shade for the bodies of the dead reflects the grim reality many Ethiopians face today. Trees should not merely be a symbol of posthumous comfort but should serve as part of a larger strategy to improve the lives of the living.

The ongoing violence and instability across the country, including kidnappings, inter-ethnic conflicts, and daily threats to personal safety, further complicate the climate change conversation. People are struggling to stay alive, and in such dire circumstances, the government's focus on planting trees without addressing the root causes of violence and instability seems disconnected from the immediate needs of the population. As the government continues to beautify cities and plant trees, it must also address the urgent need for peace, security, and stability, as these are fundamental prerequisites for any long-term climate action to succeed.

While addressing climate change through large-scale tree planting and environmental projects is important, the government must first ensure that the basic needs of its citizens are met. Safety, security, and peace must be the primary focus before advancing other initiatives like greening the country. Without stability, efforts to combat climate change and enhance environmental sustainability will remain hollow. People cannot protect the environment if they are not safe, and they will not care for the trees if their lives are in constant danger. Therefore, Abiy's administration must balance its climate goals with a strong, concerted effort to bring peace and order to Ethiopia, ensuring that people's survival and well-being come first.

Abiy's efforts to combat climate change through massive tree planting initiatives are commendable and should be supported, these efforts cannot be successful without a more integrated approach that includes peacebuilding and the protection of citizens. By focusing on both the immediate survival of its people and long-term environmental sustainability, Abiy's government can create a balanced and effective strategy that secures a better future for both the environment and the citizens of Ethiopia.

***

Prioritizing Cosmetic Development Over Real Economic Diversification

Under Abiy Ahmed's administration, Ethiopia's economy continues to face serious challenges, despite billions of dollars in foreign loans and significant resources directed toward urban beautification projects in Addis Ababa. While the government focuses on flashy infrastructure, such as parks, modern roads, hotels, and well-lit streets, the fundamental sectors of the economy, such as manufacturing and industry, have stalled. The beautification efforts, which are aimed at polishing the country's image, do not address the structural issues of Ethiopia's economy, which remains heavily dependent on agriculture. Abiy's government's focus on image-building rather than economic transformation is hindering the country's long-term growth prospects.

Ethiopia's economy has been primarily reliant on agriculture, with over 80% of the population depending on the sector for their livelihoods. However, this over-reliance on agriculture exposes the country to significant vulnerabilities, especially in the face of climate change, political instability, and global market fluctuations. Abiy's administration, instead of promoting economic diversification to mitigate these risks, continues to neglect key sectors such as manufacturing, which is essential for long-term economic stability. For instance, out of the many sugar factories in the country, only one or two are functioning, and the broader industrial sector is underdeveloped. These shortcomings reflect a broader failure to invest in the core areas that could drive sustainable growth and job creation.

The administration has failed to effectively utilize the billions of dollars in loans from international institutions. Despite receiving substantial funds, no new factories have been built, and the country's industrial base remains weak. Instead, Abiy's government has poured money into infrastructure projects in Addis Ababa, which while aesthetically pleasing, do little to address the pressing economic needs of the population. These projects are more about creating a superficial image of prosperity than about creating real, sustainable economic opportunities for Ethiopians.

The devaluation of the Ethiopian birr by more than 75% under Abiy's leadership further highlights the failure of his administration to manage the economy effectively. This steep devaluation has contributed to inflation, making everyday goods more expensive and eroding the purchasing power of ordinary Ethiopians. Despite the growing economic difficulties, the government continues to focus on cosmetic improvements that fail to provide tangible benefits to the people.

Abiy's government's fixation on urban beautification and its failure to invest in industrialization and agriculture are creating an unbalanced economy. Ethiopia's manufacturing sector, which could reduce the country's reliance on imports and create much needed jobs, remains largely underdeveloped. The country's potential to process agricultural products and create value-added industries, such as coffee processing, remains untapped. While Abiy's government continues to promote infrastructure projects that boost the country's image, there is little attention to fostering industrial growth or increasing the capacity of the workforce to engage in meaningful, productive activities.

Additionally, the services sector, including tourism, has faced significant setbacks under Abiy's administration, primarily due to widespread insecurity and ethnic-based conflicts. While the government has invested in building beautiful resorts and hotels, these developments have not translated into a thriving tourism industry. Ethiopia's rich cultural and natural heritage holds great potential for tourism, but the lack of safety across the country has severely hindered the sector. Ongoing violence, kidnappings, and instability in regions like Amhara and Oromia have made travel unsafe for both foreigners and Ethiopians alike.

In recent years, kidnappings have become a major concern, with university students, truck drivers, and citizens of all ages being abducted and held for ransom. These incidents, often demanding millions of birr for their release, create an atmosphere of fear that deters tourists from visiting, regardless of the availability of modern facilities. Even Ethiopians are unable to travel freely between regions due to the ethnic-based politics under Abiy's administration, further exacerbating the problem. With ongoing internal conflicts and no visible solutions to restore peace and security, the promise of tourism development remains unrealized.

The failure to address safety concerns has rendered even the most luxurious resorts and hotels ineffective in attracting tourists, both international and domestic. A thriving tourism industry requires not only infrastructure but also a stable, secure environment in which people feel safe to travel. Until Abiy's government prioritizes peace, stability, and safety for all citizens, tourism will remain an underdeveloped sector, unable to contribute to Ethiopia's economic diversification.

Moreover, Abiy's government has shown little interest in addressing the education and vocational training needs of the population. With a large youth population, Ethiopia has the potential to harness its demographic dividend, but only if the government invests in creating pathways for the youth to transition from agriculture to higher productivity sectors like manufacturing, services, and technology. Instead, the government continues to underfund education, failing to equip young people with the necessary skills to thrive in a diversified economy.

The government must shift its focus from cosmetic developments in Addis Ababa to real, impactful investments in industry and education across the country. The focus should be on creating jobs, promoting manufacturing, and diversifying the economy to reduce vulnerability to agricultural shocks. To do so, Abiy's administration must make significant investments in infrastructure that supports industrialization, such as power plants, roads, and factories, rather than just roads and parks that only serve to enhance the capital's image. Additionally, greater attention must be paid to ensuring that Ethiopia's workforce is trained for the jobs of tomorrow, particularly in sectors like manufacturing, technology, and services.

Abiy's government's emphasis on image-building and cosmetic developments has come at the expense of addressing Ethiopia's underlying economic challenges. The over-reliance on agriculture, the underdeveloped manufacturing sector, and the failure to harness the potential of the services and technology sectors are significant barriers to sustainable economic growth. To achieve real economic diversification and stability, Abiy's administration must prioritize the development of industry, the creation of jobs, and the investment in education and vocational training. Without these critical steps, Ethiopia's economy will remain vulnerable and dependent on external factors, with little opportunity for long-term prosperity.

***

Social Protection Under Abiy's Government: A Weak and Divided System for Ethiopia's Vulnerable Populations

While the Productive Safety Net Program (PSNP) has made some strides in addressing food insecurity and poverty in Ethiopia, Abiy Ahmed's administration has failed to strengthen the country's social protection systems adequately. The PSNP, initiated in 2005, was designed to provide food and cash transfers to those affected by chronic food insecurity, particularly in rural areas. While it has helped stabilize the livelihoods of many Ethiopians, particularly during food shortages, Abiy's administration has been unable to address the growing challenges of poverty, climate change, and economic instability. Instead, the administration has deepened ethnic divisions, dismantled the social fabric, and weakened governance, leading to a system that fails to support the most vulnerable effectively.

Under Abiy's rule, social protection programs such as the PSNP have been undermined by an ethnically based governance structure that has created deep divisions across the country. The Prosperity Party, which dominates the political landscape, has fostered a corrupt and ineffective bureaucracy, where loyalty to the party outweighs the competence needed to manage and implement essential services. The lack of smart leadership and the prevalence of corruption in public service have crippled PSNP's effectiveness, particularly in reaching marginalized and conflict-affected areas.

Regions like Tigray and Amhara, ravaged by conflict, continue to suffer from a lack of access to food aid and basic services. Despite the PSNP's original intent to aid these areas, logistical challenges and political instability have made it difficult for the program to reach the most vulnerable populations. In these areas, where Abiy's administration has consistently failed to provide stability and support, many families continue to face severe food insecurity. To address these challenges, there must be a significant expansion of the PSNP, focusing on improving logistical infrastructure, utilizing mobile technology for cash transfers, and collaborating with local organizations to ensure more targeted interventions. Without a commitment to reaching these underserved regions, the promise of a robust social safety net will remain unmet.

Beyond geographic expansion, the PSNP must be adapted to respond to the needs of diverse populations, including women, children, the elderly, and people with disabilities. In Abiy's administration, systemic barriers, such as cultural norms and legal restrictions, limit women's access to resources like land, education, and credit. These barriers, compounded by the administration's failure to prioritize women's empowerment, make women and children even more dependent on social safety nets. The PSNP could be improved by incorporating gender-sensitive approaches, such as providing additional support to women-headed households, offering specialized training on income-generating activities, and promoting women's economic independence. However, under Abiy's government, such reforms remain largely absent. Instead, the administration's focus on ethnically divided politics has diverted attention from the need for inclusive policies that address the structural inequalities faced by marginalized groups.

Furthermore, Abiy's government has failed to integrate social protection programs like the PSNP into broader national development strategies. To break the cycle of poverty and food insecurity, the country must address structural factors such as access to quality education, healthcare, and employment opportunities. Unfortunately, the Prosperity Party's policies continue to favor ethnic and political loyalties over broad-based development. The result is an underfunded education system, a weak healthcare infrastructure, and limited job opportunities. These failures prevent vulnerable populations from achieving long-term economic independence, ultimately rendering social protection programs like the PSNP ineffective in the long run.

While the PSNP offers temporary relief, long-term solutions lie in addressing the broader economic and governance issues that perpetuate inequality. Employment opportunities must be at the core of any anti-poverty strategy, yet under Abiy's government, these opportunities remain scarce. Social protection programs should not only provide direct aid but also support livelihoods through job creation, vocational training, and entrepreneurship. The PSNP could focus on expanding small-scale business development and job placement programs to help vulnerable populations become self-sufficient. However, under Abiy's administration, the lack of investment in local economies and sustainable development has left many communities trapped in poverty, unable to break free from reliance on aid.

Another critical issue is the need for a more flexible and responsive social protection system. With the increasing frequency of natural disasters, climate change impacts, and economic crises, Ethiopia's social protection programs must be adaptable to shifting needs. Under Abiy's leadership, however, the government has shown a lack of capacity to respond to seasonal shocks or crises. The PSNP should be designed to provide flexible support during emergencies, such as cash transfers or food aid, which can be adjusted based on the severity of the crisis. But under Abiy's administration, the system remains rigid and poorly coordinated, making it difficult to effectively address sudden increases in vulnerability.

Furthermore, the success of the PSNP and other social protection programs depends on governance and accountability. Corruption, inefficiency, and political infighting under Abiy's government have severely hampered the effective delivery of aid and services to those in need. To strengthen the PSNP, the government must improve transparency, accountability, and oversight mechanisms. However, Abiy's administration has shown little commitment to these reforms, prioritizing political loyalty over effective governance. This lack of accountability undermines the program's impact, and the absence of robust monitoring mechanisms has made it difficult to ensure that aid reaches its intended recipients. Greater community involvement and better capacity-building for local governments are essential for improving the program's reach and effectiveness.

In conclusion, while the PSNP has made progress in addressing food insecurity and poverty, the failures of Abiy's administration to prioritize inclusive, transparent, and effective governance have hindered the program's success. Expanding the PSNP to reach all vulnerable populations, particularly in remote and conflict-affected areas, and integrating it into broader development strategies focused on education, healthcare, and employment, is crucial to creating a more comprehensive and sustainable social protection system. However, without significant reform in governance, accountability, and the prioritization of broad-based development, the promise of social protection under Abiy's government will continue to fall short, leaving Ethiopia's most vulnerable citizens without the support they need to thrive.

***

A Barrier to Food Security in Ethiopia

A crucial factor in improving food security in Ethiopia is the strengthening of governance structures to ensure that resources are allocated efficiently, food assistance is distributed fairly, and programs are implemented effectively. In a country where the majority of the population depends on agriculture for their livelihoods, the efficient functioning of the agriculture and food security sectors is paramount. However, under Abiy Ahmed's administration, Ethiopia's food security efforts have been undermined by weak governance, corruption, and inefficiencies in public service delivery, exacerbating the already dire situation.

The challenges to food security have grown significantly, and the root causes lie in the administration's failure to build effective governance. Abiy's ethnically based leadership has created deep divisions, as political appointments often favor those loyal to his Prosperity Party. This system of governance has not only hindered transparency but also encouraged a culture of corruption, where key sectors such as agriculture, food distribution, and humanitarian aid are plagued by fraud. Corruption has led to the misallocation of resources, and food aid often fails to reach the communities most in need, especially in rural areas, where access to basic services is already limited.

Instead of reaching the vulnerable populations it was intended for, food assistance is diverted through fraudulent practices, or it is delayed due to inefficiencies within the government's structure. This has led to widespread hunger and malnutrition, particularly in regions already suffering from economic instability. With the country's leadership failing to implement meaningful reforms, vulnerable populations continue to bear the brunt of the systemic inefficiencies.

To address these issues, Abiy's administration must take decisive steps to combat corruption within food security programs. A central aspect of this would be regular audits, greater transparency in the allocation of resources, and the establishment of independent oversight bodies to monitor food distribution. However, the lack of political will to address corruption within the administration, due to its reliance on ethnic-based loyalty, continues to exacerbate the situation. Until genuine accountability is introduced, the food security programs will remain ineffective.

In addition to corruption, the administration's weak institutional accountability makes it difficult to hold officials responsible for the failure of food security programs. The lack of transparency and oversight means that programs meant to address food insecurity often fail to achieve their intended outcomes. Public institutions involved in food security and agriculture are often unaccountable, which results in mismanagement and the perpetuation of food shortages. Moreover, the absence of meaningful local participation in decision-making has left many communities without a voice in how resources are allocated, leading to programs that fail to meet the real needs of the population.

The inefficiencies in public service delivery further exacerbate food insecurity. The bureaucratic red tape, poor coordination between government agencies, and the lack of capacity in local administrations mean that food security programs are often delayed or ineffective. For instance, food distribution might be delayed in one region because of a lack of coordination between agencies, which can worsen shortages and hunger. Abiy's administration has shown no clear plan to address these inefficiencies, and local governments lack the resources or training to properly execute national policies.

Additionally, the local capacity to manage food security programs remains severely underdeveloped. Public servants often lack the technical skills or manpower to implement food security programs effectively, which leads to waste and inefficiency. Without investments in capacity-building, the administration cannot expect to solve food insecurity through its existing programs. Local officials must be properly trained to manage and distribute resources, ensuring that food security interventions can reach those who need them most. This requires significant investment in local infrastructure and human capital, something Abiy's administration has yet to prioritize.

Abiy's government must also implement robust monitoring and evaluation mechanisms for food security programs. The lack of data-driven decision-making in food security planning means that programs often do not meet their goals, and adjustments are rarely made. The administration needs to establish systems to track the progress of food security initiatives, allowing for better policy adjustments and improvements. This will also ensure that resources are used effectively and fairly, increasing public trust in government actions.

The lack of transparency within the administration remains one of the largest obstacles to improving food security. Without an open and fair system, food distribution can be influenced by personal or political interests, which often leads to unequal access. Public information on food security, such as the allocation of resources and the outcomes of programs, should be readily available to citizens and organizations to increase accountability. Unfortunately, Abiy's administration has consistently failed to prioritize transparency, preventing citizens and civil society organizations from holding officials accountable.

International partners and donor organizations can play a role in supporting Abiy's administration in improving governance in food security. These partners can provide technical assistance and support anti-corruption initiatives, but their impact will be limited as long as the administration is not fully committed to reforming the structures that have perpetuated inefficiencies and corruption.

In conclusion, strengthening governance structures is essential for improving food security in Ethiopia. Abiy's administration has failed to address the key challenges of corruption, inefficiency, and lack of accountability within the food security sector. A more inclusive, transparent, and capable governance structure is necessary to effectively address food insecurity. Without reform, Ethiopia's food security crisis will continue to worsen, and vulnerable populations will remain at the mercy of an administration that prioritizes ethnic loyalty over the needs of the people.

***

CHAPTER 9

A Historical Context of Oromo Politics: Struggles, Identity, and Resistance.

The Oromo people, who constitute over 30% of Ethiopia's population, are the largest ethnic group in the country. Throughout Ethiopia's history, the Oromo have made significant political, cultural, and economic contributions. However, their rights have frequently been marginalized. Their political journey reflects a broader struggle for autonomy, recognition, and self-determination, which has significantly shaped Ethiopia's development.

In pre-modern Ethiopia, the Oromo people lived in decentralized communities governed by the Gadaa system, an indigenous form of democratic governance based on age-set groups. Under this system, leadership roles rotated every eight years, ensuring that power was shared across generations. It provided a framework for political autonomy, local governance, and peaceful conflict resolution. However, the expansion of the Abyssinian Empire in the 16th and 17th centuries began Oromo's long history of external domination and suppression. The rise of the Abyssinian Empire, under the Amhara-dominated monarchy, brought centralization, undermining Oromo's political structures and identity.

The imposition of the Ethiopian Orthodox Church and the imperial system further marginalized the Oromo, stripping them of their land, language, culture, and political rights. This era marked the beginning of Oromo exclusion from Ethiopia's political center. Later, under the Marxist-Leninist Derg regime, which came to power in 1974, the Oromo faced continued oppression. The Derg sought national unity but did so at the expense of ethnic autonomy, subjecting the Oromo to land nationalization policies and collectivization that deepened their marginalization.

In response, the Oromo Liberation Front (OLF) was formed in the late 1970s. It became a key political force advocating for the self-determination of the Oromo people. The OLF's resistance continued in the post-Derg era, challenging both the Derg regime and successive governments, demanding the recognition of Oromo rights and autonomy. However, the Ethiopian government viewed the OLF as a threat to national unity, further intensifying the political struggles of the Oromo.

The political landscape of Ethiopia shifted significantly with the rise of Prime Minister Abiy Ahmed in 2018. Abiy, an Oromo himself, brought a sense of hope for greater inclusion and reform. His ascent to power was seen as a victory for the Oromo people, who had long been excluded from political influence in Ethiopia. Abiy introduced a series of reforms, including the release of political prisoners, the lifting of bans on opposition parties, and the signing of peace agreements with Eritrea. These changes were initially welcomed by the Oromo, who hoped for greater political and cultural recognition.

Despite Abiy's Oromo heritage, his leadership has faced both support and criticism within the Oromo community. While many saw his rise as a chance to address historical injustices, many Oromo activists and political leaders argue that the political and cultural rights of the Oromo are still not fully respected. Despite his reforms, the ongoing challenges faced by the Oromo, particularly in areas of political participation, land rights, and economic development, continue to fuel frustration. Some feel that Abiy's government, while making strides in political inclusion, has not adequately addressed the Oromo's historical grievances.

Abiy's government has thus been met with a complex mix of hope and skepticism, as the political situation in Ethiopia remains contested. The Oromo continue to struggle for greater autonomy and recognition. Despite some gains under Abiy's leadership, the legacy of marginalization continues to influence the political realities of the Oromo people. Their aspiration for self-determination, justice, and political rights remains a central issue, shaping both their political movements within Ethiopia and in the diaspora.

The Oromo people's long history of resistance, beginning with the Gadaa system and continuing through the Abyssinian Empire, the Derg regime, and into the current era, highlights their enduring quest for autonomy and political recognition. Abiy Ahmed's rise to power offered new possibilities, but the challenges of addressing the Oromo's historical grievances and ensuring their political and cultural rights remain critical in Ethiopia's ongoing political evolution.

The political history of the Oromo people is marked by a continuous struggle for recognition, justice, and self-determination. From their pre-modern governance system through centuries of external domination to their modern-day political struggles, the Oromo have fought to shape Ethiopia's political future. While some progress has been made under Abiy Ahmed, the road to fully addressing the needs and aspirations of the Oromo people remains ongoing. The future of Ethiopia's political trajectory will continue to be influenced by the Oromo's desire for greater autonomy, recognition, and justice within the state.

***

Abiy Ahmed and the Oromo Struggle: From Historical Resistance to Contemporary Political Challenges

Mohammed Hassen's *The Oromo of Ethiopia: A History 1570-1860* provides a detailed scholarly account of the Oromo people's history during a transformative period from the late 16th to mid-19th century. As one of Ethiopia's largest ethnic groups, the Oromo's political, social, and cultural history is central to understanding the broader dynamics of Ethiopian history. Hassen's work is an essential resource that sheds light on the evolving relationship between the Oromo people, neighboring peoples, and the central Ethiopian state, a relationship that has continued to shape Ethiopian politics, especially in the context of Prime Minister Abiy Ahmed's leadership.

The Oromo, a Cushitic-speaking ethnic group, historically occupied much of present-day Ethiopia and parts of Kenya. Hassen's account begins by highlighting the distinctiveness of the Oromo, who developed a unique social and political structure based on the Gadaa system. This democratic, age-based system of governance ensured leadership rotation and collective decision-making, forming the foundation of Oromo society. Throughout the period covered in Hassen's book, the Gadaa system was crucial to maintaining Oromo autonomy, yet it faced increasing pressures from external forces, notably the Ethiopian Empire.

During the 16th century, the Oromo began migrating and expanding across central and southern Ethiopia. This "Oromo migration" significantly reshaped the political and social landscape of the region, especially as the Oromo came into contact with the Amhara-dominated Ethiopian Empire. This territorial expansion led to several conflicts, as the Oromo resisted the expansion of the Solomonic dynasty and the centralization efforts of the Ethiopian emperors. Despite the absence of a centralized state, the decentralized nature of the Oromo allowed them to form powerful nation, effectively resisting imperial control and maintaining their political autonomy for several centuries.

Hassen describes the Oromo as a people who, despite being outnumbered, managed to secure large territories in Ethiopia. Their military prowess, based on a highly organized and decentralized society, enabled them to pose a significant challenge to the Ethiopian Empire. This was especially evident during the reign of Menelik II, who, in the late 19th century, sought to centralize Ethiopian power through military conquest, which included the annexation of Oromo territories. Despite facing these external pressures, the Oromo people maintained their political independence, resisting the centralizing efforts of the Ethiopian state.

Hassen's analysis highlights the complexity of the Oromo response to the Ethiopian Empire. While resistance through armed conflict was common, there were also moments of cooperation. However, the Oromo faced increasing assimilation efforts from the Amhara elite, especially as the Ethiopian Empire expanded. These attempts included military campaigns, feudal-style governance, and forced resettlement of Oromo communities. Through these challenges, the Oromo continued to preserve their distinct identity, resisting the loss of their land and cultural practices.

In examining the cultural and religious dynamics of the period, Hassen details how the Oromo adapted to the religious influences of both Christianity and Islam. Many Oromo people in the eastern and southern regions embraced Islam, while others in the central and western areas retained their indigenous religious practices. These religious dynamics played a role in shaping the Oromo's identity and their relationship with the central Ethiopian state, which was firmly rooted in Ethiopian Orthodox Christianity. This tension between religious identities contributed to the political complexities of the time.

According to Hassen, by the mid-19th century, the expansion of the Ethiopian Empire under Menelik II began to diminish Oromo autonomy. Despite their strong resistance, the Oromo were gradually absorbed into the centralizing state through military conquest and political integration. This marked the beginning of a new era in Ethiopian history, one in which the power of the central government eclipsed the political autonomy of many ethnic groups, including the Oromo. The centralization process led to the marginalization of the Oromo, whose rights and influence within Ethiopia's political system diminished.

Hassen concludes that the period from 1570 to 1860 was one of both resilience and subjugation for the Oromo people. While they successfully maintained a degree of autonomy for much of this period, the growing influence of external forces and the centralization of the Ethiopian state eventually led to their incorporation into the larger imperial structure. Despite this, the legacy of the Oromo's resistance and their unique cultural identity persisted and continued to influence Ethiopian politics in the following centuries.

This legacy of resistance and cultural preservation has found new resonance in the contemporary political landscape, particularly under the leadership of Abiy Ahmed. Abiy, an Oromo himself, rose to power in 2018 with a promise of reform and inclusion. His ascension was seen by many as a potential turning point for the Oromo people, who had long been excluded from political power despite their significant demographic presence. Abiy's leadership has brought some hope to the Oromo community, as he made reforms that promised greater political freedom, the release of political prisoners, and the lifting of bans on opposition groups.

However, Abiy's tenure has also faced criticism, especially from Oromo activists and political leaders who argue that his reforms have not fully addressed the historical grievances of the Oromo people. Despite his Oromo heritage, Abiy has struggled to navigate the complex political realities of Ethiopia, where ethnic federalism, land rights, and political representation remain contentious issues. The Oromo, though somewhat empowered by Abiy's reforms, continue to face challenges in achieving full political recognition and self-determination.

The historical trajectory of the Oromo people, from their resistance to the Ethiopian Empire's expansion in the 16th and 17th centuries to their continued political struggles under Abiy Ahmed, reflects a long-standing quest for recognition, justice, and autonomy. Hassen's account of the Oromo people's history serves as a reminder of the deep-rooted challenges faced by the Oromo in Ethiopia's political system, and their ongoing struggle to secure their rightful place in the country's future.

In conclusion, the Oromo people's history is one of resilience, resistance, and adaptation. From their expansion and resistance against Ethiopian imperial forces in the 16th to 19th centuries, to their ongoing political struggles under Abiy Ahmed, the Oromo continue to fight for greater autonomy, recognition, and justice within Ethiopia. As Abiy's government navigates Ethiopia's complex political landscape, the legacy of the Oromo people's long-standing struggle remains a defining feature of the country's future political development.

***

Marginalization and Resistance: The Oromo Struggle from Haile Selassie to Abiy Ahmed

Emperor Haile Selassie's reign (1930–1974) marked the zenith of Ethiopia's centralized governance, a period in which the emperor sought to modernize the country while asserting strong control over its ethnic groups. However, his policies had a particularly negative impact on the Oromo people, who faced significant political, social, and cultural marginalization. Despite Haile Selassie's global reputation for his leadership in the League of Nations and his efforts to modernize the country, his administration prioritized Amhara culture and language, exacerbating the systemic discrimination that the Oromo and other ethnic groups had long faced.

Under Haile Selassie's rule, the Oromo were politically and economically marginalized. The emperor's centralization policies reinforced a hierarchical system that largely excluded the Oromo from political power. The Oromo people, who primarily lived in the southern and central regions of Ethiopia, were subjected to land dispossession and relegated to the status of peasants under the feudal system. Attempts by the Oromo to preserve their political and cultural identity were largely thwarted, and their voices were increasingly suppressed in the national political discourse.

By the mid-20th century, the Oromo's growing sense of political and cultural disenfranchisement led to the rise of intellectuals and activists within the community who called for greater representation and autonomy. The Oromo Liberation Front (OLF) emerged in the 1970s as a direct response to the policies of marginalization, advocating for self-determination and the recognition of the Oromo people's rights within Ethiopia. The OLF, alongside other resistance movements, highlighted that the Oromo struggle was not only about land rights and political representation but also about the survival of their unique cultural identity.

Asafa Jalata's *Oromo Nationalism and the Ethiopian State: A History of the Oromo Liberation Movement* provides a detailed examination of the political and historical dynamics that shaped

Oromo nationalism, particularly in the context of Ethiopia's centralization under Haile Selassie and the subsequent rise of resistance movements. Jalata critically analyzes the policies of the Haile Selassie regime, arguing that the centralization of power and the imposition of an Amhara-dominated national identity undermined the Oromo's unique cultural, social, and political systems, particularly the Gadaa system, which had long organized Oromo society on democratic, age-grade lines.

Haile Selassie's efforts to consolidate the Ethiopian state involved the suppression of indigenous languages, the imposition of Amharic as the national language, and the centralization of political and economic power in Addis Ababa. These measures, designed to assimilate non-Amhara ethnic groups, particularly the Oromo, not only disregarded their distinct identity but also subjected them to economic exploitation and social discrimination. The land tenure system, which entrenched feudal structures, left the Oromo with limited control over their land, further deepening their marginalization.

The growing discontent among the Oromo led to the emergence of the OLF and other resistance movements in the mid-20th century. These movements advocated for the recognition of Oromo cultural practices and the preservation of their unique way of life. For the Oromo, their resistance was not solely a political struggle but also an effort to safeguard their cultural survival in the face of a government that sought to erase or assimilate their identity.

Jalata's book also discusses the aftermath of Haile Selassie's rule, particularly the political landscape shaped by the Ethiopian People's Revolutionary Democratic Front (EPRDF) after the fall of the Derg regime in 1991. The EPRDF, which was dominated by the Tigray People's Liberation Front (TPLF), introduced ethnic federalism as a means to address the grievances of Ethiopia's diverse ethnic groups. On paper, this system promised greater autonomy for the Oromo and other ethnic groups, but in practice, Jalata argues that it often led to continued discrimination and exclusion from political power. Despite the formal recognition of ethnic self-determination in the 1991 constitution, the Oromo continued to face political repression, economic marginalization, and social exclusion. The TPLF-led government's approach to ethnic federalism was seen as a tool of control rather than true empowerment for the Oromo.

The challenges faced by the Oromo under the EPRDF regime have parallels with the historical experiences of exclusion and resistance during the Haile Selassie era. Despite formal recognition of their rights, the Oromo have struggled to gain meaningful political power, and their cultural identity continues to be challenged by the broader Ethiopian state. This persistent struggle for self-determination and cultural recognition has remained a defining theme in the history of the Oromo people.

In conclusion, while the reign of Haile Selassie is often remembered for efforts to modernize Ethiopia, the legacy of his centralization policies left a lasting impact on the Oromo people, whose fight for recognition, autonomy, and cultural survival continues into the present day. Jalata's work provides a critical lens through which to understand the complexities of Oromo nationalism, the historical marginalization of the Oromo, and the ongoing political struggles within Ethiopia. The story of the Oromo people, from the time of Haile Selassie to the present era under Abiy Ahmed, remains a testament to their resilience and determination to assert their rights in the face of adversity.

In 1974, the Derg, a Marxist-Leninist military junta led by Mengistu Haile Mariam, overthrew Emperor Haile Selassie. While the Derg promised social and economic reforms, it continued many of the oppressive policies of previous regimes, particularly toward the Oromo people. The Oromo, alongside other ethnic groups, faced brutal repression as the government cracked down on political dissent. The Oromo Liberation Front (OLF), which had initially gained traction in the 1970s, emerged as one of the primary resistance forces against the Derg regime. During this period, the Oromo experienced violence, forced displacements, and the suppression of their cultural expressions. The Derg's attempts to centralize power and eliminate regional autonomy were in direct opposition to the Oromo's aspirations for self-determination.

As Asafa Jalata points out, the fall of Haile Selassie and the establishment of the Derg regime in 1974 created a more favorable environment for Oromo resistance movements. Although the monarchy was overthrown, the military dictatorship that replaced it was equally repressive, particularly toward the Oromo and other marginalized ethnic groups. The OLF was founded as a political organization committed to the self-determination of the Oromo people, advocating for the promotion of their cultural, social, and political rights within Ethiopia. The OLF sought either an autonomous Oromo region or an independent Oromo state free from the control of the Amhara-dominated Ethiopian government.

Jalata emphasizes the ideological foundation of the OLF, rooted in Oromo nationalism and inspired by global national liberation struggles. The OLF's leadership articulated a clear critique of the Ethiopian state's oppressive policies, gaining substantial support among the Oromo population, especially those who had been directly impacted by Haile Selassie's centralization policies and land dispossession.

Despite the OLF's rise, it faced significant challenges. Both the Derg and later the transitional government following Mengistu's fall in 1991 treated the OLF as a threat to national unity, leading to its banning and the persecution of its leaders. Many OLF members went into exile or engaged in armed struggle. Nonetheless, the OLF remained a prominent voice for Oromo political aspirations, both in Ethiopia and in the diaspora.

Jalata further illustrates that, despite the Derg's promise of a more egalitarian society, the regime failed to improve the status of the Oromo. Instead, the Derg's Marxist-Leninist policies sought to suppress ethnic identities in favor of a singular Ethiopian identity. This was an extension of the centralization policies of Haile Selassie, but with a more overtly ideological approach. The Derg's violent repression included massacres, forced displacements, and the arrest of political activists. Despite initial support for the revolutionary forces, the OLF soon found itself in conflict with the Derg, which refused to grant autonomy to the Oromo and used military force to suppress dissent. This only strengthened the Oromo people's resolve to continue their struggle for self-determination and cultural survival.

In 1991, the Derg regime was overthrown by the Ethiopian People's Revolutionary Democratic Front (EPRDF), a coalition of ethnic-based political parties, including the Oromo Peoples' Democratic Organization (OPDO). The EPRDF promised to recognize the rights of ethnic groups through the establishment of ethnic federalism, a system that theoretically would allow each ethnic group to govern itself in its designated regional state. For many Oromos, the fall of the Derg and the rise of the EPRDF marked a new hope for addressing their long-standing grievances.

However, disillusionment soon set in. Many Oromos felt their concerns were sidelined within the EPRDF, and the OPDO, while formally representing the Oromo, was often viewed as a tool of the central government rather than a true representative of Oromo interests. This growing dissatisfaction culminated in the Oromo protests of 2014-2018. Sparked initially by a controversial land-grabbing proposal in Oromia, the protests quickly expanded into a broader movement calling for greater political representation, cultural rights, and the release of political prisoners. Led primarily by the youth, known as the Qeerroo, the protests resulted in widespread unrest and were met with violent government crackdowns.

The 2014-2018 protests laid the foundation for a new political shift, ultimately contributing to the rise of Abiy Ahmed as Prime Minister in 2018. Abiy, a former member of the OPDO, became Ethiopia's first Oromo prime minister. His rise to power was seen as a historic moment by many Oromos, signaling the possibility of greater inclusion for their people in the country's political system. Abiy promised wide-ranging reforms, including the release of political prisoners, the liberalization of the political system, and increased recognition of ethnic rights.

However, while Abiy's leadership initially raised hopes among many Oromos, his subsequent policies have sparked significant controversy. His efforts to centralize power and merge ethnic-based parties into the Prosperity Party (PP) have led to tensions within the Oromo community and other ethnic groups. Despite these challenges, Abiy remains a central figure in Ethiopia's political landscape, and his tenure represents both the ongoing struggles of the Oromo people and the complexities of achieving ethnic unity within a diverse nation.

This period, shaped by the political movements of the 20th and 21st centuries, reflects the enduring Oromo desire for self-determination, cultural preservation, and political representation. As Ethiopia moves forward under Abiy's leadership, the Oromo question remains a critical issue, one that will continue to shape the nation's future.

***

The Future of Oromo Politics: Challenges and Prospects

The future of Oromo politics remains intrinsically linked to the broader political trajectory of Ethiopia, with both opportunities and challenges ahead. Despite the political shift that brought Abiy Ahmed to power in 2018, the Oromo continue to grapple with systemic marginalization, political exclusion, and the ongoing struggle for cultural recognition. While many initially celebrated his rise as a historic moment for the Oromo people, Abiy's tenure has revealed a more complex and troubling reality.

Abiy, despite his Oromo background, has faced increasing criticism for his actions toward the Oromo community. Many Oromos feel that Abiy, once seen as a potential ally, has used the Oromo people as a political tool rather than a genuine advocate for their rights. Abiy's political maneuvers, especially his push for a unified Prosperity Party (PP), have been seen as self-serving and driven by an egotistical desire to consolidate power. This shift toward a more centralized political structure has alienated many Oromo elites, who feel sidelined or betrayed by his leadership. Abiy's policies have failed to address key issues such as land rights, political representation, and the protection of Oromo culture, leading to a growing sense of disillusionment and resentment within the community.

The Oromo's struggle for justice, self-determination, and cultural autonomy has continued to be a focal point of Ethiopian politics, but under Abiy's rule, this struggle has become even more complicated. While Abiy promised wide-ranging reforms, including the release of political prisoners and greater recognition of ethnic rights, his actions often suggest a disregard for the Oromo people's aspirations. His brutal crackdown on dissent, especially following the widespread Oromo protests of 2014-2018, further underscores the tension between his rhetoric and his actions. Abiy's government has been accused of using the Oromo as a scapegoat for political instability, disproportionately targeting the Oromo opposition and activists, further exacerbating the sense of injustice among the Oromo people.

The political elite within the Oromo community has also faced increased marginalization under Abiy's leadership. Key figures in the Oromo political landscape, including leaders of the OLF and other Oromo organizations, have found themselves excluded from the power structures within the Prosperity Party. This exclusion is seen by many as part of a broader effort by Abiy to consolidate his power and neutralize any potential threats to his rule, even if it means sacrificing the interests of the very people he claims to represent.

This growing sense of marginalization has led to widespread dissent among the Oromo, particularly among youth and political activists who feel that Abiy's promises have not been fulfilled. The Oromo elite, once hopeful that Abiy would bring much-needed change, now view his leadership with increasing skepticism. This division has deepened, with some advocating for continued resistance to his regime, while others search for alternative paths to achieving the political and cultural autonomy, they believe the Oromo deserve.

As Ethiopia continues to grapple with questions of ethnic federalism, unity, and decentralization, the future of Oromo politics appears uncertain. While the Oromo remain one of the largest and most politically active ethnic groups in the country, their struggle for justice and recognition is far from over. The failure of the current government to address the grievances of the Oromo people and to truly empower them within Ethiopia's political system raises questions about the prospects for lasting peace and political stability.

For the Oromo, the road ahead will require navigating a delicate balance between seeking justice within the current political framework and continuing the struggle for full political and cultural autonomy. The challenges are immense, but the desire for self-determination, political representation, and the protection of Oromo identity remains a defining feature of the Oromo struggle in Ethiopia's complex political landscape. The future of Oromo politics, shaped by the current struggles and frustrations, will continue to play a critical role in determining the direction of Ethiopia's future. The road to justice and true autonomy may still be long, but the resolve of the Oromo people to secure their rights is unwavering, even as their political landscape continues to evolve.

***

Negasso Gidada vs. Abiy Ahmed

In Ethiopia's modern political history, few figures embody integrity, humility, and genuine service to the people as much as Negasso Gidada. His life and leadership stand in stark contrast to the current administration under Prime Minister Abiy Ahmed, whose governance is often criticized for its egotistical, image-driven nature and self-serving policies.

Negasso Gidada, born in 1943, rose from modest beginnings to become one of Ethiopia's most respected Oromo political figures. His career was marked by an unwavering commitment to the Ethiopian people, exemplified by his humble leadership and intellectual rigor. He earned a doctorate in social history, was a part-time lecturer at Addis Ababa University, and became the first president of Ethiopia under the 1995 constitution. Unlike the self-serving narrative often associated with Abiy Ahmed, Negasso was deeply committed to fostering unity, democracy, and peace. He was loved by Ethiopians not because of his titles or positions, but because of his genuine connection to the people, his moderate and principled approach to politics, and his deep care for the country's welfare.

In contrast, Abiy Ahmed, since assuming office in 2018, has often been accused of using his leadership position more for self-promotion and image-building than for the genuine advancement of Ethiopia. Abiy's rise to power, marked by sweeping promises of peace and reform, soon revealed a focus on maintaining an image of a transformative leader, more concerned with global recognition than addressing the deeper issues facing the Ethiopian people. His controversial moves, such as inviting international praise with the Nobel Peace Prize while engaging in military actions against his own citizens, reflect an administration driven by ego and optics rather than authentic concern for the country's well-being.

Where Negasso Gidada lived a life of moderation, focusing on serving others and rejecting personal glory, Abiy Ahmed has been criticized for his egotistical behavior. While Negasso maintained humility throughout his life, Abiy's leadership has been marked by grand gestures and public spectacles designed to enhance his personal image. The former president of Ethiopia shunned the trappings of power, living a simple life, while Abiy's regime seems to prioritize grandiose projects, excessive military spending, and extravagant investments in Addis Ababa's aesthetics, even at the cost of basic human needs in the country.

Furthermore, Negasso's political career was grounded in principles of democracy and inclusivity. He was not afraid to admit his mistakes, apologize, and seek forgiveness from the Ethiopian people. His honesty about the flaws in Ethiopia's political process was a rare quality that made him a true statesman. Abiy, on the other hand, is often accused of using his rhetoric to manipulate and deceive the public. His government has been characterized by a lack of transparency, widespread political repression, and the silencing of critics. While Negasso fought for genuine democratic reforms and was an advocate for human rights, Abiy's administration has increasingly been seen as authoritarian, prioritizing control over the freedom and dignity of the people.

Perhaps the most telling contrast between Negasso and Abiy is their approach to the Ethiopian people. Negasso was loved because he genuinely cared for the well-being of all Ethiopians. He was a leader who sought to bridge divides, promote peace, and elevate the lives of ordinary citizens. His efforts to unite Ethiopia were driven by a sincere desire to build a better future, not to cement his own legacy. In stark contrast, Abiy's leadership is often seen as self-serving. His administration, though often praised internationally, has been plagued by internal divisions, ethnic tensions, and economic hardships, with the public bearing the brunt of policies that seem to favor political survival over genuine progress.

The life and leadership of Negasso Gidada remind Ethiopians that true leaders are those who put the needs of the people first, act with humility, and seek to serve rather than be served. Negasso's legacy stands as a beacon of what leadership should be: grounded in integrity, honesty, and the pursuit of justice for all. In contrast, Abiy Ahmed's reign continues to reveal a stark reality of a leader more focused on appearances, accolades, and consolidating power than on genuine governance and the well-being of his people.

While Negasso Gidada's humility, wisdom, and dedication to Ethiopia's democratic future remain a cherished memory for many, Abiy Ahmed's leadership will be remembered for its contradictions, self-promotion, and a broken promise of transformation. The contrast between these two leaders serves as a powerful reminder that Ethiopia deserves a future led by those who prioritize its people, their rights, and their dignity, rather than those who seek to build personal legacies at their expense.

***

Abiy and the Complex Legacy of Oromo Leadership

Abiy Ahmed's leadership of Ethiopia has been inextricably linked to the Oromo struggle for political power, with figures such as Jawar

Mohammed and the Oromo Liberation Front (OLF) playing pivotal roles in shaping the nation's political narrative. Abiy's rise to power and his ambitious vision for Ethiopia have not only shifted the political landscape but have also exacerbated divisions, particularly with the Oromo people. His tenure, which promised reform and national unity, has led to a fractured relationship between the central government and the Oromo community, with increasing disillusionment over issues like the centralization of power, economic stagnation, and political repression.

Abiy's leadership began with high hopes and significant expectations, especially from the Oromo people. His ascension to the prime ministership in 2018 was seen as a watershed moment. As the first Oromo leader to hold the position of prime minister in Ethiopia's modern history, Abiy's rise offered the promise of greater representation, political inclusion, and the opportunity for the Oromo people to reclaim some of the power and recognition that had been denied to them for centuries. His leadership represented the culmination of decades of Oromo political struggle, epitomized by movements like the Oromo Liberation Front (OLF) and the activism of figures such as Jawar Mohammed. These movements had long called for an end to the marginalization of the Oromo people and the recognition of their political, cultural, and economic rights. For many, Abiy's leadership symbolized the potential for reconciliation, justice, and a more inclusive Ethiopian state.

However, despite the initial optimism, Abiy's leadership has become increasingly contentious, particularly among the Oromo and their political leaders. Over time, Abiy's government has been accused of centralizing power in a way that undermines the democratic reforms he initially promised. His early political reforms, which included the release of political prisoners, the unbanning of opposition parties, and a peace agreement with Eritrea, were hailed as groundbreaking steps. Yet, these actions have not fully addressed the deeper political, economic, and social concerns of the Oromo people. Instead of fostering the broad-based inclusion and autonomy that many Oromo hoped for, Abiy's policies have, in many cases, exacerbated feelings of disillusionment and disenfranchisement.

One of the most significant sources of tension between Abiy's government and the Oromo community is the issue of political power. Despite Abiy's Oromo heritage, many of his policies have been perceived as undermining the political autonomy and agency of the Oromo people. His government's approach has often been viewed as top-down, where central government power remains concentrated in Addis Ababa, with little genuine decentralization or recognition of the political aspirations of the Oromo or other regional groups. This centralization of power has undermined the trust that the Oromo people had placed in Abiy's leadership, with many feeling that his reforms have served to further entrench the political dominance of the ruling elite, rather than creating a more equitable political system.

In addition to political centralization, economic stagnation has also contributed to the growing divide between the central government and the Oromo. Abiy's economic policies, while ambitious, have struggled to achieve meaningful improvements in the lives of ordinary Ethiopians, particularly those in rural areas where the majority of the Oromo population resides. Despite his efforts to attract foreign investment and modernize Ethiopia's economy, the expected benefits have not been evenly distributed, leaving many Oromos still grappling with poverty, underdevelopment, and limited access to basic services. The lack of economic opportunities, coupled with the frustration over unmet expectations, has fueled growing disillusionment among the Oromo people, who feel that Abiy's economic reforms have not adequately addressed their needs.

Furthermore, political repression has also played a crucial role in the growing tensions between Abiy's government and the Oromo. While Abiy initially promised to open up political space and reduce the repression of opposition forces, his government has been accused of clamping down on dissent, especially from Oromo political activists and leaders. Figures like Jawar Mohammed, once a close ally of Abiy, have become vocal critics of the government, accusing Abiy of betraying the Oromo cause. The treatment of opposition figures, political activists, and journalists has raised concerns about the future of democratic reforms in Ethiopia, with many arguing that the political space for dissent and debate has diminished under Abiy's leadership. The government's response to Oromo protests, including the violent repression of demonstrations, has only further alienated the Oromo people and fueled perceptions of a betrayal of the reforms that Abiy once championed.

The situation has been complicated further by the broader ethnic tensions that have plagued Ethiopia since Abiy's rise to power. While Abiy's initial reforms sought to address the grievances of marginalized ethnic groups, the decentralization of power and the opening of political space also unleashed a wave of ethnic mobilization. This has led to violent clashes between various ethnic groups, including the Oromo, Amhara, and Tigray, as each group seeks to assert its political and territorial rights. The lack of a cohesive national identity and the failure to effectively address ethnic divisions have created an environment of instability and fear, which has undermined efforts to build a unified, peaceful Ethiopia.

The relationship between Abiy Ahmed's government and the Oromo people, once hopeful and full of potential, has become strained. While Abiy's leadership has undeniably brought about some positive changes, such as his peace agreement with Eritrea, the centralization of power, economic stagnation, and political repression have made it increasingly difficult to reconcile the interests of the Oromo community with the central government. Figures like Jawar Mohammed and the Oromo Liberation Front (OLF), who once played a significant role in supporting Abiy's ascent to power, now find themselves at odds with his administration. This ongoing tension presents a major challenge for Ethiopia as it strives for unity and reconciliation.

The path forward for Ethiopia lies in its ability to address these deep divisions. The Oromo people, as the largest ethnic group in the country, must be meaningfully included in the political and economic decision-making processes. Political decentralization, genuine economic development, and the protection of political freedoms are essential for restoring the trust of the Oromo and other marginalized groups. The Ethiopian government must work to ensure that the country's development benefits all Ethiopians, not just the elites in Addis Ababa. Only by addressing the legitimate grievances of the Oromo and other ethnic groups can Ethiopia hope to achieve true unity and reconciliation, and ensure a stable, prosperous future for all its citizens.

***

CHAPTER 10

Cruelty in Power: The Price of Progress

When Abiy Ahmed assumed the office of Prime Minister of Ethiopia in 2018, his rise was met with immense hope and expectations, both from within the country and from the Ethiopian diaspora abroad. After nearly three decades of authoritarian rule by the Ethiopian People's Revolutionary Democratic Front (EPRDF), Abiy's appointment was seen as a moment of profound transformation for Ethiopia. The EPRDF had long been associated with a centralized, ethnocentric governance system that favored certain ethnic groups, particularly the Tigrayans, leading to widespread discontent and rising tensions. Abiy's ascension to the premiership came during a period of mounting political unrest, with protests erupting in various regions, notably the Oromia and Amhara regions, where marginalized ethnic groups sought greater representation and rights.

Abiy Ahmed's rise to power offered a glimmer of hope for millions of Ethiopians who had endured years of political repression, economic stagnation, and ethnic marginalization. His promises of peace, democratic reforms, and economic development resonated deeply with many who had suffered under the oppressive regime of the EPRDF. He signaled a willingness to open up the political space, releasing political prisoners, unbanning opposition parties, and allowing exiled dissidents to return. These initial actions were seen as symbolic steps toward creating a more inclusive and democratic Ethiopia. Abiy's rhetoric was inclusive, reaching out to all ethnic groups, promising a better, unified future for a country often torn apart by ethnic divisions. He promised a departure from the authoritarianism that had defined Ethiopian politics for decades, signaling a new era of openness, transparency, and freedom.

Abiy's reformist agenda seemed to be validated when he was awarded the Nobel Peace Prize in 2019 for his role in ending a two-decade-long conflict between Ethiopia and Eritrea. His role in negotiating the peace deal was widely celebrated, both within Ethiopia and internationally. The peace agreement with Eritrea, signed in 2018, marked a major diplomatic breakthrough, as it ended one of Africa's longest-standing conflicts, which had resulted in tens of thousands of deaths and led to years of stagnation and hostility between the two countries. The peace deal was widely viewed as a monumental achievement for Abiy, affirming his reputation as a statesman and a leader committed to fostering peace and stability in the Horn of Africa.

The international recognition, particularly the Nobel Peace Prize, helped solidify Abiy's image as a reformist leader. For many Ethiopians and members of the diaspora, Abiy became a symbol of hope, someone who would bring about the change that had been longed for over generations. Expectations were high that his leadership would lead Ethiopia into a new era of democratic governance, economic development, and social harmony. His promises, coupled with the positive international attention, created a sense of optimism that was difficult to ignore. It was seen as a rare opportunity for Ethiopia to break free from the chains of authoritarianism, to build a more inclusive society, and to chart a path of economic prosperity.

However, as time went on, the gap between Abiy's promises and the reality of his leadership became increasingly evident. While Abiy had promised political and economic reforms, the implementation of these reforms has been uneven, and in many cases, has not lived up to the high expectations that were set at the outset of his tenure. A significant portion of the population, particularly from ethnic groups who had long been marginalized, found that the promises of inclusion and equality were not being realized in practice. Abiy's leadership, which initially aimed to bring about national unity, began to reveal fractures, particularly along ethnic lines.

The Ethiopian political system, which had been heavily influenced by ethnic federalism under the EPRDF, became even more fragmented under Abiy's leadership. The political structure had been designed to give ethnic groups a sense of autonomy, but it also led to increasing ethnic divisions and competition for resources and power. Abiy's attempt to dismantle this ethnic federalism and create a more centralized and unified Ethiopia was met with resistance from many regional leaders and ethnic groups, particularly the Oromo, the largest ethnic group in the country, who felt that their demands for political and cultural recognition had been overlooked. Abiy's decision to abolish the long-standing ethnic federal system, in favor of a more centralized government, exacerbated tensions, and many ethnic groups saw this as a threat to their political autonomy. The resulting fragmentation fueled further ethnic violence and unrest, leading to instability in various regions of the country.

The economy, despite Abiy's attempts at liberalization and attracting foreign investment, has struggled to meet the aspirations of many Ethiopians. While there have been some successes, such as efforts to privatize state-owned enterprises and improve infrastructure, these reforms have not resulted in widespread economic benefits for the average Ethiopian citizen. Economic growth has not been felt equally, and many Ethiopians, particularly those in rural areas, continue to face poverty and unemployment. Moreover, the centralization of power and the focus on attracting foreign investment, while beneficial for some, have not addressed the structural issues of economic inequality and underdevelopment, particularly in the rural and marginalized regions.

In addition to these economic challenges, political repression under Abiy's government has grown, undermining the democratic reforms that were initially promised. Despite his initial steps to open up the political space, his government has increasingly used force against political opposition and civil society. The treatment of opposition figures, including prominent leaders such as Jawar Mohammed, who played a critical role in Abiy's rise to power, has raised alarm about the government's commitment to democracy. Political activists, journalists, and opposition leaders have been detained, and protests have been met with violent crackdowns, eroding the freedoms that Abiy had once promised. The government's increasing control over the media and its restrictions on freedom of expression have led many to question whether Ethiopia is slipping back into authoritarianism under Abiy's leadership.

Perhaps the most troubling aspect of Abiy's leadership has been the escalation of ethnic violence and the breakdown of national unity. In the wake of Abiy's reforms, tensions between ethnic groups have worsened, and violence has erupted in several regions. The country has been plagued by conflict in the Tigray region, which has become the epicenter of an ongoing war between the Ethiopian government and the Tigray People's Liberation Front (TPLF). The conflict has resulted in thousands of deaths, mass displacement, and a humanitarian crisis that has deeply affected Ethiopia's overall stability. In addition to the Tigray conflict, there has been violence in other parts of the country, including Oromia and Amhara, further exacerbating the challenges to national unity.

Abiy's leadership, once seen as a beacon of hope for Ethiopia, has been marred by political and ethnic divisions, economic stagnation, and increasing authoritarianism. His initial promises of peace, democratic reforms, and national reconciliation have not been fully realized, and the gap between the image of Abiy as a reformer and the reality of his governance has left many Ethiopians disillusioned. His efforts to unify Ethiopia have been complicated by ethnic tensions, political repression, and an inability to deliver on promises of widespread economic benefits. As Ethiopia grapples with internal conflict, economic instability, and growing political repression, Abiy's leadership will be defined by the degree to which he can navigate these challenges and restore the trust of the Ethiopian people. Ultimately, the vision of a united, democratic, and prosperous Ethiopia that many hoped for when Abiy assumed power remains elusive, leaving Ethiopia at a crossroads as it faces an uncertain future.

When Abiy Ahmed assumed power in Ethiopia in 2018, one of his central promises was the liberalization of the country's political system. For years, Ethiopia had been governed under the Ethiopian People's Revolutionary Democratic Front (EPRDF), an authoritarian regime that had relied on ethnic federalism to maintain control over the country's diverse population. While this system theoretically gave ethnic groups autonomy within their regions, it often exacerbated ethnic divisions and fueled conflict by fostering competition for power and resources among different ethnic groups. Abiy recognized the limitations and failures of this system and pledged to dismantle the ethnic federalism that had, in many ways, deepened Ethiopia's divisions. His vision was one of national unity, political inclusivity, and a more democratic future for Ethiopia.

Abiy's promises of reform were particularly resonant with many Ethiopians, both inside and outside the country. His vision for a more inclusive government was not just about policy changes; it also represented a break from the past and a new era of hope. He promised to move away from the centralized control of the EPRDF, opening up the political space for greater participation from opposition parties, civil society, and the media. His government initially took concrete steps toward liberalizing the political environment. He released thousands of political prisoners, including prominent opposition figures, and unbanned political parties that had been outlawed under the EPRDF. This move was a significant step toward creating a more open and competitive political landscape. Abiy's rhetoric, which emphasized tolerance, national reconciliation, and unity, resonated particularly well with those who had suffered under years of political repression. His government also promoted women's rights, appointing women to high-level positions in the cabinet and making significant strides in gender equality.

For Ethiopians in the diaspora, Abiy's promises of democratic reform and political liberalization were seen as a sign of hope. Many diaspora Ethiopians had fled the country during the EPRDF's brutal crackdown on dissent and opposition. They had lived in countries like the United States, Canada, and various European nations, where they witnessed the workings of stable democracies with free and fair elections, press freedom, and respect for human rights. These members of the Ethiopian diaspora, who had long been critical of the authoritarianism of the EPRDF, viewed Abiy's ascent to power as an opportunity to create a more just and democratic Ethiopia—one that could mirror the freedoms they had found abroad. The promise of a more open political system and greater opportunities for all citizens, irrespective of ethnic background, sparked great enthusiasm in the diaspora community. They hoped for the eventual return of democracy to Ethiopia, which had been denied under the previous regime.

The promise of a more democratic Ethiopia also found strong support among younger generations, both in the country and among the diasporas. These groups, many of whom had grown up under the shadow of political repression, were eager for the opportunities that democratic reforms could bring. Abiy's rhetoric on freedom of speech, human rights, and democratic participation held particular appeal to young Ethiopians who were increasingly active in political debates, social media, and civic engagement. The hope was that Abiy's leadership could usher in a more open and participatory political system, allowing for greater expression of diverse political views and addressing the grievances of marginalized groups.

The Eritrean Ethiopian War, which lasted from 1998 to 2000, resulted in tens of thousands of deaths and left both countries in a state of military and political standoff. Despite the official cessation of hostilities in 2000, there had been no peace agreement or normalization of relations for nearly two decades. Abiy's decision to engage with Eritrean President Isaias Afwerki, and to pursue peace negotiations, marked a new chapter in the Horn of Africa's geopolitical landscape.

For many members of the Ethiopian diaspora, the peace agreement with Eritrea was a sign that Abiy could bring about transformative change, not only within Ethiopia but also in the region. They saw it as the first step toward addressing the broader regional challenges in the Horn of Africa, an area often plagued by conflict and instability. The resolution of the Eritrean conflict was viewed as an important building block for fostering greater economic cooperation, cultural exchange, and stability in the region. Ethiopian expatriates, many of whom had close family ties to Eritrea, celebrated the peace agreement, hoping that it would lead to greater unity among Ethiopians and Eritreans alike, and contribute to long-term prosperity for both nations.

Moreover, the peace deal was seen as a potential model for resolving other regional conflicts, demonstrating that diplomacy and dialogue could replace the entrenched cycles of war and mistrust that had characterized the Horn of Africa for decades. Abiy's diplomatic success bolstered his image as a transformative leader, someone who could bring lasting peace not just to Ethiopia but to a volatile region that had long been torn by war, poverty, and political tension. The subsequent opening of borders between Ethiopia and Eritrea, the resumption of air travel, and the restoration of people-to-people ties were hailed as signs of progress and reconciliation.

Despite the initial optimism surrounding Abiy's promises and reforms, the reality of his leadership has proven more complicated. While some of the changes he implemented were undoubtedly positive, his efforts to liberalize Ethiopia's political system and unite the country have been met with resistance, both from within and outside the government. The dismantling of the EPRDF's ethnic federal system, for example, led to significant pushback from regional leaders who feared a loss of political power and autonomy. Abiy's move toward a more centralized government structure, while intended to foster national unity, was seen by many as a threat to the delicate balance of power among Ethiopia's diverse ethnic groups. The political tensions that have erupted in response to these changes have fueled ethnic violence, civil unrest, and widespread instability in various parts of the country.

In addition, Abiy's approach to opposition politics has been criticized for increasingly authoritarian tendencies. Although opposition parties were allowed to return and engage in the political process, political repression, including the arrest of opposition leaders and the silencing of dissent, has risen under Abiy's leadership. While he initially embraced political liberalization, the political space has narrowed as Abiy has consolidated power, and his government has increasingly cracked down on protests, media freedoms, and opposition figures. These actions have caused growing disillusionment among many Ethiopians, both within the country and in the diaspora, who had hoped for a true democratic transformation.

Thus, while Abiy Ahmed's rise to power promised a new era of peace, democratic reform, and economic development, the path to realizing these promises has been fraught with challenges. His efforts to break from the past and create a more inclusive Ethiopia have been undermined by ethnic tensions, political opposition, and growing authoritarianism. The peace agreement with Eritrea remains a significant achievement, but it has not been enough to overcome the internal political and social divisions that continue to plague Ethiopia. For Ethiopians in the diaspora, the hope for a democratic, peaceful, and prosperous Ethiopia remains, but the gap between Abiy's promises and the current realities of governance has left many wondering whether the dream of a reformed Ethiopia will ever be realized.

***

The Collapse of Hope: From Promises to Betrayal

As time passed, the reality of Abiy's leadership began to starkly contrast with the hopeful expectations that many had for him. Rather than ushering in a new era of democracy, Abiy's tenure has been marked by an increasing authoritarian shift, with violent military campaigns in regions like Tigray, Amhara, and Oromia. The Ethiopian government, under Abiy's leadership, has engaged in brutal crackdowns on political opposition, media freedom, and ethnic minorities, actions that are difficult to reconcile with his early claims of a more open and democratic government.

One of the most glaring contradictions in Abiy's leadership was his promise to never imprison citizens without due process. Early in his rule, he claimed that Ethiopia would not be a country where people were imprisoned without examination, suggesting that his government would uphold basic rule of law and human rights. However, as political tensions rose, Abiy's government has detained opposition leaders, activists, and journalists without trial, some even disappearing for long periods. The arbitrary arrests of political opponents, especially those critical of Abiy's handling of ethnic violence and the war in Tigray and Amhara, have shattered the image of a progressive leader. Abiy's administration has also been accused of curbing freedom of expression, with journalists and media outlets critical of the government being harassed, arrested, or forced into exile.

For many members of the Ethiopian diaspora, these shifts have been nothing short of disheartening. The diaspora community had placed their trust in Abiy as a beacon of change—a leader who would end years of political persecution, offer freedom and prosperity, and create a unified nation. They hoped that Abiy would fulfill the dreams of those who had fled the country in search of better opportunities and safety. Diaspora Ethiopians, particularly those from Amhara, Oromia, and Tigray, pinned their hopes on a unified Ethiopia, free from the internal divisions that had caused years of suffering.

However, the outbreak of the Tigray conflict in 2020, which involved severe human rights violations and the displacement of millions, shocked the diaspora. The brutality of the Ethiopian military's actions in Tigray and Amhara, including the targeting of civilians, the destruction of religious sites, and widespread sexual violence, made it clear that Abiy's regime was willing to pursue violent methods to maintain control. Many in the diaspora felt betrayed, especially given Abiy's previous image as a peacemaker. The war exposed the flaws in his leadership and raised serious concerns about his true intentions.

In the face of this, many Ethiopians abroad began to feel that Abiy was merely using the language of peace and democratic reform to mask a deeper, more authoritarian agenda. His growing ties with military elites, the militarization of the Ethiopian state, and the centralization of power suggested that Abiy was, in fact, moving further away from democracy and freedom. Some in the diaspora began to draw comparisons between Abiy and dictatorial leaders, seeing his approach to governance as strikingly similar to that of authoritarian regimes around the world.

The disappointment among the diaspora has been palpable. For many, Abiy's failure to live up to his promises has created a sense of betrayal. People who had hoped for an Ethiopia free from ethnic violence, where democracy and human rights would be respected, now face the reality of ethnic conflict, military violence, and political repression. The initial excitement over his Nobel Peace

Prize win has long since faded, replaced by growing concern and frustration.

In the diaspora, the sense of hope that Abiy sparked turned to disillusionment. Amharas, Oromos, Tigrayans, and others, once hopeful that their homeland would be transformed, now watch in horror as their loved ones suffer and die in a civil war that seems to have no end. Ethiopian activists abroad who had once campaigned for the change that Abiy promised to have now shifted to advocacy for peace, human rights, and justice in Ethiopia.

Abiy's failure to meet the expectations of Ethiopians, especially those living outside the country, has sparked calls for a return to true democratic reforms, an end to ethnic violence, and a commitment to justice for those harmed by his regime's actions. The diaspora remains a crucial voice in advocating for these changes, but their trust in Abiy has been irrevocably broken. Many now fear that Ethiopia may be on the path to greater authoritarianism, rather than the democratic transformation they had hoped for.

For the Ethiopian diaspora, the betrayal of Abiy's leadership serves as a reminder of the dangers of placing too much hope in a single leader, especially when that leader has not demonstrated a commitment to true change. Ethiopians both at home and abroad are left grappling with a sense of loss and disillusionment, questioning whether peace, democracy, and unity are even possible under Abiy's rule.

***

The Postponement of the 2020 Elections and Rising Criticism

In June 2020, the National Election Board of Ethiopia (NEBE) and Prime Minister Abiy Ahmed announced the decision to postpone the country's parliamentary elections, initially scheduled for August of that year. The stated reason for the delay was the outbreak of the COVID-19 pandemic, which posed a significant public health threat both within Ethiopia and globally. The government's position was that holding the election during a time of widespread illness and restrictions would compromise the safety of voters and undermine the integrity of the electoral process. On the surface, this rationale seemed reasonable, as countries around the world grappled with similar dilemmas regarding public health and electoral processes. However, the decision quickly became controversial, with accusations from opposition groups, civil society organizations, and international observers that the government was using the pandemic as a pretext to extend its rule and undermine the democratic process.

At the heart of the criticism was the claim that the decision to delay the election was not driven by the pandemic but by Abiy's desire to consolidate political power. The Ethiopian constitution mandates that elections be held within a five-year cycle, and Abiy's tenure was due to end in August 2020. For many, the postponement of the election raised serious constitutional concerns. Critics argued that by unilaterally delaying the election, Abiy was effectively bypassing the constitution's stipulation for regular, democratic elections. This view was particularly concerning because it was not the first instance in which the government had taken actions that seemed to undermine Ethiopia's democratic institutions.

Opposition parties and civil society groups were quick to accuse Abiy's government of using the pandemic as a cover to extend its time in power. They argued that the government had not taken adequate steps to prepare for the election under pandemic conditions, such as implementing measures to ensure safe voting or adjusting the electoral timeline. Instead, they claimed, the government chose to delay the election without offering a clear alternative plan for restoring democratic processes. Many opposition leaders pointed out that the government had previously held elections under less-than-ideal conditions, citing the 2015 election as an example. The 2015 elections, which were widely criticized for their lack of transparency and fairness, had been marred by allegations of voter suppression, intimidation, and fraud. The international community had condemned the elections, but Abiy's government had previously promised to make significant reforms in order to establish a more transparent, free, and fair political system.

This contrast between Abiy's promises of democratic reform and the reality of his actions contributed to growing disillusionment both within Ethiopia and among the Ethiopian diasporas. Opposition groups feared that the postponement of the 2020 elections was the first step in a broader campaign to suppress political opposition, eliminate dissent, and solidify Abiy's control over the country. The postponement was also seen as a failure to deliver on Abiy's promise of a democratic transition for Ethiopia, undermining the credibility of his government's reformist image. For many Ethiopians who had welcomed Abiy's ascension to power in 2018 as a beacon of hope for democracy, the delay was a sign that the prime minister's reforms were more rhetoric than substance.

The criticisms of the government's decision to delay the election were not limited to domestic opposition. International observers, including the United Nations and foreign governments, expressed concern about the impact of the delay on Ethiopia's democratic future. While many acknowledged the health risks posed by the COVID-19 pandemic, they also emphasized that delays in holding elections could destabilize the political environment, erode public trust in democratic institutions, and perpetuate Ethiopia's authoritarian legacy. Ethiopia's international partners, many of whom had supported Abiy's earlier reform efforts, were concerned that the delay would undermine his credibility and signal a retreat from the democratic path that had been charted in 2018.

Despite these concerns, the Ethiopian government maintained that the postponement was in the best interest of public health. In response to mounting criticisms, Abiy and his officials defended their decision by pointing to the necessity of protecting citizens from the spread of COVID-19. The government argued that it was prioritizing the well-being of the Ethiopian people over political considerations, and that the electoral process would not be meaningful if held under conditions that jeopardized public health. For the Ethiopian government, the decision to delay the election was presented as an exceptional measure in extraordinary circumstances.

In the end, the parliamentary elections were rescheduled for June 2021, nearly a full year after the initial date. In the lead-up to the election, the government engaged in a campaign to reassure the public that the voting process would be conducted with greater transparency and fairness than in previous years. The Ethiopian government promised to ensure the safety of voters by implementing COVID-19 precautions, such as social distancing, sanitization of polling stations, and the provision of personal protective equipment (PPE). Additionally, the government insisted that political opponents would be able to participate in the elections and that no party would be excluded from the political process.

When the election finally took place in June 2021, the African Union (AU) issued a statement praising the elections as an improvement over previous ones, particularly when compared to the 2015 elections, which had been marred by widespread allegations of fraud, voter suppression, and violence. The AU noted that the election had been conducted in a more peaceful and orderly manner, with fewer reports of violence and intimidation than in previous years. However, the AU's positive assessment was met with skepticism, both within Ethiopia and abroad. While some hailed the elections as a step forward, many Ethiopians and international observers questioned the legitimacy of the process.

In particular, the election was marred by widespread instability and violence in several regions, including the northern Tigray region, where a brutal conflict between the Ethiopian government and the Tigray People's Liberation Front (TPLF) had been ongoing since late 2020. As a result of the conflict, the election could not be held in Tigray, and millions of people there were unable to participate in the democratic process. The absence of elections in Tigray raised serious concerns about the inclusivity and fairness of the process, as a significant portion of the population was effectively disenfranchised.

In addition, opposition groups and civil society organizations accused the government of using the electoral process as a tool to consolidate its power and suppress opposition. These groups alleged that the government had engaged in voter suppression tactics, including limiting the ability of opposition parties to campaign freely and intimidating voters in regions with strong opposition support. The ruling party, the Prosperity Party, which was founded by Abiy after the dissolution of the EPRDF, was accused of using state resources to secure an electoral advantage, including the manipulation of media coverage and the restriction of opposition access to the political sphere.

Despite the government's attempts to present the election as a democratic milestone, the outcome was deeply contentious. The Prosperity Party emerged victorious, securing a significant majority in the parliament. However, the legitimacy of the election was called into question by both domestic and international observers. Many Ethiopians, particularly those in opposition-controlled regions or those who had been displaced by the Tigray conflict, felt that the election did not represent the will of the people and that the democratic process had been compromised. The postponement of the election, combined with the lack of inclusivity and ongoing political repression, led to a deepening of the political crisis in Ethiopia, raising questions about Abiy Ahmed's commitment to democratic reform.

In conclusion, the postponement of Ethiopia's 2020 elections marked a turning point in Abiy Ahmed's leadership and in the country's political trajectory. Initially viewed as a necessary measure to protect public health during the COVID-19 pandemic, the delay quickly became a flashpoint for criticism, both within Ethiopia and internationally. The decision raised serious constitutional and democratic concerns, with opposition groups accusing the government of using the pandemic as an excuse to prolong its hold on power. While the 2021 election took place, it was marred by conflict, violence, and allegations of electoral fraud, leaving many Ethiopians and international observers questioning the legitimacy of the process. The delay and the subsequent election reflected the complex and often contradictory nature of Abiy Ahmed's leadership, which has alternated between moments of reform and attempts to consolidate power, raising critical questions about Ethiopia's democratic future.

***

Opposition to the Postponement of Ethiopia's 2020 Election

Jawar Mohammed, a prominent Ethiopian political figure, and Lidetu Ayalew, a long-time opposition leader, both emerged as key voices in opposition to Prime Minister Abiy Ahmed's decision to delay Ethiopia's 2020 parliamentary elections due to the COVID-19 pandemic. While the Ethiopian government defended the delay as a necessary measure to protect public health, many political parties and civil society groups, including Jawar and Lidetu, viewed the postponement as a strategic move by Abiy to consolidate power and avoid electoral defeat. Both leaders argued that the delay was a direct threat to Ethiopia's democratic aspirations, marking a shift toward authoritarianism.

Jawar, who had played a pivotal role in the 2014–2016 Oromo protests, was initially a supporter of Abiy Ahmed, believing that Abiy's promise of reform would benefit the historically marginalized Oromo people. However, as Abiy's policies shifted, particularly regarding ethnic federalism and political freedoms, Jawar became one of Abiy's most vocal critics. His opposition became more pronounced following the election delay. Jawar and his political allies, including the Oromo Federalist Congress (OFC), argued that the postponement was part of a broader effort to suppress growing political opposition and maintain control over the political landscape. They believed Abiy was using the COVID-19 crisis as an excuse to extend his time in office, undermining the democratic process in the process.

Jawar's criticisms of the government went beyond the election delay. He accused Abiy of stifling opposition, curtailing political freedoms, and consolidating power at the expense of Ethiopia's democratic institutions. His activism, particularly through his media platform, the Oromia Media Network (OMN), fueled public opposition to Abiy's government and called for a transition to a more inclusive and democratic governance structure. Jawar advocated for a transitional government that would lead Ethiopia toward fair and democratic elections, a stance that placed him in direct conflict with the Abiy administration.

Similarly, Lidetu Ayalew, a former leader of the Coalition for Unity and Democracy (CUD) and now head of the Democratic Party (DP), also opposed the election delay. Lidetu, who had been a vocal critic of Ethiopia's political establishment since the 2005 elections, viewed the postponement as an illegal and unconstitutional act that undermined the constitutional mandate for elections to be held within five years. He, like Jawar, believed that the government was exploiting the pandemic to extend its control, and that the lack of a clear plan for when elections would be held only deepened public mistrust in Abiy's leadership.

Lidetu and Jawar's calls for a transitional government, with the aim of ensuring a fair and transparent electoral process, put them at odds with Abiy's administration. Both men argued that Ethiopia needed a fresh political start to address deep-rooted issues of ethnic division and authoritarianism. Their advocacy for dialogue and reconciliation to resolve Ethiopia's political crises further complicated their relationship with the government, as it highlighted their opposition to Abiy's consolidation of power.

As a result of their outspoken criticism and advocacy for change, both Jawar and Lidetu found themselves in exile. Jawar, who was arrested in 2020 in connection with violence in Oromia, fled the country after his release from prison, and now resides in Kenya. Lidetu, who had long been an advocate for democratic reforms, also went into exile in the United States. Despite being in exile, both continue to actively promote peace, dialogue, and reconciliation as crucial pathways to resolving Ethiopia's ongoing political crises. They advocate for a peaceful transition to a more inclusive government and call for a return to the democratic principles that they believe have been undermined by Abiy's administration.

However, despite their advocacy for peace, both Jawar and Lidetu are viewed with skepticism by many Ethiopians. Some see them as opportunists, whose actions are driven more by personal ambition than by a genuine desire to bring about change. Their history of political engagement, particularly their involvement in high-profile movements and criticisms of the current government, has led some to question their motives and trustworthiness. Many perceive their calls for a transitional government as self-serving, believing that their leadership would be a way to gain political power rather than contribute to Ethiopia's long-term stability.

Nevertheless, Jawar and Lidetu continue to have significant followings among certain political factions and the Ethiopian diaspora. They remain influential figures in the opposition movement, and their calls for a peaceful, democratic transition resonate with those who are disillusioned with the current government. Despite the challenges they face, both Jawar and Lidetu persist in their advocacy for dialogue and reconciliation, believing that Ethiopia's future depends on addressing its political and ethnic divisions through peaceful means. Whether they can regain the trust of the Ethiopian people and play a role in the country's political future remains uncertain, as the country grapples with deep political divisions and an uncertain path forward.

In response to Prime Minister Abiy Ahmed's decision to delay Ethiopia's scheduled parliamentary elections in 2020, a range of opposition parties from diverse ethnic, political, and regional backgrounds voiced their strong disapproval. These parties had eagerly anticipated the opportunity to contest the elections, hoping to challenge Abiy's leadership amid growing political tensions, particularly around issues of ethnic representation and democratic governance. The delay, which the government justified on the grounds of the COVID-19 pandemic, was seen by many in the opposition as a transparent and self-serving tactic to maintain political control in the face of mounting dissent. With Abiy's reforms facing increasing opposition, the delay exacerbated already existing tensions in the country and led to widespread accusations of authoritarianism.

While the COVID-19 pandemic undeniably posed significant challenges globally, including in Ethiopia, critics within the opposition contended that the government's decision to postpone the elections was politically motivated. The postponement was announced at a time when ethnic and regional tensions were rapidly intensifying across the country, and many opposition parties felt that Abiy's government was using the pandemic as a cover for consolidating power. From their perspective, the delay reflected a growing authoritarianism that sought to stifle opposition and suppress popular discontent. The opposition argued that the real crisis facing Ethiopia was not the pandemic but the political and ethnic divisions that had worsened under Abiy's leadership. The need for a free and fair election, they contended, was essential to address these divisions and restore the country's credibility as a democratic state.

This sense of urgency was rooted in the perception that Abiy's leadership had increasingly alienated many groups, particularly ethnic minorities and political dissidents, who felt that their concerns were being ignored by the government. Ethiopia's ethnic federalism system, which had allowed for a degree of regional autonomy, was becoming a focal point of political struggle. Many opposition leaders feared that if elections were postponed indefinitely, Ethiopia would face deeper fragmentation along ethnic lines, further polarizing an already divided society. The postponement was seen as an opportunity for Abiy to maintain power while delaying necessary reforms that could address grievances related to ethnic representation and political participation. For these critics, the election delay represented an ongoing failure to move beyond the ethnic-based politics that had defined the Ethiopian People's Revolutionary Democratic Front (EPRDF) era, and they viewed it as a critical step backward in Ethiopia's democratic transition.

One of the central criticisms of Abiy's decision to delay the elections was that it reinforced a pattern of political exclusion and disenfranchisement. Opposition leaders argued that Ethiopia's political crisis was already marked by the marginalization of key groups, including those from the Tigray region, Oromo activists, and other political factions who had been excluded from the political process. They believed that a timely election could serve as a much-needed mechanism for reconciliation and representational fairness. The delay, in their view, only exacerbated these issues, leaving the grievances of Ethiopia's marginalized communities unaddressed and further deepening the divisions between the central government and various opposition groups.

The opposition was also deeply concerned about the broader political environment, which they argued had become increasingly hostile to dissent and opposition activity. Many opposition leaders, including well-known figures like Jawar Mohammed and Lidetu Ayalew, found themselves facing a growing crackdown on political freedoms. The political space for dialogue and contestation had been shrinking since Abiy's rise to power. Opposition parties, once hopeful that Abiy's reform agenda would lead to a more open political environment, were increasingly alarmed by government actions aimed at stifling opposition voices. Media censorship, political arrests, and the targeting of opposition activists became more prevalent as the government sought to control the narrative and suppress criticism. Critics pointed to a growing pattern of repression, where opposition leaders and political activists were harassed, imprisoned, or subjected to violent repression.

For many opposition figures, the situation became untenable as they found themselves fighting not only for political space but also for basic freedoms such as the right to free speech and political assembly. These attacks on opposition leaders, which included the targeting of figures like Jawar Mohammed, who was a prominent Oromo media mogul and political figure, were seen as clear signals that Abiy's government was no longer committed to the promises of democratic reform. Instead, the government appeared to be doubling down on efforts to silence its critics and maintain control over political power. Opposition leaders were quick to highlight the contradiction between Abiy's early rhetoric of political openness and the actual policies being pursued by his government. They argued that Abiy's promise of democratic reform had become increasingly hollow as he resorted to increasingly authoritarian tactics to maintain his grip on power.

The impact of these developments on the political climate in Ethiopia was profound. As opposition leaders faced imprisonment and harassment, the overall trust between the government and the opposition continued to deteriorate. The relationship between Abiy's government and the opposition became marked by deepening distrust, with each side accusing the other of undermining Ethiopia's democratic future. This mistrust made it increasingly difficult to create a political space where meaningful dialogue could occur, and the growing repression on both sides further entrenched political divisions. The country, once hopeful of a new era of democracy and political reform under Abiy, found itself mired in a political climate of distrust, ethnic polarization, and political repression.

The political fallout from the election delay also had serious consequences for Abiy's international standing. As Ethiopia's internal political crisis deepened, the government's reputation for democratic reform, which had been one of the key aspects of Abiy's rise to power, began to erode. The international community, which had largely supported Abiy's initial promises of reform, began to question his commitment to democracy. International human rights organizations and foreign governments expressed increasing concern about the erosion of political freedoms in Ethiopia. The delay of the elections, followed by crackdowns on opposition figures, raised alarm bells for many international observers who had once heralded Abiy as a beacon of hope for Ethiopia and the Horn of Africa. For these observers, the delay was not just a political misstep, it was a significant setback for Ethiopia's democratic aspirations and raised questions about the sustainability of Abiy's reform agenda.

This erosion of trust between the government and the opposition, coupled with mounting political repression, set the stage for a broader political crisis. As the government delayed elections and silenced dissent, opposition parties and civil society organizations began to argue that the democratic transition Abiy had promised was increasingly unlikely. In the eyes of many, Ethiopia's hopes for democratic reform had been dashed, and the country seemed poised for further instability.

In conclusion, Abiy Ahmed's decision to postpone Ethiopia's 2020 parliamentary elections became a flashpoint for opposition groups and civil society organizations, who saw the delay as a blatant attempt to consolidate political power and extend Abiy's rule. The delay exacerbated the already tense political climate in Ethiopia, where ethnic tensions, political repression, and the crisis in Tigray had created a volatile environment. For opposition leaders, the delay was a clear indication that Abiy's government was unwilling to deliver on its promises of democratic reform, and that the political space for free and fair elections had been narrowed even further. The mounting pressure from opposition groups, coupled with widespread concerns about the growing authoritarianism of the government, left Ethiopia facing an uncertain political future, with few signs of resolution on the horizon. The political challenges confronting Ethiopia under Abiy's leadership illustrated the fragile nature of the country's transition and the obstacles to achieving a truly democratic and inclusive political system.

***

The Idea of a Transitional Government

In the wake of the postponement of elections and the growing authoritarian trend under Abiy Ahmed, calls for a transitional government grew louder from opposition figures and civil society. A transitional government, according to these critics, would serve as an interim political structure designed to navigate Ethiopia through the crisis by stabilizing the country and ensuring free and fair elections once the political and security situation permitted.

Proponents of a transitional government argued that the Abiy administration had become increasingly incapable of managing Ethiopia's political and ethnic conflicts. Given the war in Tigray, the ongoing ethnic tensions, and the government's authoritarian turn, the establishment of a transitional government was seen as a way to ensure the peaceful transfer of power and the restoration of democratic governance.

A transitional government, in theory, would be composed of representatives from various ethnic and political groups, including opposition parties, civil society, and independent actors. The goal would be to create an inclusive, neutral body that could oversee the implementation of democratic reforms, address the humanitarian crises resulting from the war in Tigray, and organize credible elections once conditions were conducive. Such a government would also aim to restore the rule of law and address the human rights violations that had been perpetrated by both the state and armed opposition groups.

However, Abiy Ahmed and his government were opposed to the idea of a transitional government, viewing it as a threat to their political control. Abiy's rejection of the transitional government proposal reflected his increasing centralization of power and his belief that his leadership was essential to Ethiopia's stability. From his perspective, calls for a transitional government were tantamount to a challenge to his legitimacy and authority.

***

Abiy's Threats Against Jawar, Lidetu, and Other Opposition Leaders

Abiy's response to critics like Jawar Mohammed, Lidetu Ayalew, and other opposition figures became increasingly hostile. In the years following his rise to power, Abiy had initially sought to present himself as a reformist leader, eager to open up the political space. However, as opposition to his government grew, especially over issues like the Tigray conflict and the delay of elections, Abiy's rhetoric became more aggressive and his actions more repressive.

One of the most significant moments of tension came in 2020 when Abiy's government began targeting Jawar Mohammed and his media network, Oromia Media Network (OMN). Jawar was accused of inciting violence and unrest, particularly following the death of the popular Oromo singer Hachalu Hundessa in June 2020. Jawar and other Oromo leaders were arrested in connection with the protests that erupted after Hachalu's death. Abiy's government also accused Jawar and Lidetu of undermining the stability of the country by promoting divisive rhetoric and organizing opposition movements aimed at destabilizing the government.

Abiy's threats against opposition leaders were not limited to rhetoric. There were reports of arrests, detentions, and targeted crackdowns on opposition figures and activists, particularly in the aftermath of the 2020 election delay and the outbreak of the Tigray War. The government's use of military force and state security apparatus to suppress dissent grew more pronounced, with accusations of extrajudicial killings, torture, and unlawful detentions becoming widespread.

These actions served as a warning to other opposition leaders: dissent against Abiy's leadership would be met with force. Critics and opposition parties were silenced, media outlets were shut down, and protests were violently suppressed, with little recourse for legal challenges or accountability.

The opposition to the postponement of the 2020 election, led by figures such as Jawar Mohammed, Lidetu Ayalew, and other political parties, highlighted the growing disillusionment with Abiy Ahmed's leadership. While initially heralded as a reformer, Abiy's decision to delay the election, combined with his increasing authoritarianism, human rights abuses, and the brutal suppression of dissent, marked a significant shift in Ethiopia's political landscape.

The call for a transitional government, though not heeded by Abiy, reflected the deepening political crisis in Ethiopia. The opposition's criticisms of Abiy's leadership, coupled with the government's threats and crackdowns on political figures, suggested that Ethiopia's path toward democracy was in jeopardy. As the country continued to grapple with internal conflicts, ethnic divisions, and authoritarian tendencies under Abiy's rule, the prospects for democratic reform appeared increasingly uncertain.

***

The Tigray War: Ethiopia's Descent into Conflict and Crisis

The Tigray War, which erupted in November 2020, marks a devastating chapter in Ethiopia's modern history, plunging the country into one of its worst humanitarian crises. The conflict began when the Tigray People's Liberation Front (TPLF), the former dominant party in Ethiopia's ruling coalition, the Ethiopian People's Revolutionary Democratic Front (EPRDF), clashed with the federal government under Prime Minister Abiy Ahmed. The Ethiopian government labeled the TPLF's attack on federal military bases in the Tigray region as an act of treason, leading to a swift military response. This was initially presented as a "law enforcement operation" by Abiy's government, intended to neutralize the TPLF and restore order. However, the situation rapidly escalated, transforming into a full-scale war that would have far-reaching consequences for the country.

The violence, which began as an internal Ethiopian conflict, soon spiraled into a catastrophic humanitarian disaster. Both Ethiopian and Eritrean forces, alongside Amhara militias, launched coordinated attacks on Tigray, targeting civilian infrastructure and committing widespread atrocities. Human rights organizations, including Amnesty International and Human Rights Watch, documented extensive violations by both sides, including mass killings, sexual violence, forced displacement, and the deliberate targeting of civilians. Thousands of lives were lost, and millions of people were displaced, many fleeing to neighboring Sudan or living in dire conditions within Ethiopia.

As the war continued, the government's promises of a brief, surgical operation were exposed as false. Instead, the violence expanded beyond the Tigray region, with civilians suffering tremendously as they became the primary targets of the conflict. The Ethiopian government's initial portrayal of the TPLF as a "criminal clique" and its subsequent military offensive alienated large sections of the population, particularly in Tigray. Abiy's rhetoric, which labeled the TPLF as terrorists and dismissed any calls for dialogue, deepened ethnic divisions within the country, exacerbating tensions that had long been present in Ethiopia's political landscape.

International condemnation of the conflict grew as reports of atrocities continued to emerge, yet the Ethiopian government refused to allow unrestricted humanitarian access to the region. The blockade imposed on Tigray further worsened the crisis, as food, medicine, and other essential supplies were denied to millions of civilians. The United Nations and other humanitarian organizations struggled to provide aid, with famine and disease spreading rapidly throughout the region. At the height of the conflict, over 5 million people in Tigray required emergency food assistance, with approximately 400,000 facing famine-like conditions. The widespread displacement also created a refugee crisis, with millions fleeing the conflict and struggling to survive in overcrowded camps in Sudan and within Ethiopia.

The involvement of Eritrean forces, with a history of hostility toward Tigray, compounded the violence. As the Ethiopian National Defense Force (ENDF) and Eritrean soldiers carried out widespread massacres and sexual violence, the war became an ethnic conflict, with Tigrayans disproportionately targeted based on their ethnic identity. The systematic nature of these abuses, including the mass rape of women and girls, was widely condemned by human rights groups. These forces also destroyed vital infrastructure, such as healthcare facilities and schools, further crippling the region's ability to respond to humanitarian disasters.

Abiy's handling of the war has led to a rapid decline in his international standing. Once celebrated as a reformist leader who won the Nobel Peace Prize for his efforts to normalize relations with Eritrea, his image was shattered as the brutal realities of the Tigray War unfolded. His government's refusal to acknowledge the scale of the atrocities and its obstruction of independent investigations has only worsened the situation. As reports of war crimes and human rights violations continued to surface, international pressure on the Ethiopian government grew, yet Abiy's administration maintained a defensive posture, denying accusations and portraying the conflict as a response to rebellion rather than a broader humanitarian crisis.

The Tigray War has exposed the deep ethnic and political divisions within Ethiopia, highlighting the fragility of the country's political and social fabric. Despite Abiy's promises of unity and reform, the war has left the country more divided than ever. The legacy of the conflict is one of immense suffering, destruction, and mistrust. Ethiopia's path to peace and reconciliation has become more uncertain, as the ethnic and political tensions that fueled the war remain unresolved.

The war's impact on Ethiopia has been profound. It has devastated the lives of millions, leaving a legacy of pain, displacement, and ethnic animosity that will take years to heal. Abiy's leadership, which was once seen as a beacon of hope for reform and peace, is now defined by the brutal response to the Tigray conflict. The failure to address the underlying political and ethnic issues, combined with the disproportionate military response, has left Ethiopia on the brink of further instability. The Tigray War is a stark reminder of the challenges faced by countries with diverse ethnic groups trying to build a unified government, and it underscores the difficulties in reconciling deeply entrenched political and ethnic divisions.

In the wake of the Tigray War, Ethiopia faces a long road to recovery. The conflict has torn apart the nation's social fabric and undermined its political stability. The humanitarian toll is staggering, and the human rights abuses committed by all sides in the conflict will leave scars that will take decades to heal. The international community's role in holding those responsible for the atrocities accountable remains uncertain, as Ethiopia continues to resist calls for an independent investigation. For many, the war marks the collapse of hope for Ethiopia's peaceful and prosperous future under Abiy's leadership, and the country now stands at a crossroads, with its future uncertain and its people deeply scarred by the horrors of war.

***

Abiy Ahmed's War on Amhara: An Erosion of Identity, Rights, and Justice

When Abiy Ahmed took office as Ethiopia's Prime Minister, his initial reforms were met with widespread optimism, hailed as steps toward uniting the nation's ethnically diverse society. His actions, releasing political prisoners, easing media restrictions, and signing a peace agreement with Eritrea, seemed to promise a new era for Ethiopia. However, these reforms, while lauded initially, set the stage for a series of conflicts, particularly with the Amhara people. Abiy's centralization of power, his advocacy for a "greater Ethiopian unity," and his move away from Ethiopia's entrenched ethnic federalism eroded the Amhara's historical political influence and territorial integrity.

For the Amhara, Abiy's government signaled the erosion of their political voice. Policies framed as efforts for "reconciliation" and "unity" seemed to overlook the Amhara people's concerns about security, cultural preservation, and political representation. The shift from ethnic federalism to a more centralized form of governance sidelined the Amhara, reducing their role in national politics. Abiy's failure to engage the Amhara meaningfully in the political process bred disenchantment, contributing to the fracturing of Ethiopia's political landscape.

Historically, the Amhara people were central to Ethiopia's political and cultural identity. They formed the backbone of the country's centralized monarchy, with a rich tradition of Christian heritage and governance through the Ethiopian Orthodox Church and military. However, Ethiopia's ethnic federal system, established during the Tigray People's Liberation Front (TPLF)-led government, marginalized the Amhara, fostering an environment where ethnic identities, rather than a shared national identity, became the basis for political power.

Under this system, other ethnic groups like the Tigray, Oromo, and Sidama were granted regional autonomy, while the Amhara were treated as a "default" ethnic group, contributing to their sense of exclusion. Abiy's rhetoric, which promised national unity and de-emphasized ethnic federalism, only deepened tensions, further undermining the Amhara's sense of belonging in the broader political sphere. This erosion of Amhara identity under Abiy's leadership was a key factor in the rise of Fano, a militia that has come to symbolize the resistance of the Amhara people determined to protect their heritage and rights.

***

Fano: The Heart of Amhara Resistance

Fano, which translates to "the people" or "resistance," holds significant cultural and historical meaning for the Amhara. Traditionally, Fano referred to local militias defending Amhara lands during times of crisis, especially during foreign invasions such as the Italian occupation in the late 19th and early 20th centuries. In the current context, Fano has evolved into a powerful symbol of resistance against marginalization and perceived betrayal by Abiy's government.

The strength of Fano lies in its deep connection to Amhara identity, rooted in the Ethiopian Orthodox Church, literature, and the Ge'ez language. However, this same connection also serves as its vulnerability, as Fano operates outside of formal state structures, leading to internal divisions, inconsistent leadership, and difficulties navigating Ethiopia's complex political environment. Despite these challenges, Fano has become a crucial part of the Amhara narrative of resilience, driven by the collective desire for self-preservation, justice, and the protection of cultural identity.

Prime Minister Abiy's public statements, alongside those of military leaders such as Marshal Berhanu Jula, have only exacerbated tensions by belittling the Amhara's historical contributions to Ethiopia's political landscape. These dismissive remarks, combined with violent military actions against the Amhara, including atrocities committed during the Tigray conflict, have fostered deep resentment and anger. To many Amhara, Fano is not merely a militia, but a symbol of their struggle for survival, dignity, and justice.

Abiy's response to Amhara resistance has been marked by the extensive use of military force, including drone strikes and aerial bombardments. These tactics have led to significant civilian casualties, particularly among Amhara women and children. Reports from organizations such as Amnesty International and Human Rights Watch document numerous atrocities, including the targeted killing of Amhara civilians in areas suspected of harboring Fano fighters. These actions have sparked accusations of war crimes and genocide, as civilians, rather than combatants, have borne the brunt of the government's military campaign.

The lack of international intervention or accountability has intensified the sense of betrayal within the Amhara community. Many view the Ethiopian government's actions as an attempt to erase their culture, land, and identity. The ongoing conflict has prompted widespread allegations of ethnic cleansing and genocide, with human rights organizations documenting mass killings, sexual violence, and forced displacement of Amhara civilians. The destruction of homes and properties, coupled with the denial of humanitarian aid, has created dire conditions for the Amhara people. Despite this, the international community has been slow to act, often citing Ethiopia's sovereignty as a reason for inaction.

This international apathy has only deepened frustration and fear among the Amhara, who feel that their suffering is being ignored on the global stage.

***

Amhara's Struggle for Autonomy

The grievances of the Amhara people with Abiy's government are deeply tied to the political landscape shaped by the TPLF's 1995 constitution, which enshrined ethnic federalism and allowed for self-determination up to secession. Amhara elites argue that TPLF's control over the federal government marginalized them, economically crippled their region, and excluded them from political power. The Amhara also view the demarcation of disputed territories such as Welkait and Tegede, claimed by Tigray, as a direct challenge to their historical territorial rights.

Though many Amhara initially supported Abiy, hoping for national unity and progress, his policies have increasingly favored the Oromo, leaving the Amhara feeling betrayed. The Pretoria Peace Agreement between Abiy's government and Tigray, which excluded

Amhara from negotiations, deepened these feelings, particularly regarding disputed territories.

The Fano militia, which has resisted government suppression, controls large swaths of rural Amhara, although it has struggled to gain control of major cities. The militia sees its fight as an existential struggle to defend Amhara culture, history, and identity against what they perceive as an existential threat. Government efforts to suppress Fano have resulted in heavy civilian casualties, with drone strikes killing dozens and injuring many more.

Abiy's leadership has increasingly veered toward authoritarianism. His government has cracked down on opposition groups, journalists, and activists through arbitrary arrests, harassment, and violence. Repression of free speech, including the detention of journalists and internet shutdowns, has stifled independent journalism and created a climate of fear. Additionally, security forces have been accused of extrajudicial killings, torture, and unlawful detentions, particularly in the Oromia region where political dissidents and activists have been targeted.

The Amhara people's struggle reflects Ethiopia's broader challenges—deep divisions along political, ethnic, and historical lines. The marginalization of the Amhara, coupled with the authoritarian policies of Abiy's government, has created a cycle of resentment, violence, and instability. The demand for autonomy, justice, and recognition of Amhara rights remains at the heart of this conflict.

Ethiopia's future hinges on overcoming these divisions and fostering unity, equality, and peace, where no ethnic group feels marginalized or excluded. Only through genuine political dialogue, accountability, and reconciliation can Ethiopia hope to move beyond its fractured past and build a more inclusive future for all its people.

***

Koree Nageenyaa

Koree Nageenyaa is a secret Ethiopian government agency believed to be responsible for orchestrating executions and unlawful detentions, primarily within the Oromia region. The committee is alleged to have been formed in response to growing security concerns but has since become notorious for carrying out extrajudicial killings, arrests, and suppressing political dissent.

The head of Koree Nageenyaa is Shimelis Abdisa, the president of Oromia, and it includes several high-ranking officials from the Prosperity Party, such as Fekadu Tessema, and Ararsa Merdasa, head of security for Oromia. The group reportedly operates out of the Prosperity Party's premises, where meetings are held.

Initially created to address security issues in Oromia, Koree Nageenyaa quickly expanded its scope beyond its original mandate. The committee has been accused of interfering in the justice system, directing operations against political opponents, and executing unlawful actions under the guise of combating "enemy cells." Shimelis Abdisa, the leader, stated that Koree Nageenyaa would target "enemy elements," signaling a shift toward widespread repression.

According to a former judge of the Oromia Supreme Court, the committee's practices are deeply undemocratic. Individuals are often arrested without warrants, investigation, or due process. The committee allegedly decides on detentions without judicial oversight, leading to numerous human rights violations.

The operations of Koree Nageenyaa began shortly after Prime Minister Abiy Ahmed assumed power in 2018. The agency is believed to have orchestrated numerous killings, with reports linking it to at least a dozen deaths, including the massacre of 14 shepherds in Oromia in 2021. Initially attributed to fighters from the Oromo Liberation Army (OLA), the incident is now thought to have been the result of the committee's covert operations.

In early 2024, Taye Dendea, a former ally of Prime Minister Abiy Ahmed and Minister of Peace, was forced to resign after publicly criticizing the government's refusal to allow protests in Addis Ababa. In a series of tweets, Taye accused Abiy Ahmed of being responsible for civilian deaths and linked the prime minister to the Koree Nageenyaa's brutal actions.

One of the most high-profile cases involving Koree Nageenyaa occurred in April 2024 with the assassination of Bate Urgessa, a prominent opposition leader. Bate, who had long been a vocal advocate for Oromo rights, was fatally shot in his hometown of Meki, Oromia. Though the government claimed his death was due to family disputes, many believe that Koree Nageenyaa orchestrated his killing. Bate had been repeatedly arrested and mistreated by security forces, and shortly before his death, he had been detained again after speaking with a French journalist.

Bate's assassination sparked widespread condemnation, particularly among Oromo scholars and professionals who strongly denounced the politically motivated killing. Bate had dedicated his life to defending the rights of the Oromo people and had long been an outspoken critic of the illegal arrests and killings carried out by the government. His death serves as a grim reminder of the continuing political repression and the lengths to which the Ethiopian government may go to silence its critics.

Koree Nageenyaa's actions have left a trail of fear and suffering throughout Oromia, raising serious concerns about the erosion of democratic principles and the rise of authoritarianism in Ethiopia. The agency's ongoing operations are seen as part of a broader strategy to suppress political opposition and stifle dissent, with tragic consequences for many innocent lives.

***

Abiy Ahmed: The Cruelty Behind the Façade of Reform

Abiy Ahmed's leadership of Ethiopia has become a tragic case study in the dangers of ego-driven, authoritarian rule. A man who once projected himself as a reformer, a harbinger of peace, and a symbol of democratic change has evolved into a leader whose cruelty, apathy, and self-interest have overshadowed the promises he made to his people. His image, carefully crafted and maintained, is one of prosperity, unity, and progress. Yet beneath this facade lies a leader whose egocentric and authoritarian tendencies have destabilized Ethiopia, deepened its ethnic divisions, and caused widespread human suffering.

At the heart of Abiy's rule is an insatiable desire for power, coupled with a willingness to betray those who helped elevate him. His manipulation of public perception, particularly in the aftermath of the Tigray War, reflects a leader consumed by his image and the need to present himself as a hero. He promised peace, democracy, and reconciliation, yet the reality has been one of brutal repression, military crackdowns, and violations of human rights. Abiy's inability to reconcile Ethiopia's deeply rooted ethnic divisions and his increasingly authoritarian methods have only intensified the suffering of millions.

The Tigray War, which erupted in 2020, is a glaring example of Abiy's cruelty and indifference to the human cost of his decisions. Initially, he framed the conflict as a brief operation to restore order, but it soon escalated into a devastating war marked by widespread atrocities. Extrajudicial killings, sexual violence, and starvation were used as weapons of war. Abiy's government, despite mounting evidence, consistently denied the scale of the violence, blocking independent investigations and deflecting blame onto foreign actors. His response was not one of humility or accountability but of deflection and deceit, protecting his image rather than acknowledging the suffering of the Ethiopian people.

Abiy's leadership is also marked by an alarming disregard for human rights and the rule of law. His treatment of opposition parties, journalists, and ethnic minorities reveals an authoritarian mindset, one that uses violence and intimidation to suppress dissent. The crackdown on the media, the targeting of political opponents, and the silencing of activists all point to a leader who values control and stability over democracy and justice. His actions in the Tigray region, where he refused to allow humanitarian aid, obstructed media access, and ordered the destruction of civilian infrastructure, show a man willing to sacrifice human lives for the sake of political power.

Moreover, Abiy's growing reliance on military force to resolve Ethiopia's complex political challenges highlights his egocentric belief in his ability to control the country through sheer might. Instead of pursuing dialogue, Abiy has responded to ethnic tensions with violence, turning the country into a battlefield where civilians are caught in the crossfire of his ambition. His authoritarian methods have only deepened Ethiopia's internal divisions, alienating ethnic groups like the Oromo, Amhara, and Tigray, who feel increasingly marginalized by a government that claims to represent all Ethiopians while targeting those who disagree with him.

Abiy's actions reveal a leader more concerned with his image and personal power than with the well-being of the people he governs. His promises of prosperity and national unity were quickly overshadowed by his authoritarian rule, and the international community, which once hailed him as a beacon of hope in Africa, now questions his commitment to the democratic principles he once championed. Abiy's failure to address the root causes of Ethiopia's internal conflicts and his tendency to rely on military solutions rather than meaningful dialogue have left the country teetering on the brink of collapse.

In the end, Abiy Ahmed's leadership will be remembered for its contradictions, the promises of peace and democracy destroyed by the reality of cruelty, betrayal, and apathy. His legacy is one of a leader who deceived both his people and the world, using his image as a reformer to mask his authoritarian tendencies and the immense human suffering he caused. The political and social fabric of Ethiopia, once fragile, has been further torn apart by his actions, leaving the country with deep divisions, unhealed wounds, and an uncertain future.

***

CHAPTER 11

Divided Faith: The Ethiopian Orthodox Church and Abiy Ahmed's Power Struggle

The Ethiopian Orthodox Tewahedo Church, one of the most ancient and influential institutions in Ethiopia, has long been a pillar of unity, especially in times of crisis. For centuries, it has served as a stabilizing force in a country marked by ethnic and political divisions, providing a shared sense of identity and faith to a population of over 45 million followers. Its role as both a religious and socio-political institution has been vital to Ethiopia's cohesion. However, in recent years, the Church has faced internal fractures, exacerbated by political struggles, ethnic tensions, and the interference of the state under Prime Minister Abiy Ahmed's leadership.

Abiy's early tenure was initially perceived as a moment of hope for Ethiopia, especially among the Orthodox Christian community. He presented himself as a reformer and a peacemaker, even positioning himself as a savior of the Ethiopian Orthodox Church.

Abune Merkorios, the 4th Patriarch of the Ethiopian Orthodox Church, returned to Ethiopia after 27 years in exile, marking a significant moment in both the history of the Church and the political landscape of Ethiopia. His return was made possible by a historic reconciliation process spearheaded by Prime Minister Abiy Ahmed. Abune Merkorios was forced into exile in 1991, following the political changes that saw the fall of the Derg regime and the rise of the Ethiopian People's Revolutionary Democratic Front (EPRDF). His departure was the result of what many perceived as political interferences in Church affairs, a move that led to a division among the clergy. The exiled faction of the Church declared itself a separate Synod, and both Synods excommunicated each other, leading to years of tension and division. This schism within the Church reflected the broader instability in Ethiopia, where politics and religion were increasingly intertwined.

In an effort to heal this divide, Prime Minister Abiy Ahmed intervened, bringing the two factions together. Through diplomatic efforts in Washington, D.C., a groundbreaking agreement was reached. Patriarch Abune Mathias would retain his administrative role, while Abune Merkorios would resume his spiritual leadership, with both leaders holding equal authority in the Church. Initially, the reconciliation was seen as a hopeful moment, a sign of peace, not just within the Church, but for a country deeply fractured by ethnic tensions and political unrest. The Ethiopian Orthodox Church, which had traditionally played a role in uniting the diverse peoples of Ethiopia, was expected to help heal the nation's wounds.

A highly symbolic gesture came when Abiy personally flew Patriarch Abune Merkorios to Ethiopia, a move that underscored the Prime Minister's support for the Church and its role in Ethiopia's political and social cohesion. This act was seen as a public affirmation of Abiy's commitment to peace, not only within the Church but also across the broader Ethiopian society. His leadership in the reconciliation process resonated with many Ethiopians who viewed it as an important step toward healing the rifts within the Church and uniting the country's diverse communities.

The return of Abune Merkorios after 27 years in exile was not just a personal homecoming for the Patriarch, but a moment of spiritual and political significance. It symbolized the possibility of overcoming deep divisions, both within the Church and in Ethiopian society at large. As the Ethiopian Orthodox Church strives to rebuild and strengthen its role as a unifying force in the country, the return of Abune Merkorios and the agreement between the two Synods offer hope for a more peaceful and united future for Ethiopia.

However, Abiy's later actions revealed a more complicated and less supportive relationship with the Church. As tensions within the Ethiopian Orthodox Tewahedo Church grew, particularly with the Oromo bishops challenging the authority of Abune Matthias and ordaining their own bishops in defiance of the central Church leadership, Abiy's role became more contentious. The conflict was largely centered around accusations from the Oromia region that the Orthodox Church had neglected the region's needs, leaving it marginalized. The Oromia bishops, therefore, sought to assert their independence and establish their own ecclesiastical hierarchy, disregarding the central authority of Abune Matthias, who had been at the helm of the Church for decades.

Abiy's response to this situation was nuanced and, in many ways, strategically silent. While some believed that he was trying to mediate and protect the unity of the Church, others viewed his position as one of quiet complicity. As the divisions within the Church became more pronounced and violent clashes occurred between the factions, with at least 30 people killed and hundreds wounded in February 2024, there were growing suspicions that Abiy was not just a bystander but an active participant in the division. The timing of these divisions was significant; it occurred at a moment when Abiy's political authority was becoming more authoritarian, and his relationship with key religious institutions like the Church and with ethnic groups like the Amhara and Oromo was increasingly strained.

The Oromia-based bishops' challenge to the authority of the Church was, in part, seen as a reflection of the broader political dynamics in Ethiopia. Abiy, particularly in the context of his political relationship with the Oromo elite, may have seen the Church as a powerful, independent institution that could challenge his growing control over the state. Abiy's government had already come into conflict with other centers of power, especially those representing the Amhara region, who historically saw the Church as an integral part of Ethiopian identity. By undermining the Church's unity, Abiy appeared to weaken one of the most powerful and symbolic institutions in the country, potentially reducing its ability to challenge his authority.

Furthermore, as the Ethiopian Orthodox Tewahedo Church grappled with these internal challenges, the situation in the northern Tigray region added further complications. The Tigray War, which began in November 2020, caused immense suffering to the Orthodox Church in Tigray, with churches being looted, bombed, and burned. Priests were killed, and Church leaders, including the patriarch's chief of staff, who was from Tigray, were subjected to multiple arrests. This led to further divisions, as the Church's leadership in Tigray accused the central Church of complicity in the conflict and silence regarding crimes against civilians. For many in the Tigray region, the Church's failure to take a stand during the war was a significant betrayal, further deepening the rift between the northern and central Church leadership.

As the war reached its conclusion with a peace deal in November 2022, the impact on the Church was devastating. Church leaders in Tigray declared that the Church had not only failed to condemn the atrocities committed during the war but had also been complicit in the actions of the government. This accusation was a blow to the Church's moral authority and exacerbated the split within the Ethiopian Orthodox Tewahedo Church. The conflict resulted in the establishment of a separate Orthodox Church faction in Tigray, under the leadership of Abune Selama, further disintegrating the historic unity of the Church. This fictionalization was a direct result of the war and the political and religious divisions that had become increasingly entrenched under Abiy's government.

Abiy's handling of the Church's divisions, particularly in the context of his broader authoritarian tendencies, raises critical questions about his long-term goals and vision for the country. The Orthodox Church, once a unifying force, now finds itself weakened and fragmented, unable to provide the same level of guidance and cohesion it once did. Abiy's political agenda, which increasingly centers on consolidating his own power, seems to have been at odds with the Church's traditional role as an independent institution that could hold the government accountable. His interactions with the Church, particularly in the context of the divisions with the Oromo bishops and the Tigray faction, have left the Church in a vulnerable position, unable to effectively address the needs of its followers or the country as a whole.

In essence, Abiy's political maneuvers, which have undermined both the Orthodox Church and the Amhara elite, have contributed to the fragmentation of one of Ethiopia's most important institutions. The Church, once a pillar of unity, now finds itself embroiled in bitter internal divisions that reflect the broader fragmentation of Ethiopian society. The price of Abiy's pursuit of power and control has been paid by the Church, which is now in its weakest position in centuries. Its ability to heal the wounds of the nation, both spiritual and political, is now in doubt. Without a strong, united Church, Ethiopia faces a future of continued political instability, ethnic fragmentation, and social unrest, with the Church itself weakened by the very forces that it once helped to bind together.

Abiy's attempts to assert control over the Church and its leaders have had far-reaching consequences, and as Ethiopia moves forward, the Church's ability to recover from this crisis will be crucial. The Ethiopian Orthodox Tewahedo Church, like the nation itself, stands at a crossroads. Whether it can heal its divisions and reclaim its place as a unifying force in Ethiopian society depends largely on how its leaders respond to the current crisis, and whether they can regain the trust of the Ethiopian people after years of manipulation and betrayal. In the end, the future of Ethiopia may very well depend on the future of its Church.

Under Prime Minister Abiy Ahmed's leadership, Ethiopia's secular framework, which guarantees religious freedom and the separation of state and religion, has been severely strained by rising religious tensions and conflicts. While Abiy came to power with promises of peace and national reconciliation, his administration has struggled to manage the growing rifts between the state and religious communities, particularly between the Ethiopian Orthodox Tewahedo Church (EOTC) and other faith groups.

Abiy's involvement in religious affairs, despite the constitutional mandate for government non-interference, has become increasingly controversial. His administration has been accused of manipulating religious institutions for political gain, particularly in relation to the EOTC. The tensions within the Church deepened in 2023 when three archbishops from the EOTC ordained 27 bishops without approval from the central leadership. This move, seen as an attempt by splinter groups to assert independence, has been linked to growing government-backed factions, raising concerns that the government is exacerbating religious divisions to maintain control.

One of the most violent incidents occurred in February 2023, when security forces in Oromia clashed with EOTC parishioners in Shashemene over an attempted seizure of a church building by the Holy Synod of Oromia Nations and Nationalities (HSONN), a splinter group. The excessive force used by security forces resulted in the deaths of several parishioners, highlighting the government's heavy-handed approach to religious disputes. The Ethiopian Human Rights Commission (EHRC) condemned the violence, but the underlying divisions within the Church were not fully addressed, fueling the perception that the government's interference in religious matters is worsening, rather than resolving, the crisis.

In addition to these internal conflicts, Abiy's administration has faced criticism for its treatment of religious minorities. In 2023, the Oromia regional government demolished mosques in Sheger City, sparking protests and violent clashes with security forces. The Ethiopian Islamic Affairs Supreme Council (EIASC) appealed to Abiy for intervention, but their pleas were ignored. This incident, alongside reports of excessive force used against protestors, reflects the government's inability or unwillingness to protect religious minorities, further deepening grievances within Ethiopia's Muslim community.

The government's interference has also extended to religious practices, with several incidents underscoring its growing control over religious expression. For example, the government suspended employees who participated in the EOTC's call to wear black during the Nineveh fast in January 2023, a move seen by many as an overreach into religious practices. These actions have created an atmosphere of fear and mistrust, where religious expression is increasingly viewed as a threat to the government's authority.

Abiy's efforts to mediate religious disputes and promote interfaith dialogue have yielded limited results. While he has facilitated meetings with religious leaders and made gestures of peace, such as calling for unity during the Tigray conflict, these actions have failed to ease the mounting tensions. In September 2023, an inter-religious conflict between Muslims and Orthodox Christians led to violence, including the burning of homes and the displacement of Orthodox

Christians, further highlighting the challenges Abiy faces in promoting religious harmony.

The government's handling of religious diversity has come under increasing scrutiny, as Ethiopia's constitution guarantees religious freedom but is often undermined by state interference in religious affairs. Abiy's administration, while attempting to mediate between religious groups, has been perceived as using religion as a tool for political control. This manipulation of religious institutions for political purposes has deepened sectarian divides, undermining efforts to build a united, pluralistic society.

As the situation unfolds, the role of Prime Minister Abiy Ahmed in shaping Ethiopia's religious and political landscape remains deeply contentious. While he has made progress in other areas of peacebuilding, his administration's involvement in religious matters has exacerbated tensions, fueling divisions rather than fostering coexistence. The secular framework, intended to protect religious independence, has been tested by Abiy's actions, as the lines between religion and politics continue to blur under his leadership. The religious unrest in Ethiopia, affecting both Christian and Muslim communities, highlights the broader challenges the country faces in balancing state power with the protection of religious freedoms.

***

CHAPTER 12

Abiy Ahmed and the Nobel Peace Prize

When comparing historical Nobel Peace Prize winners to Abiy Ahmed, it becomes apparent that while the prize is intended to recognize efforts toward peace, stability, and human rights, not all recipients have maintained these principles consistently. Abiy Ahmed's leadership, despite his Nobel Peace Prize in 2019, has been marred by numerous allegations of human rights violations, authoritarian practices, and a violent military crackdown on dissent, particularly in the Tigray and Amhara regions of Ethiopia. This comparison to other historical figures—some of whom were later seen as authoritarian leaders responsible for widespread human rights abuses—raises critical questions about the true nature of Abiy's leadership and the credibility of awarding the Peace Prize to figures who later engage in brutal actions.

Abiy Ahmed was awarded the Nobel Peace Prize in 2019 primarily for his efforts to resolve the two-decade-long border conflict with Eritrea. His peace agreement with Eritrean President Isaias Afwerki was hailed as a groundbreaking diplomatic achievement, marking an end to the "no war, no peace" stalemate between the two nations. Additionally, Abiy's early reforms, such as releasing political prisoners, lifting restrictions on opposition groups, and increasing media freedoms, contributed to his international acclaim.

However, the years following his award have painted a very different picture. Abiy's leadership has been marred by growing ethnic tensions, violent military crackdowns, and a disregard for human rights. The Tigray war, which broke out in late 2020, has been one of the most significant events that has raised serious concerns about Abiy's authoritarian style and willingness to use extreme measures to suppress opposition. The Ethiopian government's use of drones and airstrikes in Tigray and Amhara, reports of mass killings, sexual violence, and forced displacement of civilians, and the blockade of humanitarian aid to these regions have led to widespread accusations of war crimes and crimes against humanity.

Moreover, press freedom has been severely restricted, with journalists facing imprisonment, harassment, and threats. The international community has expressed concerns about Abiy's growing authoritarianism and the suppression of dissent, undermining the very values of peace and democracy that the Nobel Peace Prize is supposed to celebrate. His government has been criticized for silencing opposition voices and curtailing freedom of expression, and his efforts at reconciliation have been overshadowed by violence, making the peace prize increasingly contentious.

Several past Nobel Peace Prize laureates, such as Stalin, Kissinger, and others, later came to embody controversial or authoritarian actions that contradicted the ideals of peace, human rights, and democracy. Comparing Abiy Ahmed to these figures provides context for understanding the complexities of awarding such a prestigious prize, as the actions of recipients can sometimes diverge significantly from the values they were initially recognized for.

Joseph Stalin (1945 Nobel Peace Prize Nominee):

Although Joseph Stalin never won the Nobel Peace Prize, he was nominated in 1945 due to his role in defeating Nazi Germany during World War II. Despite this recognition, Stalin's legacy is one of brutal repression, widespread purges, and the deaths of millions of his own citizens through famine, forced labor camps, and political executions. Stalin's policies, including the forced collectivization of agriculture, resulted in the deaths of millions, particularly through the Holodomor famine in Ukraine, where millions perished from starvation caused by state policies. His totalitarian regime imposed strict controls over the Soviet people, eliminating any form of dissent and forcing the population into submission through violence and intimidation.

***

Henry Kissinger (1973 Nobel Peace Prize):

Henry Kissinger, U.S. Secretary of State and National Security Advisor under Presidents Nixon and Ford, was awarded the Nobel Peace Prize in 1973 for his role in negotiating a ceasefire and peace agreement to end the Vietnam War. However, Kissinger's legacy is highly controversial due to his involvement in the U.S. bombing campaigns in Southeast Asia, including Cambodia and Laos, and his support for repressive regimes, such as the military dictatorship in Chile (following the coup against Salvador Allende). His role in authorizing actions that led to the deaths of thousands has led to accusations that his Peace Prize was an inappropriate acknowledgment of his policies, which were at odds with the principles of peace and human rights.

***

Aung San Suu Kyi (1991 Nobel Peace Prize):

Aung San Suu Kyi was awarded the Nobel Peace Prize in 1991 for her non-violent struggle for democracy and human rights in Myanmar. However, after coming to power as the country's leader, she faced international criticism for her failure to intervene in the military's crackdown on the Rohingya Muslim minority. Under her leadership, the military was accused of committing genocide, forcing hundreds of thousands of Rohingya into refugee camps, and carrying out mass killings and rapes. Suu Kyi's silence on these atrocities, and her subsequent defense of the military, has tarnished her legacy, with many questioning the legitimacy of her Peace Prize.

Abiy's transformation from a reformer to a leader associated with authoritarianism and violence mirrors the trajectory of some other controversial Nobel laureates. Initially viewed as a reformist, Abiy's consolidation of power and suppression of political dissent, including curbing press freedom and arresting opposition leaders, reflects a disturbing trend in his governance. His response to the Tigray conflict, which includes widespread reports of extrajudicial killings, sexual violence, and the use of drones against civilians, paints a picture of a leader more inclined toward violent suppression than peaceful reconciliation.

His actions in the Amhara and Tigray regions, which have led to allegations of ethnic cleansing and even genocide, sharply contrast with the values espoused by the Nobel Peace Prize. The lack of press freedom under his government, the imprisonment of journalists, and the systematic silencing of dissent all point to a shift toward authoritarianism that undermines his earlier claims of being a reformist. The starvation and displacement of millions, particularly in Tigray and Amhara, echo the kind of repression that has been seen in other authoritarian regimes throughout history.

***

The Irony of the Nobel Peace Prize:

The irony of Abiy Ahmed receiving the Nobel Peace Prize lies in the disparity between his initial promises and the reality of his governance. While the Nobel Committee awarded him the Peace Prize for what seemed like a genuine effort to bring peace between Ethiopia and Eritrea, his subsequent actions have undermined the values of peace, justice, and human dignity. The brutal treatment of civilians, the use of military drones against non-combatants, and the military's disregard for humanitarian aid reflect a disregard for human rights that stands in direct contrast to the ideals for which the Peace Prize is awarded.

Just as leaders like Stalin, Kissinger, and Suu Kyi later became symbols of authoritarianism and human rights violations, Abiy's actions have cast doubt on the credibility of the Nobel Peace Prize as an indicator of moral leadership. In awarding the prize to figures who later turn authoritarian, the Nobel Committee raises questions about the efficacy of recognizing leaders based on a single diplomatic achievement without a deeper assessment of their commitment to human rights and peace over the long term.

The comparison of Abiy Ahmed to historical Nobel Peace Prize winners like Joseph Stalin, Henry Kissinger, and Aung San Suu Kyi underscores the complexities and contradictions inherent in awarding such a prestigious prize. While Abiy's initial peace efforts were groundbreaking, his later actions, particularly in relation to human rights violations, drone attacks on civilians, and his authoritarian turn, demonstrate a stark contrast to the ideals of peace, democracy, and human rights that the Nobel Peace Prize is meant to celebrate. The case of Abiy Ahmed serves as a powerful reminder that leadership must be continuously scrutinized, and that the Nobel Peace Prize should not be seen as an endorsement of a leader's entire legacy but rather as a momentary recognition of efforts that must be validated over time with tangible commitments to peace and justice

***

CHAPTER 13

From Allies to Adversaries: The Betrayal of Trust in Abiy Ahmed's Leadership

Taye Dendeha: From Ally to Adversary in Ethiopia's Political Landscape

Taye Dendeha's political journey is one of dramatic shifts, marked by his initial alliance with Prime Minister Abiy Ahmed and his eventual fall from grace as a staunch critic of the government. Once a close ally and supporter of Abiy's early reforms, Taye's experience reveals the complexities of Ethiopia's evolving political environment and his deep commitment to defending ethnic federalism, which ultimately set him at odds with the centralizing policies of the very government he had once helped to build.

Taye began his political career as a supporter of the system of ethnic federalism. This federal system, which granted significant autonomy to Ethiopia's diverse ethnic groups, resonated deeply with Taye, as he believed it was crucial for preserving the rights and self-determination of regional communities.

When Abiy Ahmed came to power in 2018, Taye initially supported the prime minister's reforms, which were seen by many as a much-needed break from the country's long-standing political struggles. Abiy's early actions, such as releasing political prisoners and pursuing peace with Eritrea, earned him widespread praise, and Taye stood by him, believing that Abiy's leadership could bring about lasting positive change. Taye was appointed as State Minister of Peace in 2021, solidifying his role within Abiy's government. However, as time passed, it became clear that Taye's vision for Ethiopia differed sharply from Abiy's.

Abiy's shift toward centralizing power, particularly with the formation of the Prosperity Party in 2019, began to alarm Taye and many others who feared that it would dismantle the very federal system that had helped maintain Ethiopia's fragile peace. Taye believed that ethnic federalism, with its focus on regional autonomy, was essential for preventing ethnic conflicts and preserving the country's cultural diversity. As Abiy sought to weaken regional powers and consolidate authority under a single party, Taye grew increasingly disillusioned with the direction of the government.

Taye's opposition to Abiy's policies became more vocal, culminating in his eventual betrayal by the very government he had supported. In December 2023, Taye was removed from his position as State Minister of Peace, a move that marked a clear break between him and the prime minister. The following day, he was arrested by federal security forces, who accused him of collaborating with "anti-peace forces." By mid-2024, Taye was charged with terrorism, accused of having connections to the Oromo Liberation Army (OLA), a group that has been engaged in an insurgency against the Ethiopian government.

The betrayal of Taye by Abiy Ahmed, once a close ally, underscores the complex and often perilous nature of Ethiopian politics. Taye's arrest and charges reflect the broader tension between Ethiopia's regional autonomy advocates and the centralizing vision of Abiy's government. For Taye, the political struggle was never just about personal ambition but about defending the rights of Ethiopia's ethnic communities, which he believed were under threat.

Taye's fall from grace is a poignant reminder of how quickly political alliances can shift in Ethiopia's volatile political landscape. From an insider in Abiy's government to a vocal critic and political prisoner, Taye's trajectory symbolizes the risks faced by those who challenge the consolidation of power in Ethiopia's increasingly centralized government. His story raises important questions about the future of Ethiopia's ethnic federalism and the political freedoms that have been progressively curtailed under Abiy Ahmed's leadership.

As of December 2024, Taye remains in custody, having been granted bail but reportedly abducted by armed men upon his release. His continued detention and abduction only add to the mounting concerns about the safety of political dissidents in Ethiopia, where the government's response to opposition has become increasingly heavy-handed.

Taye Dendeha's legacy will likely be defined by his transformation from a trusted ally of Abiy Ahmed to one of his most prominent critics. His unwavering support for ethnic federalism, despite the high personal cost, ensures that his influence will continue to shape Ethiopia's political discourse as the country grapples with questions of unity, autonomy, and the future of its diverse ethnic communities.

***

Gedu Andargachew: From Trusted Advisor to Exiled Opposition Leader

The political trajectory of Gedu Andargachew and Abiy Ahmed, two prominent Ethiopian leaders, is deeply intertwined with the fate of the Amhara people. Both initially represented hope for the Amhara region's political future, but over time, their leadership has come to be marked by betrayal, shifting alliances, and disillusionment. Their roles in Ethiopia's political landscape have been characterized by a complex relationship with ethnic identity, regional power struggles, and authoritarianism. This piece explores their legacies, examining how both figures initially emerged as champions of reform, only to later be seen as betrayers of their people, particularly in the context of their handling of the Amhara identity, political ambitions, and alliances within Ethiopia's ethnically charged political environment.

Gedu Andargachew, a former president of the Amhara region and a key figure in Ethiopian politics, is often viewed as one of the most prominent political figures to rise from the Amhara ethnic group during the early 21st century. Initially, Gedu was a symbol of hope for the Amhara people, who had long felt marginalized in Ethiopia's political system, especially after the establishment of the ethnically based federalism that sidelined their historical dominance.

Gedu's early tenure as the head of the Amhara region, particularly before Abiy Ahmed's rise to power, marked a period of relative stability and political engagement for the Amhara people. He was seen as someone who could bring development and progress to the region, focusing on the welfare of Amhara people while negotiating the complex dynamics between the Amhara region and the central government.

However, as Abiy Ahmed ascended to the national stage in 2018 and embarked on his ambitious program of reform and national reconciliation, Gedu's role in Amhara politics started to shift. While initially part of Abiy's political alliance, Gedu's political future became tied to the changing tides of Ethiopian ethnic politics. Gedu, despite his political acumen, became entangled in Abiy's rapidly centralizing regime, which sought to undermine the very ethnic federal system that had given the Amhara a degree of regional autonomy. As Abiy consolidated power, Gedu was relegated to a secondary position, and the promises of progress and development for the Amhara people began to fade.

Gedu's support for Abiy, who was hailed as a reformer, became increasingly controversial as Abiy's policies alienated the Amhara population, particularly with regard to the rising tensions with the Tigray region and the perceived marginalization of Amhara political interests. Gedu's betrayal of the Amhara people became evident when he, too, became complicit in supporting Abiy's authoritarian measures, including the suppression of political dissent and the violent crackdown on the Tigray region.

Despite his previous support for Abiy's reforms, Gedu's inability or unwillingness to stand against Abiy's increasingly autocratic leadership left the Amhara people feeling abandoned. His failure to protect Amhara interests during this turbulent period led to his eventual alienation from the very people he was meant to represent, marking him as a symbol of political betrayal.

***

Brigadier General Asaminew Tsige: From Ally to Martyr in the Struggle for Amhara Autonomy

Brigadier General Asaminew Tsige (1958 – 24 June 2019) was a prominent Ethiopian military officer who served as the chief of regional security forces in the Amhara Region in 2019. His rise to power came after a tumultuous period in his life. Previously, he had been imprisoned for his alleged involvement in a coup attempt by the opposition group Ginbot 7. During his time in prison, Asaminew was subjected to torture, which resulted in the loss of sight in one of his eyes. Despite these hardships, he was released in 2018 and reinstated to his former rank and pension, marking a dramatic return to public life.

Asaminew hailed from the Amhara ethnic group and he became known for his hardline stance on Amhara nationalism. He was particularly admired by a segment of the Amhara youth, who viewed him as a symbol of their aspirations for greater political autonomy and the preservation of their cultural heritage. Upon his release and subsequent appointment to a government position, Asaminew advocated for more self-rule for the Amhara Region and even encouraged his people to take up arms and form local militias to defend their rights.

Asaminew's political stance, however, came into direct conflict with the policies of Prime Minister Abiy Ahmed, who was pushing for a more centralized government in Ethiopia. Asaminew's growing influence fueled the rise of the National Movement of Amhara (NaMA), a political organization that sought to challenge the dominance of the Amhara Democratic Party (ADP), which had been closely aligned with Abiy's government. Though NaMA had existed before Asaminew's return to power, his involvement provided it with greater legitimacy and momentum.

In 2019, the relationship between Asaminew and Abiy took a deadly turn. Asaminew was accused of masterminding an attempted coup in the Amhara Region, which led to the tragic assassination of Amhara Region President Ambachew Mekonnen and General Se'are

Mekonnen, the Chief of Staff of the Ethiopian National Defense Force. Both men were allies of Prime Minister Abiy. The killings sent shockwaves through the country and raised suspicions of a wider conspiracy.

The events surrounding Asaminew's death remain shrouded in mystery and controversy. After the failed coup, Asaminew went into hiding, evading capture for 36 hours before being shot dead by the Ethiopian police on 24 June 2019. The circumstances of his death remain highly suspicious, with eyewitnesses claiming that Prime Minister Abiy had ordered that Asaminew should not be captured alive. There are reports suggesting that Abiy, seeing Asaminew as a growing threat to his own authoritarian rule, wanted the general silenced rather than imprisoned.

On the same evening that Asaminew was killed, Prime Minister Abiy appeared on national television, dressed in a military uniform, and addressed the nation about the so-called coup attempt. His statements were met with skepticism, as he claimed that Asaminew had been plotting to overthrow his government. However, at the time of his death, Asaminew was reportedly in Bahir Dar, far from the capital Addis Ababa, raising further doubts about the validity of Abiy's narrative.

Asaminew's journey was a testament to the deepening divisions within Ethiopia's complex ethnic and political landscape. His death not only highlighted the ruthlessness of Abiy's regime but also underscored the growing tensions between centralization and regional autonomy in Ethiopia.

For many Amhara people, Asaminew Tsige became a martyr, a symbol of their struggle for freedom, autonomy, and justice in the face of a government they viewed as increasingly authoritarian and dismissive of their cultural and political rights. His legacy lives on as a reminder of the deep fractures within Ethiopia's political system and the high price paid by those who dared to challenge the status quo.

***

Andargachew Tsegie: From Ally to Outcast in Ethiopia's Struggle for Democracy

Ethiopia's political landscape has been shaped by a complex tapestry of ethnic identities, historical grievances, and national aspirations. Among the key figures who have influenced this journey are Andargachew Tsegie and Abiy Ahmed. Andargachew, an opposition leader and former member of the armed resistance group Ginbot 7, and Abiy, Ethiopia's Prime Minister and Nobel Peace Prize laureate, have played pivotal roles in the nation's political development. However, their legacies are marred by their divergent paths, marked by shifting alliances, political compromises, and a broader struggle for the soul of the Ethiopian state. Both Andargachew and Abiy emerged as symbols of hope for a more inclusive Ethiopia, promising reform and freedom from authoritarianism. Yet, as political ambitions and ethnic tensions unfolded, both men's actions eventually betrayed the very promises they had made to their people.

Andargachew Tsegie's political journey began with his deep-rooted opposition to Ethiopia's entrenched political order. As a founding member of Ginbot 7, an organization dedicated to overthrowing the Tigray People's Liberation Front (TPLF)-dominated Ethiopian People's Revolutionary Democratic Front (EPRDF) regime, Andargachew represented a voice for many Ethiopians dissatisfied with the authoritarian government. Ginbot 7 sought to replace the TPLF-led government with a more inclusive, democratic system, advocating for the protection of political rights, freedoms, and the unity of Ethiopia's diverse ethnic groups. In 2014, Andargachew was arrested while in Yemen and later extradited to Ethiopia, where he was sentenced to death in absentia. His arrest became an international cause célèbre, symbolizing the political repression faced by opposition leaders in Ethiopia. But his story took a dramatic turn in 2018, when Abiy Ahmed, then newly appointed Prime Minister, initiated a series of political reforms, including releasing political prisoners like Andargachew. His release was hailed as a breakthrough, and many believed that the country was entering a new era of democratic governance.

However, Andargachew's return to Ethiopia and subsequent alignment with Abiy's reformist government did not lead to the broad-based change that many had hoped for. Initially, Andargachew supported Abiy's vision of national reconciliation, but as Abiy's centralizing policies began to take shape, Andargachew and his supporters began to feel sidelined. The promise of national unity and freedom was quickly overshadowed by Abiy's turn toward authoritarian rule, with his increasing control over the military, security apparatus, and political structures. For Andargachew, the betrayal came not from the central government's political changes but from Abiy's actions, which threatened the freedoms he had fought for. Andargachew found himself caught between supporting a government that promised national unity and the reality of ethnic tensions that were intensifying under Abiy's leadership. His loyalty to Abiy, driven by his desire for peace and unity, became increasingly difficult to justify as Abiy's policies marginalized Ethiopia's ethnic minorities and concentrated power in the hands of a small elite.

Ethiopia's ethnic diversity has long been a defining feature of its social and political fabric. The tension between different ethnic groups, each with their own aspirations, cultural values, and historical experiences, has shaped the country's political history. Both Andargachew and Abiy, in their respective political trajectories, were caught in the midst of these ethnic tensions. Andargachew's early political stance was one of opposition to the TPLF-dominated government, which was seen as disproportionately favoring the Tigray people at the expense of other ethnic groups, particularly the Amhara. His advocacy for a democratic Ethiopia that would allow equal rights for all ethnic groups resonated with many who were dissatisfied with the political hegemony of the TPLF. However, his eventual alignment with Abiy, whose administration began to prioritize national unity over ethnic federalism, meant that Andargachew, too, became entangled in the growing political tensions that arose from the centralization of power.

Abiy's leadership, on the other hand, exemplified the difficulty of balancing Ethiopia's ethnic diversity with the desire for national unity. While Abiy initially embraced the idea of ethnic autonomy, his subsequent push for a unified Ethiopia under the Prosperity Party left ethnic groups like the Amhara, Tigray, and Oromo feeling marginalized. His failure to reconcile these competing aspirations and his authoritarian response to political unrest exacerbated the ethnic tensions that had simmered under the surface for decades. The struggle for Ethiopian identity, particularly in the context of its ethnic composition, is central to understanding the legacies of both Andargachew and Abiy. The Amhara, in particular, have faced a unique dilemma. Historically one of the dominant ethnic groups in Ethiopia, the Amhara have seen their political power wane under both the TPLF-led government and Abiy's push for national unity. Their sense of political and cultural identity has been tested as the country navigates its future in a post-EPRDF landscape.

As Abiy's government began to take shape, the reforms promised during his early tenure were overshadowed by increasing authoritarianism and political centralization. Though Abiy initially gained support for his promises of freedom and peace, most notably through the peace agreement with Eritrea, his approach to governance soon demonstrated a stark contrast to the democratic ideals he once championed. Abiy's centralizing policies, combined with his increasingly authoritarian methods of governance, caused significant concern among opposition groups, including those within the Amhara community. The very political freedoms Andargachew had fought for seemed to be eroding under Abiy's leadership, and the promise of democratic reforms appeared to be unraveling.

Andargachew's disillusionment deepened as he realized that Abiy's reforms were not as inclusive as they appeared. The failure to address the Amhara's political aspirations and the ongoing ethnic tensions in the country led to a growing sense of betrayal. What was initially seen as a fight against the TPLF became, in the eyes of many, a brutal civil war marked by atrocities, mass displacement, and a humanitarian disaster. For Andargachew, the tipping point came when Abiy's government failed to protect the political rights and identity of the Amhara people, and instead, perpetuated policies that deepened the ethnic divisions in the country. His political idealism, which once sought to change Ethiopia through reform, was crushed by the authoritarian trajectory of Abiy's regime.

Andargachew's departure from Abiy's orbit marked the beginning of his vocal opposition, as he sought to rally other Ethiopians to resist Abiy's increasingly autocratic rule.

In the broader political context, Andargachew's disillusionment with Abiy's leadership mirrors the trajectory of his long-time ally, Berhanu Nega. Once a fellow revolutionary within Ginbot 7, Berhanu Nega has increasingly aligned himself with Abiy Ahmed's Prosperity Party, a move that has led to accusations of betrayal from many in the Ethiopian opposition, especially among the Amhara elite. Berhanu, a charismatic leader who once advocated for a democratic, inclusive Ethiopia, is now serving as Ethiopia's Minister of Education under Abiy's government. His decision to join the Prosperity Party, despite his past opposition to the TPLF-led government and his close relationship with Andargachew, has been seen by many as an opportunistic betrayal. In the eyes of his former supporters, Berhanu's shift toward Abiy's increasingly authoritarian government represents a stark departure from the principles of freedom and democracy that once defined his political career.

For many in the Amhara community, Berhanu Nega's alignment with Abiy signals a painful abandonment of the struggle for Ethiopia's diverse communities. His strong rhetoric in support of a unified Ethiopia once captured the imagination of many, including Amhara intellectuals and activists, who believed that his vision of national unity would bring stability to the country. However, now, as Berhanu serves in Abiy's cabinet, his credibility among those who once saw him as a champion for the oppressed has eroded. Andargachew's friendship with Berhanu Nega, once close as brothers in arms, now stands as a reminder of the harsh realities of Ethiopian politics. While Andargachew continues to resist the centralizing, authoritarian policies of Abiy's government, Berhanu has embraced them, leaving his former comrade and long-time friend behind. This shift has become emblematic of the broader betrayal many feel in Ethiopia's political landscape, where loyalty to ideals has given way to political pragmatism, often at the expense of the democratic aspirations that first brought these men to prominence.

Both Andargachew Tsegie and Berhanu Nega have seen their political trajectories defined by their once-shared vision of an inclusive Ethiopia. However, as they have taken divergent paths, their legacies have become deeply intertwined with the disappointments and betrayals that have characterized the country's struggle for democracy, peace, and national unity.

***

Tyie Bogale's Advocacy for Democracy and Human Rights: The Capture, Torture, and Escape

Tyie Bogale, a prominent Ethiopian historian, teacher, and democracy advocate, is yet another example of the widespread political repression under Prime Minister Abiy Ahmed's government. As a committed advocate for democracy, human rights, and the rule of law, Tyie Bogale's activism placed him in direct opposition to the authoritarian tendencies of Abiy's administration. His capture, torture, and eventual flight from Ethiopia embody the broader crackdown on dissent that has characterized Abiy's leadership, leaving countless Ethiopians silenced, imprisoned, or forced into exile.

Tyie Bogale was known for his intellectual contributions as a historian and teacher, where he focused on historical justice and the restoration of Ethiopia's democratic principles. His work and advocacy often emphasized the importance of accountability for past injustices and the need for a pluralistic, democratic society in Ethiopia. In particular, he was an outspoken critic of the ethnic-based political system and the authoritarian practices that had dominated Ethiopian politics for decades.

As a prominent member of the intellectual community, Tyie advocated for the creation of an Ethiopia where free speech and political freedoms were respected, and he consistently challenged those in power, including Prime Minister Abiy Ahmed. His political views and activities, which included public speaking and involvement in opposition movements, made him a target for government surveillance and repression.

Tyie's criticism of Abiy's political trajectory, especially his centralization of power and attempts to curtail the influence of regional political structures, put him at odds with a regime that was becoming increasingly authoritarian. His beliefs were rooted in the ideal that Ethiopia's future depended on inclusive politics, ethnic harmony, and democratic reform, values that were rapidly being undermined under Abiy's leadership.

Tyie Bogale's capture in the summer of 2019 by Ethiopian security forces marked a dark turn in the escalating political repression under Prime Minister Abiy Ahmed. The exact circumstances surrounding his arrest remain unclear, but his imprisonment is a direct result of his outspoken stance against the government's policies, which included criticism of Abiy's military actions, crackdown on opposition, and the ongoing ethnic violence.

Like many others who have challenged the government, Tyie was detained by the security apparatus, a force increasingly accused of operating with impunity under Abiy's regime. His torture during his detention was a stark reflection of the brutal tactics used by the Ethiopian government to intimidate and silence its critics. Tyie, along with other political prisoners, was subjected to physical and psychological abuse in an attempt to break his spirit and prevent him from continuing his activism.

His ordeal is not unique; it mirrors the experiences of many Ethiopians who have found themselves caught in Abiy Ahmed's authoritarian grip. Journalists, activists, opposition leaders, and intellectuals critical of the government have been arrested, detained, and tortured. Many of them are subjected to harsh conditions in Ethiopian prisons, where reports of abuse, starvation, and denial of medical care are commonplace.

For Tyie Bogale, the harsh realities of Ethiopia's prison system and the threat to his life and safety became unbearable. His detention under Abiy's rule exemplified the growing climate of fear in Ethiopia, where political dissent was increasingly met with violence, and individuals who dared to speak out were deemed enemies of the state.

After enduring months of torture and harassment, Tyie Bogale was finally released from prison, but the conditions under which he was released were far from ideal. His health had been severely impacted by the brutal treatment he had suffered, and the threats to his life remained constant. Tyie, like many others who have been politically persecuted under Abiy's regime, had little choice but to flee the country.

Tyie's escape was not an easy one. He had to make the difficult decision to abandon his home, his work as a teacher, and his intellectual contributions to Ethiopia. But the repressive political environment, targeted harassment, and physical harm made it impossible for him to stay in the country any longer.

Upon leaving Ethiopia, Tyie, like many other Ethiopians who have been forced into exile, joined the growing ranks of those who have fled the country to escape political persecution. His journey into exile is a poignant reminder of the brain drain that Ethiopia has faced as a result of Abiy Ahmed's increasingly authoritarian governance. Intellectuals, human rights activists, journalists, and ordinary citizens who have had the courage to speak out against the regime find themselves living in exile, far from their homeland.

Tyie's experience is emblematic of the widespread political repression that has occurred under Abiy Ahmed's leadership. His government has faced increasing criticism for its authoritarian tendencies, especially after the initial euphoria surrounding his rise to power in 2018. While Abiy initially promised reform, peace, and democratization, his tenure has been marked by military crackdowns, human rights abuses, and the suppression of dissent.

The government's actions, such as the arrest and torture of political opponents, the shutting down of independent media, and the imprisonment of journalists and activists, are part of a broader trend of growing authoritarianism. Critics argue that Abiy's desire to centralize power has led to the erosion of democratic freedoms and the rise of political violence. Those who oppose his rule, particularly those advocating for greater democracy and human rights, face increasing risks of harassment, imprisonment, and even death.

Tyie Bogale's capture, torture, and eventual escape are just one example of how Abiy's regime has undermined the very principles of freedom of expression, democracy, and political pluralism that Ethiopians once hoped for after Abiy took power. His case is part of the broader crackdown on Ethiopia's intellectual and political elite, those who have been targeted for their dissenting views and whose voices are silenced by force and intimidation.

Tyie Bogale's exile has not only been a personal tragedy but also a loss for Ethiopia as a whole. Figures like Tyie, intellectuals, teachers, and democracy advocates, play a crucial role in shaping the political discourse and providing a voice for the voiceless. The exile of such individuals, many of whom are highly educated and committed to democratic principles, represents a significant loss for Ethiopia's future. Without these critical voices, Ethiopia's democratic struggle becomes even more difficult to achieve.

However, Tyie's escape to safety does not mark the end of his activism. From his place of exile, he continues to speak out against the human rights abuses and political repression that continue to plague Ethiopia under Abiy Ahmed. He has become part of the global diaspora of Ethiopians who are fighting for justice, accountability, and the restoration of democracy in Ethiopia.

While Abiy Ahmed's government may have successfully silenced Tyie and many others within the country, it has not silenced the broader movement for democracy. Tyie's story, like that of other exiled figures, serves as a powerful reminder of the struggle for freedom and political rights in Ethiopia, and the resilience of those who continue to fight for a better future for their homeland.

The capture, torture, and flight of Tyie Bogale reflect the broader climate of political repression and authoritarianism that has taken root in Ethiopia under Prime Minister Abiy Ahmed's leadership. His story is not just a personal one but a symbol of the challenges facing Ethiopia as a nation—a nation caught between democratic aspirations and authoritarian suppression. The ongoing struggle for freedom, justice, and democracy in Ethiopia will continue to be shaped by figures like Tyie, whose voices, though silenced within the country, are now echoing from abroad, calling for a better future for all Ethiopians.

Tyie's legacy as a democracy advocate and human rights defender will endure as an inspiration to those who remain in Ethiopia and to the growing diaspora community. His determination to continue the fight for democracy, even from exile, exemplifies the resilience of those who refuse to be silenced, no matter the cost.

***

The Betrayal of Tamagne Beyene

Tamagne Beyene is a well-known Ethiopian figure, recognized for his deep patriotism, nationalistic views, and unwavering commitment to Ethiopia's unity and sovereignty. A long-time advocate for Ethiopian national identity, Tamagne stood with Prime Minister Abiy Ahmed in the early years of his leadership, even during the height of the Tigray War. However, despite his loyalty and his public support for Abiy's government, Tamagne's relationship with the Prime Minister became a tale of betrayal, disillusionment, and eventual distancing as the true nature of Abiy's leadership and political actions unfolded.

In the years following Abiy Ahmed's rise to power in 2018, Tamagne Beyene emerged as a staunch supporter of the Prime Minister, believing that Abiy's reforms could bring about long-awaited changes in Ethiopia. At the time, Abiy promised peace, democracy, and national reconciliation, and many Ethiopians, like Tamagne, felt hope for a better future. As a fervent patriot with a deep love for Ethiopia, Tamagne believed that Abiy's unification agenda, which was supposed to bring together Ethiopia's diverse ethnic groups and create a more democratic society, was in line with his own vision for the country.

During the early days of Abiy's leadership, Tamagne did not hesitate to publicly endorse the Prime Minister, aligning himself with Abiy's promises of reform. He praised Abiy for his peace agreement with Eritrea, his efforts to open political space, and his promises to end decades of ethnic-based politics. For Tamagne, these were bold steps toward the realization of a united, peaceful Ethiopia, where all citizens, regardless of ethnic background, could coexist and thrive.

However, as time went on, it became increasingly clear that Abiy's political trajectory was not as unifying as many had hoped. Abiy's government began to display signs of centralization, authoritarianism, and ethnic favoritism, which conflicted with Tamagne's vision of a democratic Ethiopia where all groups had an equal say in the country's political and social landscape.

One of the most poignant moments in the story of Tamagne Beyene's political journey occurred when he publicly bowed down in front of Abiy Ahmed, symbolizing his complete loyalty to the Prime Minister and his belief in the man's promises for Ethiopia's future. This gesture, which many viewed as a sign of respect and devotion, marked a significant moment in Tamagne's political life, one that he would later come to regret as he distanced himself from Abiy in the face of growing disillusionment.

The bowing down before Abiy took place during a time when the Prime Minister was still regarded as a reformer, someone who had promised to heal Ethiopia's wounds, bring peace, and move the country away from the entrenched political systems that had divided Ethiopians for decades. Abiy's bold peace agreement with Eritrea, his promises to end ethnic-based politics, and his efforts to liberalize the economy inspired many Ethiopians, including Tamagne, who saw in him a leader capable of transforming the country. In many ways, Tamagne's act of bowing was a symbolic gesture of faith, marking his full endorsement of Abiy's agenda for change.

For Tamagne, this moment was about more than just public support for a political leader, it was a declaration of his unwavering belief that Abiy was the key to Ethiopia's future, a hope that the Prime Minister would rise above the challenges that had historically plagued the nation. By bowing down, Tamagne expressed his respect for Abiy as a patriot and national leader and a willingness to stand by him through the difficult road ahead.

In this moment, Tamagne felt that his loyalty to Abiy was aligned with the greater national interest. This was not just support for a political figure, it was a sacrifice of his personal views to rally behind the national agenda of unity and peace. By publicly showing his allegiance, he was saying to the Ethiopian people that he trusted Abiy's vision for the country and was willing to back him through thick and thin.

However, as Abiy's government became increasingly authoritarian and his policies began to reveal darker, more divisive tactics, Tamagne's public loyalty was severely tested. The Tigray and Amhara War, the widespread military repression, the crackdown on opposition, and the growing ethnic violence became a point of deep contention. Tamagne's trust in Abiy was shattered, especially as the Prime Minister's promises of peace and unity gave way to military conflict and the silencing of dissent.

Tamagne's moment of bowing down became a source of personal regret as he saw the government he had once supported become the very oppressor he had hoped it would overthrow. The military's brutality in Tigray and Amhara, the ethnic profiling, the targeting of civilians, and the suppressing of free speech undermined the hope that Abiy had initially inspired in Tamagne and many others. Public figures, journalists, activists, and intellectuals critical of the government were being imprisoned, tortured, or even killed.

Tamagne's support for Abiy eroded as he realized that the Prime Minister's vision of Ethiopia was no longer about unity and democracy, but rather about power and military dominance. The peace that had once been promised to Ethiopia was becoming a distant memory, replaced by a regime marked by authoritarian rule and a military-driven agenda.

Tamagne, who had once viewed Abiy as a reformer, now saw a dictator who was increasingly bending democratic norms and suppressing opposition. The centralization of power, the crackdown on dissent, the treatment of ethnic groups such as the Amhara, Oromo, and Tigray, and the military's heavy-handed tactics were stark signs that Abiy's government was not the inclusive, democratic Ethiopia Tamagne had once hoped for.

The tipping point came when Abiy's government began to target civilian populations in Amhara and across Ethiopia, with widespread displacement and starvation taking a devastating toll on the people. Tamagne could no longer ignore the mounting evidence of ethnic violence and war crimes. This disillusionment was compounded by Abiy's increasing authoritarian tactics—arbitrary arrests, violence against journalists, and the restriction of free speech. Abiy's initial promises of peace, democracy, and unity had been replaced by military rule and ethnic division.

After months of growing disillusionment, Tamagne Beyene finally distanced himself from Abiy Ahmed and became a vocal critic of the government he had once supported. His decision to break ties with Abiy was not made lightly, as it symbolized a profound shift in his belief system, a rejection of Abiy's leadership and a repudiation of the regime's increasingly authoritarian nature.

Tamagne's move to denounce Abiy was not just a personal betrayal; it reflected the broader sense of betrayal felt by many Ethiopians who had supported Abiy in the early days of his rule, only to watch him consolidate power and preside over a brutal war, widespread human rights violations, and the erosion of democratic principles. Many Ethiopians felt that Abiy's leadership had turned from a hopeful promise of national unity into a deeply divisive, militarized, and authoritarian regime.

For Tamagne, his decision to break with Abiy was a tragic realization that the man he had once believed would lead Ethiopia to a better future had become one of the key figures responsible for its deepening crisis. Patriotism, to Tamagne, meant defending Ethiopia's unity, justice, and democracy—values that were being undermined by the very leadership he had once supported.

Tamagne's decision to distance himself from Abiy Ahmed has placed him among the growing ranks of Ethiopian intellectuals, activists, and political figures who are now speaking out against the government's actions and advocating for a new, more inclusive Ethiopia. His shift reflects the deep fractures in Ethiopian society, where many Ethiopians, once hopeful about Abiy's reforms, now see him as a figure responsible for national division, ethnic violence, and the undermining of democracy.

As a patriot and democracy advocate, Tamagne's next steps are focused on promoting peace, unity, and political reform for Ethiopia. His journey from support for Abiy to disillusionment and criticism underscores the complexities of Ethiopia's political struggle. The ongoing Amhara War, ethnic violence, and human rights abuses have left Ethiopians with difficult questions about their future and the direction of the country.

For Tamagne Beyene, his story is one of betrayal, not just by Abiy Ahmed, but by the system that he hoped would deliver democracy and unity to Ethiopia. Yet his growing role as a critic of Abiy's regime is also a testament to the enduring struggle for justice, accountability, and a democratic Ethiopia. In the years to come, Tamagne's voice will continue to be an important one in the conversation about Ethiopia's future, a future he hopes will one day be shaped by peace, freedom, and unity, rather than the divisions and turmoil of today.

***

Bekele Gerba and the Fall of OFC

The political journey of Bekele Gerba, the prominent leader of the Oromo Federalist Congress (OFC), and his eventual break with Abiy Ahmed serves as a poignant example of the disillusionment and betrayal felt by many Oromo elites during Abiy's rule. Bekele, once a key figure in the opposition to Ethiopia's previous regimes, found himself caught in a political storm as Abiy's leadership, which initially promised change and democracy, gradually turned authoritarian. This shift ultimately led to Bekele's exile, the disbandment of the OFC, and the collapse of hope for many in the Oromo political elite who had trusted Abiy.

When Abiy Ahmed first came to power in 2018, his promises of reconciliation, democracy, and political openness resonated deeply with many Ethiopians, particularly in the Oromo region—the largest ethnic group in the country. For the Oromo political elite, including figures like Bekele Gerba and Professor Merera Gudina, Abiy represented a fresh start after decades of perceived marginalization under the previous regimes.

As a leading figure in the Oromo Federalist Congress (OFC), Bekele Gerba had long been a voice for Oromo self-determination and federalism, advocating for political change within Ethiopia that would allow the Oromo people to have a more meaningful role in the governance of the country. The OFC, a party with roots in the broader Oromo Liberation Front (OLF), was focused on promoting the interests of the Oromo people while also contributing to the broader democratic process of Ethiopia.

Abiy's rise to power brought about political reforms that included the release of political prisoners (including Bekele Gerba) and a promise to dismantle the ethnic federalism that had previously divided Ethiopia. The inclusion of the Oromo elite in the political process after years of oppression sparked a wave of optimism among many within the Oromo community, including those in the OFC.

Bekele Gerba, for his part, cautiously welcomed Abiy's early moves, including the opening of political space for parties like the OFC. He returned to Ethiopia after his release from prison, eager to engage in the political reform process. At that point, many believed that the Oromo struggle for equality had found a champion in Abiy, someone who would, in time, honor the promises of national unity while respecting the rights and autonomy of Ethiopia's ethnic groups.

However, as time passed, it became increasingly clear that Abiy Ahmed's reforms were not as inclusive and democratic as they initially appeared. The centralization of power under Abiy's rule became more apparent, especially as the Prime Minister began consolidating control over key political and military institutions. Abiy's rhetoric of unity soon began to clash with the reality of his increasingly authoritarian leadership, leading to growing ethnic tensions and political repression.

For Bekele Gerba and the OFC, this shift was deeply troubling. Abiy, who had initially appeared open to political dialogue, began to marginalize opposition voices and suppress dissent. The government's crackdown on Oromo opposition, coupled with the targeting of Oromo activists and leaders, signaled to many that Abiy's commitment to democratic reform was increasingly hollow. Instead of embracing federalism and ethnic equality, Abiy's administration began to show signs of ethnic favoritism, prioritizing the Amhara and Tigray regions in ways that sidelined Oromo interests.

The Tigray War further strained relations, as Oromo civilians and political leaders, including Bekele Gerba, found themselves caught between a violent conflict and the authoritarian policies of the Abiy government. Bekele's position within the OFC and the broader Oromo political landscape grew untenable as his calls for peace and democratic reform clashed with the government's increasingly militarized response to the crisis.

As the political situation in Ethiopia deteriorated, the Oromo Federalist Congress (OFC) and its leadership found themselves in direct opposition to Abiy's government. Bekele Gerba, once a key ally of Abiy's promises, found his role in the political process increasingly marginalized. Political persecution and the criminalization of opposition figures became commonplace, and the OFC was subjected to increasing pressure and intimidation.

By 2020, Bekele Gerba made the difficult decision to leave Ethiopia for exile, unable to continue his political activities in a country where the space for dissent had shrunk dramatically. His departure from the OFC symbolized a broader disillusionment within the Oromo political elite, many of whom had placed their hopes in Abiy's leadership only to see their aspirations for a more democratic Ethiopia dashed.

The OFC, once seen as a vehicle for promoting Oromo political aspirations, began to disintegrate under the growing pressures from the government. Its leaders were forced to either go into exile, like Bekele, or remain silenced under the weight of Abiy's crackdown. The collapse of the OFC and the exile of key leaders marked a tragic moment for the Oromo elites, who had long fought for greater political inclusion and autonomy.

The exodus of Bekele Gerba and other Oromo leaders into exile, as well as the downfall of the Oromo Federalist Congress, highlighted a growing sense of betrayal among the Oromo elite. Many had aligned themselves with Abiy, believing that his leadership would address the historical grievances of the Oromo people. However, Abiy's shift towards a centralized, authoritarian state left many Oromo leaders disillusioned and disempowered.

Bekele Gerba's departure from the OFC and his exile served as a bitter reminder of the false hope many had placed in Abiy's leadership. The Oromo elites, once hopeful for the realization of their vision for a democratic Ethiopia, now faced a grim reality in which their voices were silenced, and their political struggle was further undermined by a regime that increasingly embraced authoritarianism over democracy.

The Oromo people, who had long struggled for equality and political representation, found themselves once again marginalized, with their political elite either in exile, imprisoned, or oppressed under Abiy's rule. Bekele's decision to leave the country was not only a personal sacrifice but also a symbolic moment for many Oromos who had once placed their faith in Abiy and his promises of reconciliation and democratic governance.

For many in the Oromo elite, the political landscape under Abiy became a time of sorrow and disappointment. Leaders like Bekele Gerba and Professor Merera Gudina, once considered to be the torchbearers of the Oromo political struggle, found themselves sidelined and politically irrelevant under the very government they had hoped would lead Ethiopia to a more democratic future. The centralization of power, the militarization of the state, and the persecution of opposition figures shattered the dreams of a peaceful, unified, and democratic Ethiopia.

The Oromo elite's political power was fractured, with many fleeing to exile as their voices and political agendas were pushed aside. This represents a tragic shift in Ethiopia's political landscape, where those who had once championed freedom, democracy, and federalism found themselves increasingly alienated by a regime that promised much but delivered little.

As Bekele Gerba and other political leaders now find themselves in exile, it remains unclear whether the Oromo political struggle will ever regain the momentum it had under the initial years of Abiy Ahmed's leadership. The betrayal of these leaders and the collapse of OFC stand as a harsh reminder of the risks and realities of political loyalty in a regime that has grown increasingly autocratic and repressive. For many in the Oromo elite, the era of hope has faded, leaving behind a sad legacy of broken promises and lost political power.

***

Mesay Mekonnen: A Voice for Truth and Ethiopian Nationalism

Mesay Mekonnen is an Ethiopian journalist known for his outspoken criticism of both the Ethiopian government and the broader political status quo. He has worked for years with independent media outlets like ESAT (Ethiopian Satellite Television) and Deutsche Welle (DW), both of which have provided platforms for critical voices within Ethiopia.

ESAT, in particular, has been a thorn in the side of the Ethiopian government, especially after Abiy Ahmed came to power. The station's independent reporting on Ethiopian affairs, often critical of Abiy's government, has led to accusations of "terrorism" from the government. Mesay Mekonnen, as a prominent journalist at ESAT, has faced direct persecution from the state, with the government labeling him as a "terrorist" for his critical coverage. The government's use of such labels, often applied to opposition journalists and activists, is a tactic aimed at discrediting and silencing dissenting voices.

Mesay, like many journalists such as Dereje Habtewold, working with independent media in Ethiopia, has been a target of harassment, including arbitrary arrests, threats, and intimidation. Despite the government's attempts to discredit him, Mesay has remained a staunch advocate for press freedom and the rights of Ethiopians to access independent, unbiased news. His work highlights the growing struggle between the Ethiopian government's narrative and the independent media that seeks to challenge it.

The term "terrorist" has been weaponized by Abiy Ahmed's government to discredit opposition groups, journalists, and activists. This labeling strategy is not new to Ethiopia's political history, but under Abiy's leadership, its use has intensified. Many critics, including opposition leaders, journalists like Mesay Mekonnen, and media organizations like Ethio360 have been unfairly labeled as terrorists, a tactic that delegitimizes their work and creates a climate of fear.

For Mesay Mekonnen and others in the Ethiopian diaspora, the government's accusations have created a dangerous and oppressive environment in which journalists are forced to navigate the fine line between reporting the truth and risking imprisonment, exile, or worse. The labeling of independent journalists as terrorists serves a dual purpose: it undermines their credibility while simultaneously justifying government crackdowns on media outlets that provide coverage counter to the government's official narrative.

The government's use of this label also plays into the larger struggle over Ethiopia's national identity. Abiy's administration has positioned itself as the defender of Ethiopia's unity, and those critical of his rule are often framed as enemies of the state, accused of undermining national security. The accusation of terrorism serves to rally the public behind the government by painting opponents as threats to national peace and stability, despite the fact that many of these "terrorists" are simply advocates for democracy and human rights.

The government's treatment of Mesay Mekonnen and independent media outlets highlights the ongoing battle for press freedom and democratic principles in Ethiopia. Abiy Ahmed's government, which once promised reform and national reconciliation, has increasingly been characterized by authoritarian practices that limit free speech, crack down on opposition voices, and silence critical media outlets.

The labeling of journalists and opposition members as terrorists is part of a broader strategy to stifle dissent and maintain control over the political narrative in Ethiopia. This attack on independent journalism not only threatens the future of Ethiopian democracy but also undermines the public's ability to access diverse perspectives on the nation's political realities.

Mesay Mekonnen's continued work, despite the threats and harassment he faces, exemplifies the resilience of independent media and the ongoing struggle for Ethiopia's future. His commitment to truth and press freedom, alongside his dedication to a peaceful and democratic Ethiopia, stands in stark contrast to the authoritarian tendencies of Abiy's government. The relationship between Abiy Ahmed, Mesay Mekonnen, and the broader struggle for press freedom in Ethiopia is emblematic of the country's deepening political crisis. As Abiy's government has become more authoritarian, figures like Mesay Mekonnen, working through independent outlets like ESAT and DW, have become central to the fight for truth, democracy, and national unity. The government's use of the "terrorist" label against journalists and activists only serves to further isolate Ethiopia from global norms of press freedom and human rights.

The legacy of Abiy's leadership, particularly in terms of his treatment of independent media and opposition voices, will be remembered as a pivotal moment in the struggle for Ethiopia's future. As Mesay Mekonnen and other journalists continue to stand for truth, the future of Ethiopia's democracy and national identity remains uncertain, with the fight for press freedom standing at the heart of this ongoing struggle.

***

CHAPTER 14

Unsolved Killings During Abiy Ahmed's Era: A Nation in Mourning and Suspicion

Prime Minister Abiy Ahmed's tenure since 2018 has been marked by numerous political and social challenges, including significant reforms, the outbreak of war, and escalating ethnic tensions. While his rise to power was initially heralded as a beacon of hope for peace and democratic reform, his leadership has also been associated with several high-profile killings and disappearances that remain unsolved. These killings have fueled suspicions of political repression, ethnic violence, and the centralization of power. Among the most notable unsolved murders during Abiy Ahmed's leadership are those of Engineer Semegnew Bekele, Hachalu Hundessa, General Saere (or Sarra), President of Amhara Region Ambachew Mekonnen, and others. These tragic deaths have raised serious questions about the stability of Ethiopia and the role of the state in these violent incidents.

The unsolved killings during Abiy Ahmed's leadership have raised serious questions about the level of political violence and repression in Ethiopia under his rule. While Abiy came to power with promises of reform and democratization, his tenure has been marked by increasing authoritarianism, ethnic violence, and a crackdown on opposition voices.

One of the central themes that emerges from these killings is impunity. The Ethiopian government's failure to provide transparency in investigating these deaths or to hold accountable those responsible for them has raised alarm among Ethiopians and the international community. The killing of individuals such as Semegnew, Hachalu, and Ambachew appears to fit into a broader pattern of targeted assassinations and political violence that seeks to eliminate perceived threats to the government's power.

Abiy's government has been criticized for its centralization of authority, undermining the ethnic federalism that had been a hallmark of Ethiopian governance. This centralization has led to increased ethnic tensions, with various ethnic groups, including the Oromo, Amhara, and Tigray, accusing the government of favoring certain groups over others. The government's failure to address these grievances has led to increased disillusionment and violence, particularly in regions like Amhara and Oromia, where political leaders and activists have been targeted for their opposition to Abiy's policies.

Moreover, the lack of independent media and the crackdown on free speech under Abiy's government has exacerbated the sense of distrust and suspicion. Journalists and opposition figures critical of the government have been harassed, imprisoned, or silenced, making it even more difficult for the public to access reliable information about the true nature of these killings.

The unsolved killings of high-profile figures such as Semegnew Bekele, Hachalu Hundessa, General Saere, and Ambachew Mekonnen have left deep scars on Ethiopia's political landscape. These deaths, and the surrounding conspiracy theories, paint a troubling picture of a government that is struggling with ethnic divisions, authoritarian tendencies, and a failure to promote justice and accountability.

As Ethiopia continues to grapple with internal conflicts, including the ongoing Tigray War and escalating ethnic violence, the legacy of these unsolved killings will likely continue to haunt Abiy Ahmed's leadership. The lack of transparency, the suppression of opposition voices, and the political use of violence have undermined the credibility of the government and deepened the rifts in Ethiopian society.

For many Ethiopians, these unsolved killings are not just tragedies, but symbols of a government that has failed to address the fundamental issues of ethnic autonomy, human rights, and political freedom. Until these cases are properly investigated and justice is served, Ethiopia may continue to live in the shadow of uncertainty and suspicion, making it increasingly difficult for Abiy Ahmed's government to regain the trust of its people and the international community.

***

Engineer Semegnew Bekele: The Unsolved Death of a National Hero

Engineer Semegnew Bekele, the project manager of the Grand Ethiopian Renaissance Dam (GERD), was found dead on July 26, 2018, in Addis Ababa under suspicious circumstances. He had been one of the most visible figures in Ethiopia's ambitious hydropower project and became a symbol of national pride. His death was initially labeled a suicide by government authorities, with reports stating that he shot himself in the head. However, his family, friends, and colleagues quickly rejected this claim, questioning the plausibility of such an act given his professional achievements and public persona.

Conspiracy theories about his death soon surfaced, with many alleging that Semegnew may have been silenced due to his knowledge of sensitive information regarding the GERD, possible corruption in the project, or even broader political tensions surrounding the construction. The Ethiopian government's failure to conduct a thorough and independent investigation only fueled these suspicions. As Ethiopia's political climate grew increasingly volatile under Abiy's leadership, questions about whether Semegnew's death was a targeted killing for political reasons remained unanswered.

***

Hachalu Hundessa: The Killing that Sparked Nationwide Protests

On June 29, 2020, the assassination of Hachalu Hundessa, a prominent Oromo singer and activist, sent shockwaves through Ethiopia and ignited massive protests. Hachalu, whose music had become a rallying cry for the Oromo people's struggle for equality and justice, was shot dead in Addis Ababa. His death triggered violent unrest across Ethiopia, particularly in the Oromia region, where his supporters believed the government may have been involved.

Hachalu's murder has remained a subject of intense political controversy. Many Oromos and opposition groups suspect that Abiy Ahmed's government or factions within it were behind the killing, viewing him as a threat to their rule. His death was seen by many as an attempt to stifle the Oromo protest movement, which had gained significant momentum in the years leading up to his death. The Ethiopian government has repeatedly claimed that Hachalu's death was the result of an ethnic conflict and criminal elements, but these explanations have not been convincing to many Ethiopians, who see it as part of a broader campaign of suppression against those critical of Abiy's government.

Despite multiple arrests and investigations, the true motives behind Hachalu's assassination remain unclear. The failure to fully resolve his killing has left the Oromo community and other Ethiopians with deep suspicions about the government's role in the tragedy.

***

General Saere: The Death of a High-ranking Military Officer

General Saere, an influential military officer, was killed in an attack on June 22, 2019, along with several of his colleagues, during a coup attempt in the Amhara region. The attempted coup, which resulted in the death of Amhara's regional president, Ambachew Mekonnen, and his advisor, Ezez Wasse, has been widely discussed in Ethiopia and beyond.

While the Ethiopian government labeled the coup as the result of rogue elements within the Amhara region, many saw the deaths of General Saere and others as an act orchestrated by more powerful political factions. Some analysts and opposition figures speculate that Abiy Ahmed's government may have played a role in the assassination of General Saere and his colleagues to eliminate powerful opponents in the Amhara region. Others argue that the situation was a result of internal divisions within the military or regional political rivalries. The true cause of his death has not been definitively determined, and the lack of transparency around the coup's events has led to further speculation and distrust in Abiy's government.

*****

Ambachew Mekonnen: President of Amhara Region

On the same day that General Saere was killed, Ambachew Mekonnen, the President of the Amhara Region, was assassinated in what appeared to be part of the larger coup attempt. Mekonnen, a former ally of Abiy Ahmed, was seen as a key figure in the central government's efforts to consolidate power in the wake of the 2018 reforms. His death, along with that of his advisor Ezez Wasse, was portrayed by the government as an act of regional insurrection.

However, questions have been raised about the true nature of the coup. Some observers argue that Ambachew's death was not just the result of a military uprising but possibly linked to broader power struggles between Ethiopia's ethnic-based political factions. The Amhara region has often felt marginalized in Ethiopia's political landscape, and Ambachew was seen as a prominent representative of Amhara interests. His assassination has left many questioning whether the coup was a calculated move by rivals to weaken Amhara power and influence within the government, or whether it was part of a broader effort to manipulate ethnic divisions in Ethiopia.

*****

Bate Urgessa's Killing: Another Tragic Chapter in Ethiopia's Unresolved Deaths

Bate Urgessa stands out as another high-profile victim whose killing during Abiy Ahmed's era remains shrouded in mystery and suspicion. Bate Urgessa was a prominent Oromo businessman and a former member of the Oromo Liberation Front (OLF), who later became a critic of both the government and the OLF's leadership.

His death, like many others, highlights the ongoing political tensions and power struggles that have been amplified under Abiy's leadership. The circumstances surrounding his killing have added to the growing list of unresolved political murders that have left Ethiopians with more questions than answers.

Bate Urgessa was not only a businessman but also a vocal advocate for Oromo rights and a former member of the Oromo Liberation Front (OLF), which had long been engaged in an armed struggle against the Ethiopian government. As a critic of both the government and OLF leadership, Bate became a controversial figure in Ethiopia's complex political landscape. After his time with the OLF, Bate became an influential member of the Oromo diaspora, living abroad and engaging in public commentary on the political and social issues facing his people in Ethiopia.

His vocal criticism of the political elite, including those in the Abiy Ahmed administration and his call for greater Oromo autonomy and a more inclusive political structure, made him an important figure in the Oromo political movement. His killing on August 25, 2020, came at a time when Ethiopia was already facing intense internal conflict, and it sent ripples through the Oromo community, which was already reeling from the assassination of Hachalu Hundessa.

Bate Urgessa was killed in a violent attack, and just like the other high-profile murders under Abiy Ahmed's leadership, the exact details surrounding his death remain unclear. Some reports indicated that Bate was gunned down by unidentified assailants in a drive-by shooting, which fits a pattern of targeted attacks on political figures, activists, and critics.

***

CHAPTER 15

The Rediscovery of Ethiopia's Lost Cities: A Comparison of Addis Ababa, Finfinne, and Barara

The rediscovery of Ethiopia's lost cities has brought new perspectives on the country's rich historical tapestry, challenging modern interpretations of its urban and political evolution. Addis Ababa, known today as Ethiopia's political and cultural capital, stands in stark contrast to the long-forgotten medieval cities such as Barara. The search for lost cities like Barara and Tegulet, while deeply rooted in Ethiopia's medieval period, reveals a complex urban landscape that predates the modern era. As these ancient sites come to light, it becomes evident that Ethiopia's history, and particularly that of Addis Ababa and the ancient city of Barara, is far more intricate than previously thought.

Addis Ababa, located at the base of Mount Entoto, was founded in 1886 by Emperor Menelik II and has since become Ethiopia's capital. Originally a resort town with mineral springs, the city quickly grew into the heart of the Ethiopian Empire, serving as the center of administration, commerce, and culture. Over the years, Addis Ababa evolved into a bustling metropolis, symbolizing the modernization and centralization of Ethiopia under Menelik and his successors.

However, the modern-day prominence of Addis Ababa should not overshadow the historical and cultural layers embedded in its land. The city was founded upon land once known as **Finfinne**, a term meaning "natural spring" in the Oromo language. Before its transformation into the capital of Ethiopia, the region surrounding Finfinne had been a place of spiritual and cultural significance to the Oromo people. While the modern Addis Ababa reflects a more imperial narrative, the indigenous roots of Finfinne remain a key aspect of the area's identity, connecting the city's present with its pre-imperial past.

*****

Barara: The Lost Medieval City of Abyssinia

In contrast to the modern development of Addis Ababa, the city of **Barara** represents an entirely different period in Ethiopian history. Described by Fra Mauro in his 15th-century map as a prominent city in the Kingdom of Abyssinia, Barara was once a powerful center of trade, culture, and religion, especially during the medieval period. The city was mentioned frequently in European sources but remained largely mysterious due to the lack of detailed local records.

Recent archaeological research, especially around the Germama and Kessem river valleys, has identified a site that might correspond to the lost city of Barara. The site includes large cemeteries, pottery, and architectural remains, providing evidence of a thriving urban center. Despite the devastation of the religious wars of the 16th century, which led to the destruction and abandonment of many Ethiopian cities, Barara's importance can still be traced through historical and archaeological data. The discoveries at Barara suggest it was a vibrant city, serving as the capital of Abyssinia and a point of interaction between Christian and Islamic kingdoms in the region.

***

Finfinne: The Sacred Roots Beneath Addis Ababa's Development

Before it was renamed Addis Ababa, the area had been known as **Finfinne**, a name still held dear by the Oromo people. The region was recognized for its healing waters and its significance in Oromo spirituality. While the Oromo people had long inhabited the area around Finfinne, the establishment of Addis Ababa as the capital shifted the political landscape of the region, gradually erasing much of the local cultural narrative.

The modern city of Addis Ababa, however, does not entirely erase the influence of Finfinne. While Menelik II's founding of Addis Ababa in 1886 marked a new political chapter for Ethiopia, it also introduced the idea of centralization, particularly in the context of the Empire's relationships with European colonial powers. Yet the historical name of Finfinne and its connection to the Oromo identity continue to play an essential role in discussions surrounding the city's heritage and cultural significance, pointing to a deeper and more indigenous history that predates Menelik's vision of a modern Ethiopian state.

***

Contrasting Addis Ababa, Finfinne, and Barara

The comparison of **Addis Ababa**, **Finfinne**, and **Barara** illustrates the rich and evolving historical narrative of Ethiopia. Addis Ababa, as the modern capital, represents the political and cultural center of contemporary Ethiopia. Its rise in the late 19th century is a testament to Ethiopia's resilience against European imperialism and its vision of a unified modern state. However, Addis Ababa's roots lie in the region historically known as Finfinne, an area that had been sacred to the Oromo people for centuries before Menelik II's establishment of the capital and Barara, Ethiopia's medieval history.

Ultimately, the rediscovery of cities such as Barara, the historical significance of Finfinne, and the modern developments of Addis Ababa suggest that Ethiopia's identity is not confined to a singular city or historical period. From the ancient trade routes and cities of the Aksumite Empire to the dynamic political center of Addis Ababa, the story of Ethiopia is one of continuity, transformation, and resilience.

As investigations into Ethiopia's lost cities continue, it becomes increasingly clear that the country's history is far richer and more complex than what is often portrayed. The cities of Barara, Finfinne, and Addis Ababa represent different epochs in Ethiopia's ongoing narrative, illustrating the deep layers of cultural, political, and social development that have shaped the modern Ethiopian state. Through careful archaeological research and historical inquiry, these lost cities offer crucial insights into the development of Ethiopian civilization and its enduring legacy.

***

Addis Ababa under Abiy Ahmed: A City Divided by Identity and Leadership

Addis Ababa is central to the nation's political, cultural, and economic landscape. Known as "Addis Ababa" (meaning "new flower" in Amharic), the city has long been a symbol of Ethiopia's unity and modernity. As the seat of government and a major diplomatic hub, Addis Ababa has historically been viewed as a space representing all Ethiopians, regardless of ethnic background. However, under the leadership of Prime Minister Abiy Ahmed, the city's identity has become more contested, reflecting a broader national struggle over ethnic federalism, national unity, and the role of Ethiopia's various ethnic groups in shaping the future of the country.

Addis Ababa, situated at an elevation of 2,355 meters (7,726 feet) above sea level, lies within the Awash River basin, at the base of Mount Entoto. The city's terrain is varied, rising gradually from the lowland areas near Bole International Airport (2,326 meters) to the over 3,000 meters in the Entoto Mountains. The city's modern history traces back to 1886, when Menelik II, the Negus of Shewa, founded the settlement. Initially, Addis Ababa was a small resort town for the Ethiopian nobility, gradually growing into the political, administrative, and commercial center of the Ethiopian Empire.

However, the city's significance has taken on new layers of meaning under the rule of Abiy Ahmed. His approach to the identity of Addis Ababa and its status within the larger Ethiopian federation has sparked tension and controversy. Under Abiy Ahmed, Addis Ababa has been caught in a web of conflicting identities. On one hand, Abiy's rhetoric positions Addis Ababa as the capital of all Ethiopians, emphasizing unity and collective belonging. On the other hand, his policies and public statements often seem to prioritize the interests of the Oromo ethnic group, particularly in relation to the city's status and governance. As an Oromo leader, Abiy has voiced his belief that Addis Ababa, historically linked to the Oromo people through its original name "Finfinne," should reflect their significance in Ethiopian history and society.

Despite his calls for unity, Abiy's approach has sometimes been seen as favoring the Oromo, leading to criticisms that he is overly focused on the Oromo cause, even at the expense of national cohesion. For example, his appointment of an Oromo mayor for Addis Ababa, despite the city having a predominantly Amhara population, has raised questions about his commitment to maintaining the city as a neutral, pan-Ethiopian capital. Critics argue that such appointments reflect a bias that undermines the sense of inclusivity and balance that Addis Ababa historically represented.

Furthermore, Abiy's refusal to grant Addis Ababa its own regional status, a proposal that would separate the city from the Oromia Region and make it a federal entity under direct control of the central government, has led to further frustration. This indecision over the city's future status has created uncertainty about whether Addis Ababa will remain an independent capital or be absorbed more fully into Oromia. While Abiy has repeatedly stated that Addis Ababa belongs to all Ethiopians, his political actions often appear to favor the Oromo community, raising concerns among other ethnic groups, particularly the Amhara, about the true intentions behind these decisions.

The issue of Addis Ababa's governance has deepened ethnic tensions in Ethiopia. The Amhara community, which constitutes the largest ethnic group in the city, has expressed discontent with Abiy's leadership, perceiving his actions as being too heavily influenced by his Oromo background. The perception among many Amhara is that Abiy, who came to power on a platform of national reconciliation, is now too focused on promoting Oromo interests, leaving other ethnic groups feeling marginalized and excluded from the decision-making process.

The appointment of an Oromo mayor and the support for Oromo-centric policies, such as calls to integrate Addis Ababa more closely with Oromia, have been seen by some as a sign of Abiy's reluctance to maintain Addis Ababa as a truly inclusive, pan-Ethiopian city. These actions have led to suspicions that Abiy is prioritizing the Oromo identity over others, which has resulted in a loss of faith in his ability to lead Ethiopia as a unified nation. Many Amhara critics argue that Abiy's actions reflect an ethnically consumed agenda, which undermines the sense of Ethiopian nationalism and the idea of Addis Ababa as a city for all Ethiopians.

The lack of clear and decisive leadership on the issue of Addis Ababa's future has created a sense of instability and uncertainty among the Ethiopian populace. While some view Abiy as a reformer with the potential to bring about lasting peace and unity, others see his failure to address ethnic concerns, particularly the issue of Addis Ababa, as a sign of weakness and indecisiveness. As Ethiopia grapples with its identity in the context of ethnic federalism, Abiy's handling of Addis Ababa's status remains a critical issue in the broader debate over the country's future.

Addis Ababa, once considered a neutral ground for all Ethiopians, has become a microcosm of Ethiopia's larger struggles with ethnic federalism, national identity, and the balance of power between various ethnic groups. Under Abiy Ahmed's leadership, the city's future seems uncertain, as conflicting narratives about its identity, whether as a capital for all Ethiopians or as part of the Oromo region, continue to fuel division. While Abiy's rhetoric promotes unity, his policies have not fully alleviated the concerns of other ethnic groups, especially the Amhara.

The debate over Addis Ababa's future will continue to shape Ethiopia's political landscape in the coming years. Until a more balanced and inclusive approach is taken, Addis Ababa risks remaining a city divided, caught between competing national and ethnic identities and struggling to reconcile its role as the capital of a diverse and complex nation.

***

Addis Ababa: Divided and Betrayed

Addis Ababa, the beating heart of Ethiopia, was once a symbol of unity and the seat of governance for all Ethiopians. However, the city's status has become increasingly fractured in recent years, as ethnic tensions fuel divisions, turning what was once a shared capital into a battleground for political and cultural control. Under the Ethiopian People's Revolutionary Democratic Front (EPRDF), Ethiopia's 1995 constitution institutionalized ethnic federalism—a system designed to decentralize power to regional states based on ethnic lines. This system, while initially aimed at addressing the grievances of marginalized groups, has instead sown discord, especially in Addis Ababa, where the lines between ethnic identities and political power are increasingly blurred.

The constitution, which grants special privileges to the Oromo people in Addis Ababa due to its location, has led to the growing assertion that the city belongs solely to the Oromo. This claim, promoted by figures like Bekele Gerba and other prominent Oromo leaders and activists, has exacerbated the sense of exclusion and alienation among the city's other ethnic groups, particularly the Amhara, who make up the majority of the city's population. With Oromo political leaders constantly reinforcing the notion that Addis Ababa should be an Oromo city, amid ongoing calls for its incorporation into Oromia as a region, many residents feel as though they have lost their place in the very city they were born and raised in.

This tension has fostered a toxic political environment where the Oromo claim ownership over Addis Ababa, despite its diverse population. While Oromia's regional government exerts influence over the capital city, local Oromo leaders emphasize that Addis Ababa should be governed primarily by the Oromo, sidelining the interests of non-Oromo citizens. This rhetoric has not only divided the city but has also fractured the unity that once bound Ethiopians together, leaving residents feeling like strangers in their own home.

Prime Minister Abiy Ahmed, an Oromo himself, has further fueled this sense of division. Despite his rise to power being hailed as a potential bridge for Ethiopia's fractured society, his government has failed to quell the tensions surrounding Addis Ababa. Abiy's leadership has been marked by indecision and inconsistent approaches to the city's governance. While he espouses unity in public speeches, his actions often contradict his rhetoric. His failure to decisively address the issue of Addis Ababa's status, whether to make it a federal city with special autonomy or incorporate it into Oromia, has led to a growing sense of betrayal among the city's diverse population.

Abiy's appointment of Oromo leaders to key positions in Addis Ababa's administration, such as Mayor Adanech Abebe, has been perceived by some as a calculated move to placate Oromo grievances, but it has also deepened the rift between the city's ethnic groups. For many Amhara citizens, the political dominance of the Oromo in Addis Ababa feels like an imposition, reinforcing the perception that the federal government under Abiy's leadership is more concerned with appeasing one ethnic group than representing the interests of all Ethiopians. This perception has left many feeling politically marginalized and disconnected from the government, as if they have been betrayed by the very leaders they once trusted.

The EPRDF's ethnic-based federal system has only intensified these divisions, creating a governance structure that prioritizes ethnic identities over national unity. The promise of a multi-ethnic state where all citizens could coexist has been replaced by a reality where ethnic boundaries dictate access to power, resources, and even belonging. Addis Ababa, once a symbol of Ethiopian unity, has become a microcosm of Ethiopia's broader political and ethnic crises. The city's residents, regardless of their ethnic background, feel as though they are living in a city that no longer belongs to them, and they are being torn between competing forces.

The Oromo assertion of dominance in Addis Ababa, along with the federal government's failure to address this issue, has left the city's citizens feeling abandoned. Many Ethiopians in the city now experience a profound sense of displacement, having been born and raised in Addis Ababa, yet finding themselves increasingly alienated from the city's political and cultural identity. The city's residents feel as though they are children without a father, caught between conflicting narratives of ownership and belonging. They are left to navigate a city that no longer feels like their own, watching as it is claimed by one ethnic group while others are pushed to the margins.

The situation is further compounded by the broader sense of betrayal felt by many Ethiopians. Abiy's rise to power was once seen as a moment of hope for Ethiopia, a leader who would bridge divides and lead the country toward unity. Yet, his handling of the Addis Ababa issue, his indecision, his appointment of ethnically aligned leaders, and his failure to resolve the city's status, has undermined that hope.

In the end, Addis Ababa stands as a testament to the failure of Ethiopia's ethnic federalism. Rather than promoting unity, it has deepened divisions, and the city has become a symbol of the betrayal of the Ethiopian people. The citizens of Addis Ababa, who once lived in a city that embodied the hopes of all Ethiopians, now find themselves at the mercy of a political system that divides them along ethnic lines. The government, whether led by Abiy or his predecessors, has failed to deliver the unity and inclusivity that the capital city, and the country, desperately needs.

Addis Ababa, once a proud symbol of Ethiopia's unity, has become a fractured city, divided not only by political interests but also by the deep-seated ethnic divisions fostered by the country's flawed federal system. The city's citizens, whether Amhara, Oromo, or from any other ethnic group, are left searching for a sense of belonging, hoping for a government that will bridge the divisions and return Addis Ababa to its rightful place as a truly united capital for all Ethiopians. But as things stand, the city remains a painful reminder of the failure of ethnic federalism and the deep wounds it has left in the hearts of its people.

***

CHAPTER 16

Vision Alignment: Deconstructing and Reconstructing Ethiopia Along Ethnic Lines

Abiy Ahmed's vision for Ethiopia revolves around a deep transformation of the country's political, social, and economic structures, with a particular focus on the empowerment of the Oromo people. His approach aims to align the Ethiopian state with ethnic-based political dynamics, particularly the political ambitions of the Oromo people. This transformation, however, has sparked considerable debate, revealing both promises and perils for the future of the nation. Abiy's rhetoric in his speech in Nekemt, in which he presents himself as the liberator and protector of the Oromo people, marks a significant turning point in Ethiopian politics. This vision, however, must be viewed through the lens of the Oromo political discourse, which has long sought autonomy and a reimagined Ethiopian state that reflects the primacy of the Oromo identity.

***

Abiy's Alignment with Oromo Political Ambitions

Abiy's rise to power in 2018 was hailed as a potential turning point for Ethiopia, offering a glimpse of hope for marginalized groups, particularly the Oromo, the largest ethnic group in the country. In his rhetoric, Abiy positioned himself as a champion of Oromo rights and aspirations, resonating with Oromo political figures like Abo Lencho Bati, who have long advocated for greater recognition and power within the Ethiopian political system. Abiy's vision, therefore, is not merely about reconfiguring Ethiopian national identity; it is closely intertwined with the Oromo desire for autonomy, empowerment, and political recognition.

Abiy's alignment with Oromo political discourse is evident in his rhetoric, which emphasizes the importance of elevating the Oromo people within the political structure of Ethiopia. His efforts to incorporate Oromo leaders into the national conversation, his use of

Oromo language in official settings, and his focus on Oromo issues like land rights and educational reform suggest a clear intent to reshape Ethiopia in a manner that favors the Oromo. This shift towards Oromo-centered politics is significant, especially given Ethiopia's historical struggles with ethnic divisions and political inequality. For many, Abiy's approach signals a critical step toward rectifying these imbalances.

However, this focus on the Oromo also raises important questions about the broader implications for Ethiopia's unity. Ethiopia is a diverse country with over 80 ethnic groups, and Abiy's strong emphasis on Oromo politics risks alienating other groups, such as the Amhara and Tigray. These groups have long held significant political power, and Abiy's alignment with the Oromo could exacerbate existing tensions. While aligning with the Oromo may enhance Abiy's legitimacy among his core supporters, it also risks deepening ethnic divisions in an already fragmented political landscape.

The Oromo community, both within Ethiopia and in the diaspora, has long been engaged in political struggles that have shaped the nation's trajectory. The Oromo elite, activists, and diaspora populations have played pivotal roles in shaping Ethiopian politics, whether through direct involvement or through strategic advocacy for Oromo rights. Abiy's understanding of the Oromo political landscape is critical, as it informs his approach to governance. The growing strength of groups like the Oromo Liberation Front (OLF) and the Oromo Liberation Army (OLA) is a testament to the increasing political mobilization of the Oromo. These groups have evolved from political movements to armed factions, with the OLF's military wing now recognized as one of the most capable forces in Ethiopia.

The OLF's increasing military strength, combined with the growing involvement of Oromo diaspora networks, presents both a challenge and an opportunity for Abiy. While the OLF and OLA's military presence poses a threat to the stability of the Ethiopian state, it also serves as a powerful ally for Abiy as he seeks to consolidate power within Oromia. The support of Oromo elites and the Oromo diaspora provides a crucial financial and logistical base for his regime, allowing Abiy to maintain his political hold.

At the same time, the growing strength of Oromo political movements poses a challenge to the Ethiopian state. The OLF's calls for greater political autonomy and the OLA's calls for secession reflect broader aspirations for self-determination that have been long denied to the Oromo people. These demands raise important questions about the future of the Ethiopian state and the viability of a centralized, multi-ethnic Ethiopian identity.

Beneath the surface of Abiy's public persona lies a complex network of influential Oromo figures who play key roles in shaping Ethiopia's political future. Figures like Obbo Lencho Letta, Bethlehem Tafesse, and Jawar Mohammed are central to the Oromo political narrative, and their influence extends beyond the formal structures of government. These individuals, often operating behind the scenes, have been instrumental in shaping Abiy's vision for Ethiopia, which increasingly reflects Oromo-centric values and goals.

Jawar Mohammed, in particular, has become a key figure in the Oromo political movement. His advocacy for a form of "progressive patriotism" that seeks to reconcile the Oromo struggle with the broader Ethiopian state is shaping the political discourse in Ethiopia. Jawar's calls for unity, even as they distance themselves from the traditional vision of a multinational Ethiopia, reflect a shifting ideological landscape within the Oromo movement. This shift raises important questions about the future of Ethiopian unity and the role of ethnic nationalism in the nation's future.

Despite his initial popularity, Abiy faces mounting challenges both domestically and internationally. His approval has waned, particularly due to his handling of the Tigray conflict, and his domestic policies continue to sow division. In response to these challenges, Abiy appears to be shifting towards a more authoritarian style of governance. His increasing focus on consolidating power within the Oromo community may be part of this strategy, but it also risks exacerbating ethnic tensions and dividing the nation along ethnic lines.

The Politics of Deception: Abiy's Dual Strategy

Abiy's political journey has been marked by a complex relationship with Oromo activism. During the Oromo protests, Abiy covertly supported the Oromo Liberation Army (OLA), despite his public affiliation with the ruling party. This duality reflects Abiy's ability to navigate complex political dynamics while maintaining his public image as a reformer and champion of Oromo rights. His strategic use of the Afan Oromo language in public speeches serves as a tool to shield him from external criticism, allowing him to present himself as a defender of the Oromo cause while simultaneously deflecting scrutiny.

This dual strategy underscores Abiy's ability to manipulate the political narrative to his advantage. While he presents himself as a champion of Oromo rights, his true intentions often remain opaque, leading to questions about his commitment to genuine political reform. Abiy's use of language and rhetoric serves as a means of deflection, creating ambiguity that allows him to maintain his popularity among Oromo supporters while avoiding the full accountability that might come with his actions.

Abiy's political strategy hinges on cultivating fear among both his supporters and detractors. His speeches, particularly those directed at the Oromo community, often serve as psychological tools designed to instill a sense of insecurity and vulnerability. In his speech in Nekemt, for example, Abiy warned that threats to the Oromo people were mounting, while also suggesting that any resistance to his rule would result in dire consequences. This manipulation of fear is a key feature of his governance, as he seeks to consolidate power by positioning himself as the only leader capable of securing the future of the Oromo people.

Abiy's experience during the Tigray conflict has shaped his political outlook, leading him to believe that he can manage international pressure and evade consequences for any wrongdoing. This sense of impunity is reflected in his handling of accusations of human rights violations and his strategic use of international relations to bolster his legitimacy. Abiy's confidence in his ability to manipulate the international narrative underscores his belief that he can maintain power even in the face of significant criticism.

***

Abiy's Vision for Ethiopia's Future: A Divided Nation

Abiy's vision for Ethiopia increasingly appears to be one where the future of the nation is defined by ethnic divisions. His focus on the Oromo community suggests that Ethiopia's national identity will shift toward an exclusive vision of Oromo empowerment, potentially marginalizing other ethnic groups such as the Amhara. This vision poses significant risks for the future of Ethiopian unity, as it could lead to further fragmentation and conflict, particularly in regions like Addis Ababa and Oromia.

Through his strategic shifts, Abiy is steering Ethiopia toward a future in which ethnic power struggles will dominate the political landscape. While his approach may offer short-term stability for the Oromo, it risks entrenching long-term divisions that could destabilize the country. Abiy's leadership, which initially promised unity and reform, now seems to be accelerating the very ethnic tensions it sought to resolve.

The concept of the "neo-nafxanya" government is central to critiques of Abiy's regime. This term refers to the continued dominance of Amhara elites and their historical role in oppressing the Oromo and other marginalized groups. Abiy's policies, particularly his approach to land dispossession and privatization, are seen as efforts to re-establish the old power structures that perpetuated colonial oppression under the Ethiopian empire. Critics argue that Abiy's government is trying to re-establish these colonial dynamics, under the guise of modernization and national unity.

The neo-nafxanya government has also been accused of exacerbating economic inequality, particularly for the Oromo. Abiy's policies, which prioritize foreign investment and land commodification, have disproportionately impacted the Oromo people and other marginalized groups, leading to increased resistance and tension. These economic policies are seen as further entrenching the exploitation of Oromo land and resources, perpetuating a system of oppression that has existed for centuries.

***

The Repression of Oromo Nationalism and the Struggle for Self-Determination

Abiy's increasing authoritarianism has led to the suppression of Oromo nationalist movements, particularly the Oromo Liberation Army (OLA). The OLA's struggle for self-determination and political autonomy remains a central aspect of the Oromo political landscape. Abiy's attempts to dismantle the OLF and OLA have only strengthened the resolve of these movements, as the Oromo people continue to fight for their rights and liberation. The Oromo face a critical decision: whether to support Abiy's regime, which continues to perpetuate state violence and oppression, or to align with the OLF and OLA in their struggle for self-determination.

In conclusion, Abiy's vision for Ethiopia's future is marked by a shift towards ethnic-based governance, with a particular focus on the empowerment of the Oromo people. While his rhetoric aligns with Oromo political aspirations, his actions reveal a more complex and potentially dangerous strategy that risks deepening ethnic divisions and undermining Ethiopia's unity. As the Oromo continue to struggle for their rights and self-determination, they face a critical choice: either support the neo-nafxanya regime or join the fight for true liberation and sovereignty. The future of Ethiopia depends on how this struggle unfolds and whether it can be reconciled with the diverse political aspirations of the Ethiopian people.

***

Sheger City: A Vision for Urban Expansion or a Source of Ethnic Tensions?

Sheger City, a groundbreaking urban development project, has stirred controversy and debate since its inception in October 2022. Aimed at expanding Addis Ababa's influence, infrastructure, and economic capacity, the project envisions a dramatic transformation of the city's periphery and surrounding regions, potentially reshaping Ethiopia's urban landscape. But beneath the promise of growth and modernization, Sheger City has raised profound questions about its social, political, and ethnic implications, especially regarding displacement, regional inequality, and the underlying motivations of the Oromo leadership.

Sheger City is designed to encircle Addis Ababa, Ethiopia's bustling capital, creating a vast metropolitan area that stretches across three times the area of the city itself. The project aims to integrate 12 sub-cities, 36 districts, and 40 rural kebeles (villages) from the Oromia region into a larger economic and administrative framework. The project is expected to promote infrastructure development, enhance regional growth, and alleviate pressure on Addis Ababa, which has long struggled with overcrowding and inadequate infrastructure. The plan proposes the creation of a "doughnut-shaped" city around the capital, intended to boost both the city's economy and that of its neighboring towns.

Proponents of Sheger City argue that the initiative will provide much-needed modern amenities and economic opportunities to the surrounding satellite cities and districts. These new developments are anticipated to attract investment, improve transportation networks, and provide social services in previously underserved areas. Moreover, the idea behind the city's design is rooted in the "hub-and-spoke" model of urban development, which places a major city at the center of a network of smaller towns and cities, allowing for mutual growth and resource-sharing. This model has been successful in some parts of the world and is seen by supporters as a path toward sustainable urbanization in Ethiopia, which has a rapidly growing population.

However, while Sheger City's objectives seem admirable, its implementation has been deeply contentious. The project has been criticized for its methods of land acquisition and the mass displacement of thousands of residents, some of whom have lived in the area for generations. A key concern is that these displacements have disproportionately affected non-Oromo ethnic groups, particularly the Amhara population, with whom there have been historical tensions. Reports suggest that at least 100,000 people have been displaced from their homes in the name of urban development. Many of these individuals legally owned their properties, and their forced eviction, often without adequate compensation, has led to significant hardships.

In a country that has already experienced decades of ethnic-based political conflict, such actions have only fueled suspicions that the project is part of a larger agenda to "Oromize" the capital and its surrounding regions. The Oromo people, historically marginalized, have gained political prominence under Prime Minister Abiy Ahmed's leadership. However, critics argue that Abiy's government may be using Sheger City to consolidate Oromo political power at the expense of other ethnic groups, particularly the Amhara, who have long held influence in Addis Ababa.

The question of regional integrity and ethnic rights lies at the heart of the Sheger City controversy. Ethiopia is home to a diverse array of ethnic groups, and its political structure is built around a system of ethnic federalism, which grants regional autonomy to ethnic groups. This system has at times, been a source of both unity and division. The Oromo, who make up the largest ethnic group in the country, have long sought greater political representation and control over land in the regions they traditionally inhabit. The creation of Sheger City, with its expansion into Oromo-controlled areas, has been interpreted by some as an effort to secure greater Oromo dominance, leading to accusations of ethnic favoritism.

At the same time, critics argue that the project disregards the constitutional rights of other ethnic groups, particularly the Amhara, and undermines the principles of regional autonomy. The Ethiopian Constitution guarantees the right to self-determination for all ethnic groups, and forced displacements that seem to target specific communities violate these rights. For many Amharas, the destruction of their homes in the name of urban expansion is seen as an attempt to erase their presence from Addis Ababa and surrounding areas. This sense of displacement has stoked ethnic tensions, contributing to a volatile political climate.

Beyond its political and ethnic ramifications, Sheger City raises concerns about its long-term sustainability and environmental impact. The project is massive in scale, requiring extensive construction, land clearing, and resource extraction. Critics argue that such rapid urbanization could have severe consequences for the environment, particularly in a country already facing the challenges of deforestation, water scarcity, and climate change.

The environmental risks include the destruction of ecosystems, loss of biodiversity, and the potential for increased pollution. The sprawling nature of Sheger City, with its expansive urban footprint, could exacerbate these issues, further straining the already limited resources of the surrounding regions. Sustainable urban planning practices, such as prioritizing green spaces, renewable energy, and eco-friendly infrastructure, must be integrated into the design of Sheger City to mitigate these risks. Without careful planning, the project could result in a significant ecological footprint, undermining the benefits of its development.

Additionally, the forced relocation of residents, particularly those from marginalized groups, could exacerbate social inequalities. The disruption of families and communities without adequate compensation or support for resettlement could lead to greater social instability. Urban development should prioritize inclusivity and social equity, ensuring that the benefits of growth are distributed fairly across all population groups.

Prime Minister Abiy Ahmed has been at the forefront of the Sheger City initiative, and his leadership is crucial to the project's success. However, his role in the project has been scrutinized. Abiy, an Oromo leader, is seen by many as someone with a vested interest in enhancing the political power of his ethnic group. While he has championed reforms aimed at democratizing Ethiopia and fostering national unity, the implementation of Sheger City has raised doubts about the government's commitment to inclusivity.

Some view Sheger City as an extension of Abiy's efforts to consolidate Oromo political power in Ethiopia, using development projects as a means of asserting greater control over the capital and its surrounding areas. Critics argue that the project is less about urban development and more about reshaping the country's demographic and political landscape to benefit the Oromo elite. This perception has created an environment of distrust, with many citizens questioning whether their voices and rights are being fully considered in the decision-making process.

Sheger City's ambitious goals to expand Addis Ababa's influence and promote regional growth are not without merit. However, its execution has been fraught with controversy and unintended consequences. The forced displacement of residents, particularly from marginalized ethnic groups, has sparked significant opposition and raised serious concerns about social justice, ethnic equality, and political transparency.

If Sheger City is to fulfill its promise as a model of urban development, it must prioritize inclusivity, equity, and sustainability. The Ethiopian government must engage with affected communities, ensure fair compensation for displaced residents, and integrate environmental considerations into the planning process. Most importantly, the project must be viewed not just as an opportunity for growth, but as a means to foster national unity, rather than deepen ethnic divisions.

In the end, Sheger City's legacy will depend on how well it balances the goals of urban expansion with the principles of justice, environmental sustainability, and social harmony. Ethiopia stands at a crossroads, and its future urban development must be guided by the need to ensure that all citizens, regardless of ethnic background, benefit from the country's progress.

***

CHAPTER 17

The Enduring Legacy of Leadership: How Historical Figures Shape Nations

Leadership has always been one of the most crucial forces in shaping the course of history. From war to peace, economic prosperity to economic decline, and from democracy to dictatorship, leaders play a pivotal role in determining the trajectory of their nations. The choices and actions of these leaders are often irreversible, and their legacies can persist for generations, influencing the lives of their citizens and the broader global landscape. Over the last century, several historical figures have had a transformative impact on their countries, whether for better or worse. Some leaders, like Nelson Mandela, are celebrated for their dedication to peace and justice, while others, like Adolf Hitler, are remembered for the widespread devastation they caused. Here, we explore the legacies of some of these impactful leaders and their influence on history.

Winston Churchill, the Prime Minister of the United Kingdom during World War II (1940–1945) and again from 1951–1955, remains a symbol of resilience and leadership in the face of adversity. His ideological outlook was shaped by a fierce commitment to democracy, freedom, and the preservation of the British Empire. Churchill's leadership during WWII was crucial in ensuring Britain's survival against Nazi Germany, where his refusal to negotiate peace with Hitler and his focus on military strategy helped rally the nation. His famous speeches, such as "Never in the field of human conflict was so much owed by so many to so few," instilled hope and morale during the darkest days of the war. However, post-war, his influence waned as Britain grappled with economic difficulties and the process of decolonization, marking the decline of the British Empire. Churchill's post-war speeches, particularly about the Iron Curtain, would also make him an influential figure in the early stages of the Cold War.

Nelson Mandela, the first black president of South Africa (1994–1999), is globally celebrated for his leadership in ending apartheid and promoting national reconciliation. Initially a revolutionary nationalist, Mandela's views shifted towards a pragmatic approach of forgiveness and unity after his long imprisonment. He led efforts to dismantle the apartheid system peacefully, creating a multiracial democracy. His Truth and Reconciliation Commission encouraged perpetrators of apartheid-era crimes to confess in exchange for amnesty, promoting healing in a divided nation. Mandela's government focused on addressing inequality, improving education, healthcare, and land reform, although economic constraints made it difficult to achieve full transformation. His ability to negotiate a peaceful end to apartheid and transition South Africa into a democratic society made him an international symbol of peace and reconciliation.

Adolf Hitler's leadership of Nazi Germany (1933–1945) represents one of the darkest chapters in history, marked by extreme nationalism, militarism, and the belief in Aryan racial superiority. Hitler's rise to power occurred in the context of Germany's instability following World War I, the Treaty of Versailles, and the Great Depression. His economic policies, including public works programs and military rearmament, initially revived the German economy. However, his ideology of Lebensraum, or territorial expansion, led to the invasion of neighboring countries and the outbreak of World War II. Under his rule, the Holocaust led to the systematic extermination of millions of Jews, Roma, disabled individuals, and other minorities. Hitler's totalitarian regime resulted in the deaths of over 70 million people, and the war's conclusion marked the collapse of Nazi Germany, and the exposure of the atrocities committed under his regime.

Joseph Stalin's leadership of the Soviet Union (1924–1953) represents a particularly extreme form of totalitarianism, characterized by forced industrialization, political repression, and the creation of a cult of personality. Stalin's policies were rooted in Marxism-Leninism but modified to suit his vision of socialism in one country. His Five-Year Plans aimed to rapidly industrialize the Soviet Union, but they came at a human cost, with widespread famine due to forced collectivization of agriculture and the death of millions of peasants. Stalin also implemented brutal purges to eliminate political opponents, resulting in the deaths and imprisonment of millions. Despite his repressive rule, Stalin played a pivotal role in the defeat of Nazi Germany during World War II, with the Soviet Union's victory at the Battle of Stalingrad serving as a key turning point. However, Stalin's post-war leadership continued to be marked by repression, and the climate of fear he created lasted throughout the Cold War era.

Each of these leaders, Winston Churchill, Nelson Mandela, Adolf Hitler, and Joseph Stalin, had a profound impact on their nations and the world. Churchill's wartime leadership and post-war speeches set the stage for the Cold War; Mandela's efforts at reconciliation brought South Africa out of apartheid; Hitler's dictatorship plunged Europe into war and caused irreparable damage; and Stalin's rule transformed the Soviet Union into a superpower while leaving a legacy of repression. Their actions have shaped the world in lasting ways, and their legacies continue to influence global politics and the lives of those who lived through their regimes. In all, the actions of these historical figures underscore the importance of leadership in determining the fate of nations, with consequences that extend far beyond their time in power.

***

Abiy Ahmed vs. Winston Churchill

Winston Churchill was known for his decisive leadership, particularly during World War II, when the fate of the United Kingdom and much of Europe hung in the balance. Churchill's leadership was marked by bold, resolute decisions in the face of overwhelming odds, never wavering from his commitment to democratic values and freedom. He had an undeniable authenticity in his decision-making that earned him the trust of both his people and the world.

In contrast, Abiy Ahmed's leadership has been marked by hesitation and inconsistency, especially as his early reforms were followed by a growing authoritarian streak. Churchill made difficult decisions that were always geared towards national survival and global peace, even when unpopular. Abiy, on the other hand, has struggled to maintain authenticity in his decisions, often appearing to make changes that are more for international recognition than genuine political reform. While Churchill stood firm in the face of fascism and tyranny, Abiy's decisions have fluctuated between peace-building gestures and military escalation, especially regarding the Tigray and Amhara conflict. This inconsistency in decision-making weakens Abiy's leadership credibility, in stark contrast to Churchill's decisiveness and unwavering commitment to his nation and its principles.

Abiy, in a sense, is not as decisive as Churchill was, and this difference speaks to the heart of his leadership style. While Churchill's decisions were defined by action and certainty, Abiy's choices seem often shaped by political convenience or external pressures, leading to a less consistent vision for the future of Ethiopia.

***

Abiy Ahmed vs. Nelson Mandela

Nelson Mandela's leadership was authentic, deeply rooted in his moral authority, and based on the values of justice, reconciliation, and democracy. Mandela's authenticity, derived from his sacrifices during his imprisonment, gave him the credibility to unite a fractured South Africa, embracing his moral high ground even when faced with monumental challenges. His commitment to forgiveness and truth-telling in the Truth and Reconciliation Commission were testaments to his vision for nation-building.

In stark contrast, Abiy Ahmed has often been accused of being inauthentic and lacking a strong moral foundation. His early promises of political and economic reform have been overshadowed by his increasingly centralized approach to power. Critics suggest that his actions, such as his involvement in the Tigray and Amhara conflict and suppression of opposition, have exposed him as a leader who may not fully embrace the principles of reconciliation that he initially espoused. Whereas Mandela's legacy is defined by his deep sense of authenticity, integrity, and a commitment to justice, Abiy's evolving policies have given rise to the perception that he may not be as genuine in his reformist promises. His diplomatic peace with Eritrea earned him global recognition, but his domestic leadership has been marked by a growing divide between his actions and his initial image as a peace-oriented reformer.

***

Abiy Ahmed vs. Adolf Hitler

Abiy's leadership stands in stark contrast to Adolf Hitler's extremist, racist ideology and the destruction wrought by his totalitarian regime. However, the comparison between the two lies in the increasing centralization of power. While Hitler used fascism to consolidate control over Germany and pursued military expansionism, Abiy, under the guise of peace and democratic reform, has increasingly centralized authority and used the military to suppress opposition, as seen in the Tigray and Amhara conflict. Both leaders, while vastly different in their political ideologies, share a tendency to control information, silence dissent, and suppress opposition when it threatens their vision of national unity.

While Hitler's rule was driven by a toxic, radical ideology that aimed to exterminate entire populations, Abiy's leadership increasingly reflects the kind of authoritarian control that stifles **freedom of expression and democratic** governance. His shifting from a democratic reformist to a hidden dictator mirrors the way authoritarian leaders manipulate political systems for personal gain, using military and political power to maintain control.

***

Abiy Ahmed vs. Joseph Stalin

When compared to Joseph Stalin, Abiy's leadership begins to show more similarities than differences. Stalin ruled the Soviet Union with a strong hand, one marked by extreme repression, purges, and the suppression of political opposition. Abiy's leadership, despite initial reformist gestures, has increasingly mirrored Stalin's centralizing tendencies, particularly in his treatment of political rivals and his military approach to internal dissent.

Under Stalin's rule, absolute control over the state was paramount, and Stalin's use of the secret police, surveillance, and political purges were tools to maintain authority. Similarly, Abiy's government has employed military force, media censorship, and political manipulation to suppress opposition, particularly in the Tigray, Amhara, and Oromia region. While Stalin's methods were brutally repressive, Abiy's more subtle form of authoritarianism has been harder to expose, hiding behind the narrative of democratic reforms while tightening his grip on power. Like Stalin, Abiy has taken advantage of national security threats to justify repression and limit democratic freedoms, indicating the hidden dictatorship nature of his rule.

Like Stalin, Abiy appears willing to sacrifice the lives of his people for the sake of consolidating power and controlling the narrative. Stalin's purges, which saw millions executed or sent to labor camps, were justified by the claim that they were necessary for the survival of the state. Similarly, Abiy has justified his military actions in Tigray and other regions as necessary to maintain national unity and defeat terrorism, even as these actions have resulted in widespread civilian deaths and atrocities.

Abiy's leadership is increasingly characterized by centralized power, militarization, and a willingness to sacrifice innocent lives for the sake of political control. His government has been accused of war crimes, including the targeting of civilians and the destruction of religious sites, drawing parallels to Stalin's use of terror to suppress dissent and maintain absolute control.

Joseph Stalin was infamous for his use of military force, purges, and terror to secure his power and eliminate perceived enemies. Stalin used the Red Army and secret police (NKVD) to enforce his regime's authority. This included large-scale executions, mass imprisonments, and forced labor camps, which devastated millions of Soviet citizens. Stalin's Great Terror in the late 1930s saw hundreds of thousands of Soviet citizens arrested and executed on fabricated charges of treason or espionage.

Similarly, Abiy Ahmed has increasingly relied on military intervention and violent repression to suppress opposition and control the country. The Tigray and Amhara War and the military offensive in the Oromia regions are notable examples of Abiy's use of the military to deal with opposition, both ethnic and political. Under Abiy's leadership, the Ethiopian National Defense Force (ENDF), with drones and airstrikes, has targeted civilians, including women, children, and the elderly. Like Stalin, Abiy has justified these acts of repression by claiming that they are necessary for the survival of the state, while systematically violating human rights and engaging in war crimes.

Both leaders, despite their distinct historical and political contexts, share a tendency to turn to violence and military force as a primary tool to quash resistance and maintain absolute control.

One of Stalin's most notorious actions was his targeting of specific ethnic groups and political rivals. He used ethnic purges, most famously the Great Famine in Ukraine (Holodomor), to eliminate perceived threats to his regime. Stalin's policies led to the deaths of millions of Ukrainians, as well as mass deportations of groups such as the Chechens and Crimean Tatars. He also engaged in purges that wiped out intellectuals, military leaders, and politicians who could potentially challenge his authority.

Similarly, Abiy Ahmed's violent campaigns have targeted specific ethnic groups in Ethiopia. The ongoing conflict in Tigray has seen the targeted killings of Tigrayans by Ethiopian forces, with the Amhara and Oromia regions also witnessing significant violence and the targeting of ethnic groups associated with political opposition. Abiy's government has also been accused of ethnic profiling and using ethnic divisions to justify violent actions, like Stalin's policies of purging and targeting ethnic groups that were seen as potential threats to state control. Both leaders engaged in ethnic scapegoating to consolidate power and eliminate internal opposition.

Joseph Stalin was notorious for the cult of personality that he built around himself. Stalin's image was omnipresent across the Soviet Union, his portraits adorned government buildings, schools, and public spaces. His ideology became inseparable from the Soviet state, and his authority was portrayed as absolute and infallible. Dissent was equated with treason against the state and Stalin's leadership, and any opposition was brutally crushed.

Abiy Ahmed has similarly cultivated a cult of personality around himself, especially after receiving the Nobel Peace Prize in 2019. Abiy's image is often celebrated across Ethiopian media, and his reforms are presented as vital to the country's future. He has used his personal brand to shape Ethiopia's national identity, positioning himself as a reformer and visionary while presenting his critics as enemies of the state. However, beneath the image of a reformist lies the growing centralization of power around Abiy, and the suppression of any potential political threats.

Abiy's consolidation of power through the Ethiopian People's Revolutionary Democratic Front (EPRDF) and his personal authority has created a political climate where dissent is increasingly seen as an attack on both the state and Abiy himself, reinforcing his position as the unquestionable leader of Ethiopia, much like Stalin's absolute control over the Soviet Union.

Stalin maintained power by using fear, propaganda, and the suppression of free speech. He controlled the media, distorted historical narratives, and utilized the NKVD to ensure that any challenge to his authority was silenced. Those who dared to speak out against Stalin's policies were imprisoned, tortured, or executed.

Abiy Ahmed has followed a similar trajectory when it comes to controlling information and suppressing dissent. His government has cracked down on opposition leaders, journalists, and activists. There have been widespread reports of the arrest of political rivals, including those who challenge his narrative or stand against the violent repression in Amhara and other regions. Additionally, Abiy's government has imposed media blackouts and internet shutdowns in regions to control the flow of information and prevent news of atrocities from reaching the outside world. The media has been largely state-controlled, and any narrative that criticizes Abiy's actions is often censored or discredited as foreign interference or terrorism.

In both cases, these leaders have built a political climate of fear where dissent is silenced, and anyone who challenges the status quo risks being punished or eliminated. In Stalin's case, this meant purges, executions, and imprisonment; for Abiy, it often means detention, military retaliation, and political exile.

Joseph Stalin expertly used propaganda to legitimize his brutal actions. The purges, forced collectivization, and mass executions were often portrayed as necessary for the greater good of the state and in defense of the Soviet Union from internal and external enemies. Stalin's regime justified atrocities by framing them as part of a grand ideological mission, thereby diverting attention away from the violence and oppression.

Abiy has similarly utilized propaganda to frame his violent actions as part of a national struggle. For example, the conflict in Tigray has been portrayed as an essential battle against terrorism and separatism, despite the overwhelming evidence of widespread atrocities and crimes against humanity. Like Stalin's use of propaganda to justify state violence, Abiy's government has framed military intervention and attacks on civilians as part of state security efforts, while labeling dissenters and opposition groups as traitors and terrorists. This propaganda has played a key role in maintaining support for his regime and justifying its increasing authoritarian tendencies.

The comparisons between Abiy Ahmed and Joseph Stalin reveal striking similarities in how both leaders have manipulated their positions of power to consolidate control through violence, repression, and propaganda. Stalin's legacy as a brutal dictator who used fear and terror to maintain power is mirrored by Abiy's increasingly authoritarian rule, which relies on military force to suppress opposition and ethnic groups that challenge his authority. Both have created a cult of personality, suppressed dissent, and targeted those who pose a threat to their power.

Abiy Ahmed's leadership, which began with hopeful promises of democratic reform, now increasingly resembles the Stalinist model of centralization and repression, where violence and fear are used to maintain an iron grip on the country. His legacy, if left unchecked, may very well mirror that of Stalin, one of cruelty, betrayal, and mass suffering for the sake of political power.

Finally, Abiy Ahmed's leadership has taken a disturbing turn from reformist promises to authoritarian violence. His use of military force, including drone strikes and helicopter attacks on civilian populations, his targeting of religious institutions, and the mass killing of innocent people in Amhara, Tigray, and Oromia have led many to compare him to Joseph Stalin. Despite his initial image as a peacemaker, Abiy's actions reveal a hidden dictatorship that mirrors the brutal tactics of historical despots.

While the full extent of his legacy is still unfolding, the violence and destruction carried out under his regime suggest that, like Stalin, Abiy may be willing to sacrifice his people in the name of power consolidation. His growing reliance on military force, the suppression of political freedoms, and the repression of ethnic and political groups point to a tragic legacy of authoritarianism that will likely define his rule in the years to come.

***

Abiy Ahmed vs. Bashar al-Assad

The leadership of both Abiy Ahmed and Bashar al-Assad, President of Syria, offers a striking illustration of the dangers posed by authoritarian rule. While their countries are geographically and historically distinct, both leaders exhibit alarming similarities in how they maintain power, manipulate national identity, and suppress opposition. Their leadership styles are defined by a ruthless use of military force, the exploitation of nationalism and religion to bolster their image, and a pervasive disregard for human rights. Both leaders, despite initially presenting themselves as reformers, have become entrenched in a system of governance that favors the elite, silences dissent, and sacrifices the welfare of their people.

Abiy Ahmed and Bashar al-Assad initially rose to power with promises of reform. Abiy was heralded as a symbol of hope, securing the Nobel Peace Prize for his efforts to end the 20-year conflict with neighboring Eritrea. Similarly, Bashar al-Assad, who took power in Syria in 2000 after the death of his father, initially promised to modernize the country and usher in political reform. However, as their time in office progressed, both leaders revealed their authoritarian tendencies. They leveraged military power to crush dissent, restrict freedoms, and eliminate opposition. For both men, maintaining power became the central focus of their rule, achieved through force and manipulation of national narratives.

One of the most striking similarities between Abiy and Assad is their use of nationalism and religion to consolidate their power. Assad has presented himself as the protector of Syria's Arab identity, despite his Alawite minority background. By framing his leadership as a bulwark against sectarianism and foreign intervention, he has cultivated a narrative of national unity, all while systematically targeting and suppressing political opponents. Similarly, Abiy Ahmed has championed the idea of a unified Ethiopia, using *Medemer* as a justification for his increasingly authoritarian policies.

Military power is another key element in both leaders' political arsenals. Assad's leadership is inextricably linked to the use of force, particularly during the Syrian Civil War, where his regime has been accused of employing chemical weapons, indiscriminate bombings, and torture against civilians. The support of foreign powers, notably Russia and Iran, has been crucial in maintaining Assad's grip in Syria, even as international condemnation mounts. Abiy, who was initially celebrated for securing peace with Eritrea, has faced mounting criticism for his handling of the Tigray and Amhara conflict. The war in Tigray and Amhara has led to widespread atrocities, including extrajudicial killings, sexual violence, and the displacement of millions of people. While Abiy initially portrayed himself as a peacemaker, his military actions have exposed his willingness to use force to preserve his power and suppress opposition.

Both leaders have also fostered a cult of personality, surrounding themselves with loyalists who offer public displays of adoration and support. In Syria, Assad's regime stages carefully orchestrated events where crowds of loyalists are mobilized to demonstrate their allegiance, contributing to a carefully curated image of widespread national support. In Ethiopia, Abiy similarly enjoys a loyal following, with supporters presenting him as a savior of the nation. This display of loyalty is essential for both leaders, as it serves to obscure the deepening divisions and increasing repression within their countries. The loyalty of these supporters is often rewarded with political positions, economic opportunities, and public accolades, further cementing the leaders' power.

Corruption and self-enrichment are also hallmarks of both regimes. Bashar al-Assad's family and close allies have amassed significant wealth by controlling key sectors of Syria's economy, including the military-industrial complex and the oil trade. His rule has been characterized by rampant corruption, with state resources used to enrich the Assad family and its supporters. Similarly, Abiy Ahmed's government has faced accusations of cronyism, with many of his supporters benefiting from political and business opportunities linked to his rule. While Abiy initially promised economic reform, his administration has been accused of sidelining ordinary Ethiopians while catering to a small elite that helps sustain his power.

The most disturbing similarity between Abiy and Assad is their shared disregard for human rights. Under Assad's regime, millions of Syrians have suffered from violence, displacement, and loss of life. The Syrian government has been accused of committing war crimes, including the use of chemical weapons, targeting civilian infrastructure, and executing political dissidents. In Ethiopia, Abiy's government has faced allegations of war crimes, including massacres, the targeting of civilians, and the obstruction of humanitarian aid during the Tigray conflict. Both leaders have engaged in large-scale repression, with critics and opposition figures either silenced or eliminated. The use of violence against civilians has become a tool for both leaders to maintain control and suppress any challenge to their authority.

Ultimately, the leadership of Abiy Ahmed and Bashar al-Assad highlights the dangers of authoritarianism and the ways in which power can be maintained through military force, manipulation of national identity, and suppression of human rights. Both men, despite their initial promises of reform, have shown a willingness to resort to violence and corruption to preserve their hold on power. They have used religion and nationalism as tools to unite their populations under a banner of loyalty, while their regimes have become increasingly defined by brutality, repression, and self-interest. In both Syria and Ethiopia, the true cost of their leadership has been borne by the people, whose lives have been shattered by war, corruption, and the relentless pursuit of power.

***

CHAPTER 18

Ethiopia's Path Forward: A Nation at a Crossroads.

Ethiopia, once hailed as a beacon of progress and potential in Africa, now finds itself at a critical juncture in its history. Prime Minister Abiy Ahmed, who rose to power in 2018 with promises of reform, peace, and unity, was initially met with widespread hope. His leadership was seen as an opportunity to break free from the political stagnation and ethnic tensions that had long characterized the country. However, under his rule, Ethiopia has witnessed profound changes, many of which have left the nation deeply divided, economically fragile, and politically unstable. The future of Ethiopia, once imagined unified, is now uncertain, with many wondering whether the country can overcome its profound crises or if it is on the brink of disintegration.

Under Abiy's leadership, Ethiopia underwent significant political changes, the most notable being the dissolution of the Ethiopian People's Revolutionary Democratic Front (EPRDF) in favor of the Prosperity Party. This shift, which was intended to create a more centralized and unified government, instead deepened Ethiopia's ethnic divisions. The EPRDF had allowed for a delicate balance of power between the country's various ethnic groups, but the move toward a more centralized party alienated key groups, particularly the Tigrayans. The result was a surge in ethnic nationalism and regionalism, leading to violent clashes and political fragmentation. The eruption of the Tigray War in November 2020, which has continued to devastate the northern part of the country, marked a stark turning point in Ethiopia's descent into a civil conflict. The war has claimed thousands of lives, displaced millions, and left the Tigray region in ruins. The Ethiopian government's military response to the conflict has exacerbated social divisions, and the humanitarian situation remains dire, with widespread suffering and deprivation.

The Tigray War is emblematic of a broader political crisis in Ethiopia, one in which Abiy's government has increasingly relied on authoritarian measures. Despite his early promises of democratic reform, human rights abuses, media censorship, and the suppression of dissent have become commonplace. Political opposition, journalists, and civil society activists have been targeted, arrested, or silenced. Abiy's response to unrest in regions like Oromia and Amhara has been marked by violence, with the government using heavy-handed tactics to quell protests and dissent. His leadership, once seen as a symbol of hope, has increasingly been viewed as repressive and intolerant of opposition. The question remains: can Abiy steer the country back toward unity and democracy, or has his government exacerbated Ethiopia's divisions to the point of no return?

Socially, Ethiopia has become a country deeply fragmented along ethnic lines. Under the EPRDF's system of ethnic federalism, Ethiopia's various ethnic groups were given a degree of autonomy, but this model also contributed to a sense of division and competition for resources. Abiy's push to dismantle the ethnic federalism system, while well-intentioned in promoting national unity, has instead fueled ethnic nationalism and competition between groups. The result has been an increase in violent clashes between ethnic militias, further destabilizing the country. More than 2.9 million people are currently displaced within Ethiopia, while many others have sought refuge in neighboring countries. The country's youth, once optimistic about Abiy's promise of a new Ethiopia, have become disillusioned as they face high unemployment, limited opportunities, and a lack of political voice. Their growing frustration and political apathy are a reflection of the broader discontent with the government's failure to address the needs of the population, particularly the most marginalized groups.

Economically, Ethiopia has faced significant setbacks under Abiy's leadership. The country, once lauded for its rapid economic growth, is now struggling with high inflation, rising costs of living, and increasing poverty. Abiy's ambitious plans to privatize state-owned enterprises and attract foreign investment have largely faltered, hindered by resistance from entrenched political elites and the centralization of power. Key sectors, such as telecommunications and energy, remain under state control, and the private sector has struggled to develop in a business environment characterized by political instability. The ongoing conflict, particularly the Tigray War, has only worsened the economic situation. The war has drained national resources, disrupted trade, and devastated infrastructure, leaving much of northern Ethiopia in ruins. Agriculture, a cornerstone of the Ethiopian economy, has been severely impacted, and millions of people are facing hunger as food aid efforts have been disrupted. The economic damage caused by the conflict has compounded the challenges of poverty and inequality, making the prospect of recovery seem distant.

The international community has watched Ethiopia's descent into crisis with growing concern, but efforts to intervene have been met with limited success. Calls for accountability for human rights abuses, particularly those committed during the Tigray War, have been met with resistance from the Ethiopian government. Despite a 2022 cessation of hostilities agreement between the federal government and Tigray authorities, abuses have continued, and the humanitarian situation remains dire. The international community's role in supporting Ethiopia's recovery is critical, but the success of any efforts will depend on the willingness of the Ethiopian government to make meaningful changes and allow for genuine peace and reconciliation. The failure to address the root causes of the conflict, particularly ethnic tensions and political repression, risks prolonging the crisis.

Amid these profound challenges, there remains a glimmer of hope. The future of Ethiopia is not predetermined. While the country faces deep political, social, and economic crises, it is not beyond recovery. The path forward will require a concerted effort to address the deep divisions that have fragmented the country and to rebuild the trust that has been eroded by years of conflict and authoritarian rule. Political reconciliation must be at the heart of any effort to rebuild Ethiopia. A political settlement that includes all ethnic groups and political factions is essential to ending the conflict and promoting national unity. The government must also allow for greater political freedoms, respect for human rights, and the active participation of civil society in decision-making processes.

Ethiopia's economic recovery will depend on both internal reforms and external support. The privatization of key sectors should be pursued, but in a way that ensures fairness and reduces the influence of powerful elites. Efforts to rebuild infrastructure and revitalize agriculture and industry will be crucial to the country's long-term growth. The focus must be on sustainable development, and there is an opportunity to harness Ethiopia's rich natural resources to build a more diversified economy that can provide jobs and opportunities for its growing population.

Finally, Ethiopia's youth must be empowered to lead the country into the future. With a population that is overwhelmingly young, the success of Ethiopia's recovery will depend on providing the youth with opportunities for education, employment, and political engagement. Young people must be given a seat at the table in the country's future, both in terms of policymaking and in shaping the nation's economic direction.

Ethiopia's path forward is fraught with challenges, but it is not without hope. The nation's future hinges on the ability of its leaders, its people, and the international community to come together to address the deep divisions that have fractured the country. If Ethiopia can heal its ethnic divides, rebuild its economy, and restore democratic principles, it could once again emerge as a model of growth and stability in Africa. But if these issues remain unaddressed, Ethiopia may continue down a path of fragmentation and decline. The coming years will be decisive for Ethiopia, and the choices made now will determine whether the country can overcome its crises and build a more unified and prosperous future.

***

Bibliography

- Aalen, L. (2011). *Ethnic Federalism in Ethiopia: A Balance Between Unity and Diversity. African Affairs*, 110(440), 206-226.
- Aalen, Lovise. Ethnic Federalism in Ethiopia: A Response to Political Diversity. African Affairs, Vol. 104, No. 416, 2005.
- Abbink, J. (2011). *Ethnicity and Conflict in the Horn of Africa*. African Studies Review, 54(2), 121-138.
- Abbink, J. (2019). *The Tigray War and the Ethiopian State: Causes, Developments, and Consequences. African Political Science Review*, 38(2), 1-15.

- Abbink, J. (2019). *Ethiopia: The Politics of Despair and Hope*. Oxford University Press.
- Abir, M. *Ethiopia and the Red Sea: The Rise and Decline of the Aksumite Empire*. Cambridge University Press, 1974.
- "Abiy Ahmed: A Biography of Ethiopia's Reformer" The Economist, 2020. *https://www.economist.com/ethiopia/abiy-ahmed-biography*
- "Abiy Ahmed and Ethiopia's Global Positioning: A Leader in Crisis?" International Affairs Review, 2021. *https://www.iarjournal.com/abiy-ahmed-ethiopia-global-positioning*
- "Abiy Ahmed and the Philosophy of Medemer: A New Political Order?" African Review of Books, 2020. *https://africanreviewofbooks.com/articles/abiy-ahmed-philosophy-medemer*
- "Abiy Ahmed and the Prospects of Unity in Ethiopia: Political Consolidation or Authoritarianism?" International Political Science Review, 2021. *https://journals.sagepub.com/home/ips*
- "Abiy Ahmed and the Role of the Military in Ethiopian Politics" Journal of Modern African Studies, 2020. https://www.cambridge.org/core/journals/journal-of-modern-african-studies/article/abiy-ahmed-and-the-role-of-the-military-in-ethiopian-politics/9F55F4D0A8E1D426350E5FFFAED04F7

- "Abiy Ahmed's Leadership and the Tigray Crisis" Human Rights Watch, 2021. *https://www.hrw.org/ethiopia-tigray-conflict-abiy-ahmed*
- "Abiy Ahmed's Rise and Fall: The Narcissism of Leadership"
  The International Journal of Political Psychology, 2021. *https://journals.sagepub.com/home/jpp*
- "Abiy Ahmed's Rise and Controversies," The Guardian, 2021. *https://www.theguardian.com/world/abiy-ahmed-ethiopia*
- Ackroyd, Peter R. (2000). "The Biblical Representation of Ethiopia: A Cultural and Political Overview." *Journal of Biblical Literature*, 119(2), 189-204.
- Abiy Ahmed's Public Statements. "Prime Minister Abiy Ahmed's Address to Parliament on Human Rights and Security in Ethiopia." *Ethiopian Federal Parliament*, 2024.
- Adamu, S. (2021). *The Rise and Fall of Abiy Ahmed: Ethiopia's Political Crisis. Global Politics Review*, 30(3), 145-160.
- Adar, K. G. (2020). *Ethiopia's Peace Process with Eritrea: Implications for Regional Stability. Journal of African Political Economy*, 49(2), 221-240.
- "Agricultural Growth Program: Progress and Challenges," Ethiopian Ministry of Agriculture, 2021. *https://www.moa.gov.et/agriculture-programs*
- Al Jazeera. (2021). "Abiy Ahmed's Struggle: Ethiopia's War and the Future of the Horn of Africa."
- Al Jazeera. "The Rise and Fall of Abiy Ahmed." Al Jazeera, 2022.
- Aalen, Lovise. Ethnic Federalism in Ethiopia: A Response to Political Diversity. African Affairs, Vol. 104, No. 416, 2005.
- Alemu, D. (2021). *Ethiopian Elections in the Post-Abiy Era: A Democratic Outlook? Journal of Political Change*, 42(3), 212-230.
- Alemu, S. (2021). *Ethnic Federalism and the Ethiopian State: The Politics of Division.* Oxford University Press.
- Alpers, E. A. *East Africa and the Indian Ocean.* Prentice Hall, 1984.

- Al-Shehabi, T. (2020). *Regionalism and Political Stability in Ethiopia: A Study of the Abiy Ahmed Administration. African Journal of Political Economy*, 32(3), 180-198.
- "Amhara Conflict: Drone Strikes and Civilian Casualties in Mehalganat." BBC News, October 2024.
- Amnesty International. "Ethiopia: Systematic Human Rights Violations Amid Conflict." Amnesty International, 2023.
- Amnesty International. (2020). *Ethiopia: The Tigray Conflict and Human Rights Violations.*
- Ashenafi, A. (2020). *Human Rights Violations in the Tigray Conflict: A Case Study. Journal of African Conflict Resolution*, 34(1), 44-68.
- Assefa, Fisseha. Ethnic Federalism in Ethiopia: A Political History of the Oromo People. African Studies Review, 2004.
- "Drone and Airstrike Attacks on Amhara Region: Documenting the Humanitarian Crisis." Amhara Association of America, October 2024.
- Baechler, G. (2018). *The Impact of Ethnic Federalism on Ethiopian Political Stability. Journal of Peace Research*, 55(4), 487-500.
- Bahiru, Z. (2015). *A History of Modern Ethiopia, 1855–1991*. Oxford University Press.
- Balthasar, Simon. Oromo Nationalism and the Politics of Identity in Ethiopia. University of Chicago Press, 2017.
- Bauer, L. A. *The Ethiopian Orthodox Church and the Problem of Cultural Identity.* Cambridge University Press, 2001.
- BBC News. "Abiy Ahmed's Leadership: Reforms and Repression in Ethiopia." *BBC World News*, 2022. Retrieved from: https://www.bbc.com/news/ethiopia
- BBC News. (2019). "Abiy Ahmed: The Ethiopian Prime Minister Who Won the Nobel Peace Prize."
- Bekele, G. The Impact of the Ethiopian State on the Oromo: Political, Social, and Economic Dimensions. Addis Ababa University Press, 2001.
- Berhanou, A. *The History of Ethiopia: From the Aksumite Kingdom to the Modern Era.* Oxford University Press, 2007.

- Berhanu, W. (2019). *The Ethiopian People's Revolutionary Democratic Front (EPRDF) and the Crisis of Ethnic Federalism. The Journal of African History*, 60(1), 1-20.
- Binns, P. *Ethiopia: A New History.* James Currey, 2013.
- Bojórquez, A. (2020). *Oromo Political Movements and the Struggle for Self-Determination in Ethiopia.* Journal of African Political Economy, 29(1), 75-92.
- Brewer, David. (2006). *Ethiopia and the Bible: A Historical Exploration of Its Place in Biblical Texts.* Tyndale House.
- Bromwich, D. (2021). *Tigray: Ethiopia's Humanitarian Disaster and International Responses. Foreign Affairs Review*, 38(2), 122-135.
- Brown, T. (2021). *Conflict, Governance, and Human Rights in Ethiopia: Lessons Learned from the Tigray Crisis. African Governance Review*, 25(3), 120-138.
- Clapham, C. (2017). *The Horn of Africa: Politics and International Relations.* Cambridge University Press.
- Clapham, C. (2017). *The Horn of Africa: State Politics and International Relations.* Polity Press.
- Cohen, R. *The Aksumite Kingdom: A Civilization of the Red Sea.* University of Pennsylvania Press, 1978.
- de Waal, A. (2019). *The Tigray War: Ethiopia's Crisis of Sovereignty. African Affairs*, 118(472), 1-20.
- Dejene, D. (2020). *The Political Economy of Ethiopia's Development: Tensions Between Growth and Equity. Development Studies Quarterly*, 32(2), 102-120.
- Ehrlich, R. (2020). *A History of Ethiopia: From the Ancient Kingdoms to the Present.* Vintage Books.
- "ENDF Drone Strikes Create 'Living Nightmare' in Amhara Region." Addis Standard, November 2024.
- Ethiopia: Displacement and Forced Evictions," Human Rights Watch, 2023. *https://chatgpt.com/#:~:text=https%3A//www.hrw.org/world%2Dreport/2023/country%2Dchapters/ethiopia*
- Ethiopian Human Rights Commission. "2021 Report on Human Rights Violations and the Justice System in Oromiya." *Ethiopian Human Rights Commission (EHRC),* 2021.

- "Ethiopia's Prime Minister Abiy Ahmed: The Dangers of Self-Celebration and Political Narcissism" Al Jazeera, 2020. *https://www.aljazeera.com/opinions/2020/11/11/ethiopias-prime-minister-abiy-ahmed-the-dangers-of-self-celebration*
- "Fano Militia's Struggle for Survival and Its Impact on Ethiopia's Future." The Economist, October 27, 2024.
- Fekadu, A. *Ethiopia: Historical Essays on Religion, Politics, and Society.* Oxford University Press, 1998.
- Fessha, Y. T. (2020). Federalism and the Ethnic Conflict in Ethiopia: The Tigray Issue. International Journal of Constitutional Law, 18(3), 469-490.
- Fissha, A. (2020). "Abiy Ahmed's Ethiopia: From Promise to Crisis." *Journal of African Political Economy*, 15(3), 120-137.
- Fisher, H. A. S. *The History of Ethiopia: From the Earliest Times to the Rise of Aksum.* Oxford University Press, 1926.
- Fikre, T. (2020). *Ethnic Federalism and the Challenges of Unity in Ethiopia. The Journal of Political Transformation*, 36(3), 234-250.
- Fleming, Daniel E. (2004). *The Legacy of Cush: Ethiopian Influence in the Ancient World.* Oxford University Press.
- Food Insecurity and Poverty in Ethiopia," Food Security Portal, 2022.
- Gelman, V. (2017). Syria's Alawites: The Rise of the Assad Regime. The Brookings Institution.
- "Gender and Agriculture in Ethiopia: Opportunities and Challenges," Food and Agriculture Organization of the United Nations (FAO), 2022. *https://www.fao.org/ethiopia/gender*
- Getachew, M. *The Role of Ethiopia in Global History: An Overview.* Addis Ababa University, 2005.
- Girma, H. (2021). *Abiy Ahmed and the Promise of Unity: The Oromo in Ethiopian Politics.* Addis Ababa University Press.
- Hagos, W. (2021). *Ethiopia's Economic Transformation and the Abiy Ahmed Administration: Success or Failure? The Journal of African Economic Development*, 23(2), 92-110.

- Hassen, H. (2021). *Abiy Ahmed and Ethiopia's Transition: The Rise and Fall of a Political Vision. Journal of African Politics*, 40(1), 78-96.
- Habte, M. (2020). *The Impact of Conflict on Ethiopia's Economy: A Longitudinal Study. International Development Economics Journal*, 28(4), 230-249.
- Harris, Stephen L. (2014). "Ethiopia in the Biblical Tradition: From the Garden to the New Covenant." *Biblical Archaeology Review*, 40(6), 30-41.
- Hassen, Mohammed. The Oromo of Ethiopia: A History 1570-1860. Cambridge University Press, 1990.
- Heath, Derek. (2011). *Ethiopia in the Bible: A Theological and Historical Perspective.* InterVarsity Press.
- Hiruy, H. (2021). The Tigray Conflict and Ethiopia's Fragile Peace. The Ethiopian International Journal of Peace and Conflict.
- Human Rights Watch. (2021). *World Report 2021: Ethiopia.*
- International Crisis Group. "Ethiopia: A Country on the Brink." International Crisis Group, 2023.
- International Crisis Group. "Ethiopia's Complex Ethnic Politics and Abiy Ahmed's Reform Agenda." *International Crisis Group*, 2023.
  Retrieved from: https://www.crisisgroup.org/africa/ethiopia
- International Crisis Group. (2021). *Ethiopia's Tigray War: A Costly Conflict for All.*
- Jalata, Asafa. Oromo Nationalism and the Ethiopian State: The Political Legacies of Meles Zenawi and Abiy Ahmed. University of Toronto Press, 2020.
- Kadi, J. (2020). The Role of Nationalism and Religion in Middle Eastern Politics: A Comparative Study of Bashar al-Assad and Other Authoritarian Leaders. Middle East Review of International Affairs, 24(1), 45-58.
- Kassahun, G. (2022). *Abiy Ahmed: A Study of His Leadership and Vision.* Oxford University Press.
- Kassaye, G. (2022). *The Ethiopian State and Nationalism: The Rise of Abiy Ahmed and the Crisis of Federalism.* African Journal of Political Science, 34(3), 215-233.

- Kassem, F. (2019). The Political Economy of Syria: Corruption and Cronyism under Bashar al-Assad. The Middle East Journal, 73(4), 551-573.
- Kemenyi, M. S. (2021). *Ethiopian Politics and the Path to Stability: The Role of Ethnic Federalism. Journal of African Economic Studies*, 44(3), 251-270.
- Kefyalew, W. (2020). *Reforming Ethiopia's Ethnic Federalism: Challenges and Prospects. African Political Science Journal*, 19(4), 303-319.
- Kellermann, Karl. (1997). *The Nations in the Bible: A Biblical Geography of the Nations and Peoples of the Ancient World*. Baker Academic.
- Kuyper, M. *The Solomonic Dynasty and the Making of Ethiopian Culture*. University of California Press, 2010.
- Kritzeck, J. *The History of the Ethiopian Orthodox Church*. Georgetown University Press, 1963.
- Leake, L. (2020). *Ethnic Tensions and Political Crisis in Ethiopia: A Study of Abiy Ahmed's Leadership. Journal of African Politics and Governance*, 45(4), 307-320.
- Laitin, D. D. (2020). *Ethiopia's Political and Economic Transition: The Challenge of Unity and Diversity. Political Science Quarterly*, 135(4), 499-520.
- Lata, B. The Oromo People and Their Struggle for Self-Determination. The International Journal of African Historical Studies, 2015.
- Lewis, I. M. (2002). *The Ethnic Factor in Ethiopia's Politics*. Middle Eastern Studies, 38(4), 72-89.
- Lister, S. (2020). *The Tigray Crisis: Human Rights Violations and International Law. Human Rights Watch*, 32(1), 10-25.
- Lyons, T. **&** Sánchez, M. (2020). *The Ethiopian Crisis: Politics and Conflict in the Horn of Africa*. Cambridge University Press.
- Malla, K. (2020). *The Challenges of Democratization in Ethiopia: A Case Study of Abiy Ahmed's Leadership. Journal of African Political Studies*, 19(3), 245-261.
- *Markakis,* **J.** (2011). *Ethiopia: The Last Two Frontiers*. James Currey.

- "Medemer: The Ethiopian Philosophy of Abiy Ahmed" Medemer Publishing House, 2019.
- Mekonnen, T. (2019). *The Evolution of Ethiopia's Political System Under Abiy Ahmed. Review of African Political Economy*, 46(160), 171-190.
- Melles, A. (2022). Abiy Ahmed's Rise and Fall: A New Age of Authoritarianism in Ethiopia? Journal of African Politics and Society, 29(2), 87-104.
- Merera, Gudina. *The Political Economy of the Ethiopian Revolution*. Red Sea Press, 1997.
- Mesfin, G. (2020). "Abiy Ahmed and the Paradox of Political Reform in Ethiopia." *African Affairs*, 119(475), 1-22.
- Messay, K. *The Political Economy of Ethiopia*. University of Chicago Press, 2014.
- Mulugeta, K. (2021). *Ethiopia's Economic Transformation and the Abiy Ahmed Administration: Success or Failure? The Journal of African Economic Development*, 23(2), 92-110.
- Negash, E. (2021). *Abiy Ahmed's Peace Diplomacy and the Tigray Crisis. Journal of Global Politics*, 22(1), 45-63.
- Olivier, M. (2020). The Use of Military Force in Authoritarian Regimes: A Case Study of Bashar al-Assad and Abiy Ahmed. International Affairs Review, 45(3), 123-138.
- Oromo Liberation Army (OLA). "Statement on the Activities of the Koree Nageenyaa and Ethiopian Government's Response." *Oromo Liberation Army (OLA)*, 2024.
- Osman, F. (2020). *Tigray and the Future of Ethiopia: The Dynamics of Power, Ethnicity, and Conflict. Horn of Africa Review*, 48(1), 18-39.
- Pankhurst, R. *Ethiopia: A Cultural History*. Harcourt Brace, 1966.
- Pankhurst, R. *The Ethiopian Revolution: A Political History*. University of Pennsylvania Press, 1992.
- Parker, E. (2019). *Ethnic Federalism and the Challenges of State-building in Ethiopia*. Palgrave Macmillan.
- Perham, M. *Haile Selassie: The Man and the Legacy*. Faber & Faber, 1969.

- Pina, V. (2020). *The Struggles of the Oromo: Historical Background and the Role of Abiy Ahmed. Journal of African History*, 41(3), 215-240.
- Prunier, G. (2019). *Understanding the Tigray Conflict: The Struggle for Control in Northern Ethiopia. African Affairs*, 118(470), 44-60.
- Reuters. "Ethiopia's Economic Crisis and Abiy's Unfulfilled Promises." Reuters, 2023.
- Reuters Investigation on Koree Nageenyaa. "Secretive Ethiopian Security Committee Ordered Killings, Detentions." *Reuters*, 2024.
  Retrieved from: https://www.reuters.com/article/ethiopia-olaf-kills
- Safran, W. (2020). *Political Change in Ethiopia: The Rise of Abiy Ahmed and the Challenge of Reconciliation. The Journal of Conflict Resolution*, 64(3), 300-317.
- Salvadori, M. *Ethiopia: A Cultural Profile.* UNESCO, 1991.
- Schlee, G. (2020). *Ethnicity and Conflict in Ethiopia: The Roots of the Tigray War. International Journal of Ethnic Studies*, 35(2), 195-212.
- Seitz, Christopher R. (2003). "The Queen of Sheba and the Kingdom of Ethiopia in the New Testament." *Journal of Early Christian Studies*, 11(4), 457-472.
- Shinn, D. H., & Ofcansky, T. P. *Ethiopia: A Country Study.* 5th edition, Federal Research Division of the Library of Congress, 2004.
- Sidel, M. (2019). *The Role of the Military in Ethiopia's Political Evolution: From EPRDF to Abiy Ahmed. Journal of Peace and Conflict Studies*, 21(3), 98-113.
- Smith, A. (2019). *Abiy Ahmed and the Ethiopian Peace Process: What Does the Future Hold? International Security Studies*, 50(4), 319-336.
- Tadesse, A. (2020). *The Crisis in Tigray: Internal Conflict and International Involvement. Global Security Review*, 12(2), 200-213.
- Tadesse, M. The Oromo and the Christian Kingdom of Ethiopia: 1300-1700. Journal of Ethiopian Studies, Vol. 21, No. 1, 1988.

- Tadesse, T. (2020). *The Role of the Oromo in Ethiopian Politics: Historical Struggles and Modern Dilemmas.* Routledge.
- Taytu, T. *The Political and Economic Development of Ethiopia in the 20th Century.* Cambridge University Press, 1982.
- Teferra, T. *The Battle of Adwa and Its Impact on African Independence Movements.* African Studies Review, 1997.
- Teferra, T. & Alhaji, A. (2021). "Peace and Conflict in Ethiopia: Abiy Ahmed's Nobel Peace Prize and its Aftermath." *Journal of Peace Research,* 58(6), 693-711.
- Teklu, H. (2020). *Revolution and Reform in Ethiopia: The Political Economy of Abiy Ahmed's Leadership. African Review of Politics,* 31(2), 189-205.
- Teshale Tibebu. The Generation and Ideology of the Oromo Resistance in the 1960s and 1970s. East African Publishing House, 1991.
- Teshome, T. *The Ethiopian Civil War: A Study of the Political, Social, and Economic Impact.* University of London Press, 1989.
- Tewolde, H. *Revolution and Identity in Modern Ethiopia: 1974–1991.* Addis Ababa University Press, 2010.
- Tewolde, W. (2021). *Ethiopia's Tigray War: Humanitarian Disaster and Political Implications. Africa Spectrum,* 56(1), 40-56.
- "The Amhara Crisis and its Broader Implications on the Horn of Africa." Al-Ahram Weekly, November 14, 2024.
- "The Controversy Surrounding Abiy Ahmed's Nobel Peace Prize" The New Yorker, 2020. *https://www.newyorker.com/news/news-desk/ethiopia-prime-minister-abiy-ahmed-nobel-peace-prize-controversy*
- The Economist. (2020). "The Unraveling of Abiy Ahmed's Ethiopia."
- "The Formation and Challenges of the Prosperity Party under Abiy Ahmed "African Politics Review, 2020. https://www.africanpoliticsreview.com/prosperity-party-formation

- The Guardian. (2021). "Abiy Ahmed's War in Tigray: A Test of Ethiopia's Future."
- The Impact of Global Supply Chains and Inflation on Food Prices in Ethiopia," The International Food Policy Research Institute (IFPRI), 2023.
- "The Life and Legacy of Negasso Gidada: Ethiopia's Humble Leader," Ethiopian Politics Review, 2019.
- The New York Times. "Abiy Ahmed's Reforms: A Turn Towards Authoritarianism." The New York Times, 2021.
- The New York Times. (2020). "Abiy Ahmed's Struggle for Control: Ethiopia's Leader Faces Rising Ethnic Tensions."
- "The Political and Military Landscape of Ethiopia's Amhara Region." Ethiopian Political Review, 2024.
- Tsehaye, H. M. *The Struggle for Ethiopian Independence: A Historical Overview of the Battle of Adwa.* Addis Ababa University Press, 1999.
- UN Human Rights Council. (2021). Report on Human Rights Violations in Syria and Ethiopia: An Overview of the Humanitarian Crisis under Authoritarian Leadership.
- UNHCR. "Ethiopia – 2023 UNHCR Population Statistics." UNHCR, 2023.
- United Nations (2020). *Humanitarian Situation in Tigray: A Report from the UN.* United Nations Office for the Coordination of Humanitarian Affairs.
- United Nations Human Rights Council. "Report on Human Rights Violations in Ethiopia, 2024." *United Nations Human Rights Office (OHCHR).*
- Urbanization and Housing in Ethiopia," World Bank, 2020. *https://www.worldbank.org/en/country/ethiopia*
- Van de Walle, N. (2018). *Ethiopia's Development Dilemma: Balancing Growth with Inclusivity. Development Studies Quarterly*, 39(1), 134-150.
- Vaughan, S. *The Ethiopian Revolution: A History of the Derg Regime.* Oxford University Press, 1987.
- Vogel, C. (2021). The Cult of Personality: Authoritarian Leaders and Their Followers in the Middle East and Africa. Political Science Quarterly, 136(2), 177-193.

- Watson, A. E. *The Ethiopian Experience in the Early Christian Era: An Introduction to Ethiopian Christianity.* Cambridge University Press, 1995.
- Williams, D. (2019). *Ethiopia: The Fall of the Ethiopian People's Revolutionary Democratic Front (EPRDF). Journal of African Affairs*, 57(4), 275-290.
- Yusuf, A. (2019). Religion, Nationalism, and the Politics of Power in Ethiopia and Syria. International Journal of Political Science, 28(4), 69-84.
- Zewde, B. *A History of Modern Ethiopia 1855-1991.* 2nd edition, James Currey, 2001.
- Zewdie, D. (2021). *Abiy Ahmed and the Future of Ethiopian Politics: From Hope to Crisis. Global Politics Review*, 41(2), 112-125.
- Zeleke, M. (2020). *Humanitarian Responses to the Tigray Crisis: Challenges and Prospects. International Review of Humanitarian Studies*, 12(3), 202-218.
- Zelinsky, R. (2022). Dictators in Power: A Comparative Analysis of Political Repression in Ethiopia and Syria. Global Dictatorship Research Journal, 16(1), 98-112.

9 798303 286450